Praise for *Zen Under Fire*

"Not only is Marianne Elliott a beautiful writer, she's a courageous truth-teller. *Zen Under Fire* takes readers on a breathtaking adventure through war-torn Afghanistan and an equally perilous place—the human heart. I can't stop thinking about the brave stories of peace, justice, and love."

—Brené Brown, PhD, *New York Times* bestselling author of *Daring Greatly: How the Courage to be Vulnerable Transforms the Way We Live, Love, Parent, and Lead*

"This book touched my heart, soul, and intellect. Marianne is vulnerable and fearless in offering this sincere account of her experience in Afghanistan. She asks important questions and does not shy away from complex issues with no clear answers. Marianne takes the reader on an intimate journey that is raw and inspiring. I enjoyed every minute of it!"

—Hala Khouri, MA, co-founder of Off the Mat, Into the World

"This is an amazing book, kind of like if *Eat, Pray, Love* had happened in Afghanistan and the stakes were life and death. Marianne's story about diving into yoga, meditation, and compassionate action in the most war-torn parts of the world is touching, relatable, informative, and, to boot, fantastic storytelling. While falling in love with her, we learn about what stops us from putting it all out on there in the name of peace and where true courage comes from."

—Susan Piver, *New York Times* bestselling author of *The Wisdom of a Broken Heart*

"This is a poignant and uplifting story about finding resilience in the midst of intense suffering, written with genuine understanding and care. Marianne Elliott has written a very special book, both compelling and inspiring."

—Sharon Salzberg, author of
Real Happiness and *Lovingkindness*

"I could not put this book down. I could not stop thinking about it when I wasn't reading it. Marianne's story plunged into my heart but made me see I can make a difference too. There is magic in these pages."

—Jennifer Louden, author of
The Women's Comfort Book and *The Life Organizer*

ZEN
UNDER
FIRE

*How I Found Peace
in the Midst of War*

MARIANNE ELLIOTT

 sourcebooks

This book is a memoir. It reflects the author's present recollections of her experiences over a
period of years. Some names and characteristics have been changed, some events have been
compressed, and some dialogue has been re-created.

Published by Sourcebooks, Inc.
P.O. Box 4410, Naperville, Illinois 60567-4410
(630) 961-3900
Fax: (630) 961-2168
www.sourcebooks.com

Originally published in 2012 in New Zealand by Penguin Books, an imprint of the Penguin
Group, a division of Pearson New Zealand Ltd.

Library of Congress Cataloging-in-Publication Data

Elliott, Marianne
  Zen under fire : how I found peace in the midst of war / Marianne Elliott.
    pages cm
  Originally published in 2012 in New Zealand by Penguin Books.
  Includes bibliographical references.
  (pbk. : alk. paper) 1. Elliott, Marianne, 1972- 2. Afghan War, 2001---Personal narratives.
3. Afghanistan--Politics and government--20th century. I. Title.
  DS371.413.E44 2013
  958.104'7092--dc23
  [B]
                          2013010912

Printed and bound in the United States of America.
VP 10 9 8 7 6 5 4 3 2

Acknowledgments

*T*o my parents, Ian and Margaret Elliott, who taught me that life can be kind and that we all have a role to play in making it so, and who understood, long before I did, the joy of service. I know they will understand why I also dedicate this book to the people of Afghanistan, especially those who put up with my strange ways and accepted me as a colleague, a neighbor and a friend.

For this book, and for my life in general, I am in the debt of more people than I can thank here. I'd like to thank Jake Hardwig, Suraya Pakzad, Fazel Haq Fazel, and Faezeh Mohammedpoor for tolerance and generosity. Gregor Salmon and Kate Khamsi for kindness and encouragement. Alys Titchener, Jolisa and Gemma Gracewood, Rachael King, Mary Parker, Bianca Zander and Helen Heath for reading early drafts and improving them with thoughtful feedback. Susan Piver, Jen Louden, Karen Maezen Miller, and Sharon Salzberg for kind, and wise, words. My agent Laura Nolan for trust, persistence, and great advice. Shana Drehs and everyone at Sourcebooks for confidence, enthusiasm, and a lot of hard work. My family and friends for support, faith, and countless cups of tea and reassurances. And Lucas Putnam, without whom this book may never have been written, for love, immense patience, and Paekakariki.

Note on Spelling

*T*here is no standard method of transliterating from Dari into English. Where a Dari place or name is commonly used or reported in English, I have generally chosen the most common usage. Otherwise I have used the simplest spelling of words, place names, and names of people. I've also included a glossary in the back of the book for readers to reference for terminology used throughout.

Author's Note

When I lived and worked in Afghanistan I had no plans to write about the experience. This book has been written based on my personal journals, detailed notes I kept about my working days, and my memory, a tool known more for its tenacity than its precision. I've worked hard to be accurate about dates, places and names but given the conditions under which I made the initial notes, some slippage seems inevitable. Despite this, I have done my very best to "put down what really happened." As Hemingway said in *Death in the Afternoon*, aside from knowing what I really felt as opposed to what I think I ought to have felt, putting down what really happened was the hardest part.

The first precept of the yogi and the guiding principle of the humanitarian are the same: do no harm. Any book about a subject as sensitive as human rights in Afghanistan will carry some risk of doing harm. Because of the security situation in Afghanistan, and because even ex-boyfriends have rights, I've changed the names of anyone (other than public figures) who might suffer from being mentioned here. In the case of my Afghan colleagues and international colleagues still working in Afghanistan, I have sometimes gone further to disguise their identities. I've known people killed for working with foreigners, and seen a friend flee the country because of death threats based on rumors about her private life. So, to disguise the identities of two characters, I have combined them into one. Another character has been given a new ethnicity and yet another has a new hometown. None of these changes affects the substance of my story, but they allow me to send this book out into the world with less fear of its impact on the lives of the innocent (or even the not entirely innocent).

I slept, and dreamt that life was joy.
I awoke and saw that life was service.
I acted and behold, service was joy.

—Rabindranath Tagore

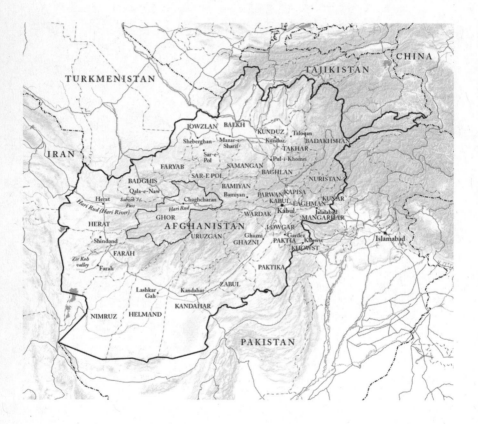

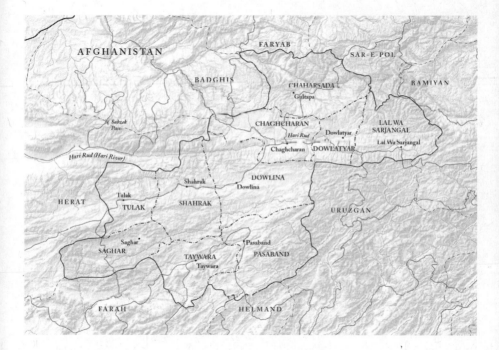

Prologue

Sunday, October 22, 2006: Herat, Afghanistan

I'm a month into my new job as a human rights officer for the United Nations Assistance Mission to Afghanistan and I'm not yet feeling on top of my game. It is Eid, the holiday that follows the end of the month of Ramadan, and my colleagues are desperate for a break. I am about to be left in charge of the office. I'm not sure I am ready for the responsibility, so I double-check with my boss.

"I'm not backing out on you," I say, "but I'm having doubts about my ability to do this."

He reassures me. "You'll be fine, Marianne. As long as no one kills Amanullah Khan, you'll be fine."

His reassurance, I think, is a joke. I have a lot to learn about Afghanistan.

My boss leaves at 9:00 a.m. on Sunday, October 22, 2006. I am now the officer in charge of a United Nations office in the middle of a war zone.

By midday, Amanullah Khan is dead.

The Road to Herat

October 2006

I came to Afghanistan almost ten months ago, in the last days of December 2005. Before that, I'd been home in New Zealand for five years since my last posting in the Gaza Strip. Having seen the struggle for dignity and justice that characterizes daily life for millions of people around the world, I found it hard to relax completely into my comfortable life in Wellington. Not that I'd been wasting my time in New Zealand. I came home from Gaza with three goals: to find a way to work on human rights issues in my own backyard, to get healthy, and to find a boyfriend.

On the first point, my job with the New Zealand Human Rights Commission had been both a challenge and a success. I'd taken on a project bigger than many people thought I was ready for, developing a national plan for human rights in New Zealand for the next ten years. Despite inevitable stumbles along the way, I did a decent job of it. The Minister of Justice even thanked me for my "steadfast and dynamic" approach. On the back of that achievement, I'd been appointed to help the government of Timor-Leste—the newest country in the world at the time—to come up with its own long-term human rights strategy.

My health goals had initially been more modest: I wanted to quit smoking and stop wheezing. Life in Gaza had been stressful and I'd adopted a typical aid-worker approach to managing that stress. I smoked an entire packet of cigarettes most days, drank coffee and Diet Coke to get through long working hours, and drank cheap Israeli wine or vodka every Thursday night to loosen the grasping fingers of anxiety from my mind. I was slim but constantly strung out, and if my jittery mind didn't keep me awake at night, my asthmatic coughing did.

Back in New Zealand I quit smoking and joined the gym in the same week, hoping to see twice the benefits in half the time. What happened was that my natural ambition and controlling tendencies flourished in my exercise regime. Within eighteen months I was running ten kilometers every morning before work, teaching aerobics several times a week and paying almost obsessive attention to what I ate and drank. By the time I left for Afghanistan, my running partner Wendie and I had won our first ten-kilometer race.

During this time I also discovered yoga, though it was mostly too slow for my liking and I resented the fact that I didn't seem to get any "better" at it no matter how hard I tried. I avoided classes with too much sitting still or breathing because they made me jittery, but I enjoyed the stretch I could get from a faster style of yoga. All told, my get-fit regime had been a resounding success.

The boyfriend project hadn't gone quite so smoothly. Before returning to New Zealand I'd dated gorgeous men from all over the world and thought I was ready to settle down. My first boyfriend back home was a handsome, kind architect who was ready to make a home, get married and have children. He should have been perfect. But I was so busy—with work, exercise, and a full social life that often didn't include him—that I struggled to make time for him and he eventually gave up on me. A better match for me was the Brazilian boyfriend who lived in Timor-Leste. We had fun whenever I visited Timor for work, and went on scuba-diving holidays together in Bali and New Zealand, but most of the time I was free to maintain my relentless schedule. In the end he went back to Brazil and I stayed on in Wellington.

A year before leaving for Afghanistan, I fell in love with a handsome Maori lawyer. Though he was only thirty-two years old, he had been selected to lead his tribe and was negotiating on their behalf with the government for settlement of historical land claims. I found his passion for justice as attractive as his physical beauty.

On our second date he told me he was married, although now separated, and had two young sons. I had also married young and divorced soon after, so I wasn't particularly shocked by his revelation. The boys and their mother were living with her family in another city.

After we'd been seeing each other for about five months I helped arrange for him to attend a workshop in the United States on community-based democracy and consensus decision-making. I drove him to the airport, kissed him good-bye, and never heard from him again.

It took me weeks to accept this was his way of ending things. I preferred to believe he had lost my phone number. Eventually I found out through a mutual friend that he had returned to live with his wife and children. Though I respected his choice, I was deeply hurt that he hadn't even spoken to me about it. I decided to take a break from dating and focus on my career.

I was in my midthirties and near the top of my professional game. When I had come home from the Gaza Strip five years earlier I'd said there was only one job worth staying in New Zealand for, and I'd now done it. I was ready for a new challenge. I was also losing patience with what I saw as a lack of perspective in my home country. After five years of biting my tongue while New Zealanders told me that our public health system was "third world," I was ready to work again with people who were facing more serious human rights challenges. I started looking for jobs in Palestine and Afghanistan.

I'd been following the work of the Afghanistan Independent Human Rights Commission (AIHRC, or the Commission) ever since it had been established in 2002. Several of the Afghan human rights commissioners had been out to visit New Zealand and I was impressed by the work they seemed to be able to do under incredibly difficult circumstances. When a job came up working with the Commission and fifteen other human rights and development organizations in Kabul, I applied.

Afghanistan wasn't much in the news before 2001, but by the time I got here, most people had heard of it, mainly as a war zone. When I arrived, in December 2005, the government of Afghanistan, with the support of hundreds of thousands of NATO soldiers from countries as diverse as the United States, Turkey and Lithuania, was fighting the Taliban for control of the country. Warfare has changed in the past few decades, and the Kabul I landed in didn't look much like the kind of war zone I'd seen in movies.

The government forces and their international allies were visible enough, rolling through the city in armored personnel carriers with young men and large guns mounted on top. Their "enemy"— antigovernment groups including the Taliban—was harder to spot, and fighting, when it happened, could just as easily take the form of a roadside bomb as an exchange of gunfire. The war in Afghanistan is a counterinsurgency and, as such, has included not only military but also political, economic, paramilitary and even psychological operations.

It's a messy kind of war, especially for civilians. In 2004, five staff members of Médecins Sans Frontières, a humanitarian medical organization, were killed while traveling in northwestern Afghanistan, resulting in the complete withdrawal of MSF from Afghanistan. Many more Afghan civilians were killed in the same year, which is precisely why human rights monitoring, the job I came here to do, is so important.

❖ ❖ ❖

You might expect people who go to live and work in war zones to be thick-skinned types for whom flak jackets and rocket fire are water off a duck's back.

Not me. As a preschooler I would get upset when other kids got hurt. I get choked up at the sight of a proud elderly man resisting help on the train. Despite my thin skin, though, I've ended up working in some of the most notorious conflict zones of our time.

I was in the Gaza Strip for two years, working for the Palestinian Center for Human Rights. My boss in Gaza was Raji Sourani, a famously resilient Palestinian human rights lawyer. The first time I burst into tears over a child killed by a "rubber bullet," Raji said, "Marianne, if you want to do this kind of work, you are going to have to toughen up." Over the two years I worked with him, Raji did his best to toughen me up, but when I left he conceded that he had failed miserably; I was as "soft-hearted" as the day I'd landed on his doorstep.

In Afghanistan I hoped to make a small but meaningful contribution to a peaceful and just resolution to one of the twenty-first century's major conflicts. After a phone interview, which was postponed twice because of changing curfews and security restrictions in Kabul, I was offered the job. On December 28, 2005, I landed in Kabul.

I had thought life in Gaza was tough. I was there in 2000 when the Al-Aqsa Intifada erupted and Gaza was shelled nightly. I got used to the sound of Israeli military helicopters overhead and to the constant fear that our apartment building would be the next hit. I was on edge and angry all the time, yet I thought I had figured out how to hold myself together in the midst of war. I thought Gaza and Timor-Leste had prepared me for pretty much any situation. But nothing had really prepared me for Afghanistan.

For my first six months in Afghanistan I worked for a group of human rights and development organizations in the capital, Kabul. These organizations formed a network to do research and advocacy on human rights issues of concern to ordinary Afghans. I was first adviser to, and then acting director of, the network.

Life in Kabul was challenging. I've struggled to explain to people what it was like. I can describe the physical desolation of the city, the houses with rocket holes in them like gaping wounds, or pockmarked by bullets. I can tell you that in winter, when I first arrived, the streets were a quagmire of cold, slushy mud through which the long-suffering citizens of Kabul picked their way in rubber clogs. I can describe the women, the hems of their dirty, ragged burqas trailing in the mud, who held their babies up to the car window for me to see as they begged for money.

But it's difficult to convey the insidious contraction that creeps into a person's body, mind and heart when she is banned from walking in the streets because of the threat of being kidnapped. It is not the same as the big explosions of fear that I felt in Gaza when the missiles were falling on the city. In Gaza, once the Israeli military helicopters were gone, the city would return to being a place where I felt safe. I could walk the streets of Gaza City alone without any sense of threat or danger. The risk there came from outside, and although when it came it wreaked havoc, when it left I felt once again at home.

In Kabul it was almost impossible to feel at home. The security situation made it dangerous for Afghan families to welcome foreigners or *khareji* into their homes. I could visit my colleagues from work, but we went to some effort to disguise my coming and going so their neighbors didn't start spreading gossip that they were harboring khareji.

So when my contract ended and I was offered my dream job as a human rights officer with the United Nations, I was relieved to learn the job would be in Herat, a large city in the west of Afghanistan, rather than Kabul. I was reluctant to leave my new boyfriend, Joel, who I had met in Kabul. Against the odds, Joel had helped me laugh and feel safe, in a place where laughter and safety were equally hard to find.

But his contract was ending and he too would be looking for a new job. Hoping Joel would be able to follow me to Herat soon, I took the job.

Herat is no walk in the park. In fact, the security risk even here means I am forbidden to walk anywhere. But at least there is a park where local residents can walk and I will be able to watch them from the window of the car, trying to absorb a vicarious sense of freedom.

The UN recruitment process is infamously slow. It took three months for me to jump through the bureaucratic hoops, and by the time I arrived in Herat I'd been in Afghanistan almost nine months. I was no longer a newcomer to the country; but a new job in a new city had me feeling almost as green as the day I first arrived.

2
What Could Possibly Go Wrong?

October 2006: Herat, Afghanistan

I've been in Herat a month now, and I'm struggling to find my feet. I've moved a lot with my job but I've never gotten used to saying good-bye to all my friends and starting over again. Despite all my traveling, I am a homebody at heart, and the first thing I do when I arrive in a new place is try to make my room as cozy as possible.

Here in Herat, this has proven challenging. I live in a shared guesthouse with my UN colleagues. The streets of Afghanistan are dusty, colorful and full of life—groups of giggling *chador*-clad teenage girls on foot, young men on bicycles, entire families on motorbikes and donkey-drawn carts laden with fruit and vegetables jostle for position with brightly colored three-wheeled taxis. These Afghan tuk-tuks make their Thai brethren look dull, with scenic murals painted on their walls, fluorescent pink fabric guitars sewn onto their covers and orange, purple and green tassels hanging from every corner. The interior of my guesthouse, in contrast, is austere. The walls and floor are scrubbed white plaster and tile. My bedroom is decorated with explosions of gaudy color. The effect is like a sterile hospital room festooned with bouquets of plastic flowers. There are none of the traditional Afghan fabrics and handcrafts that I love.

Instead of a traditional wool carpet, my floor is covered with a machine-woven synthetic rug. In place of one of the delightful brightly colored hand-painted metal trunks I've seen in the market in Herat, I have a set of drawers covered in a faux-wood plastic veneer, with an elaborately carved gilt mirror. Perhaps whoever decorated my room was trying to make it more attractive to its foreign occupant. I appreciate the effort made on my behalf, but if I wasn't so busy with my work, buying an Afghan wool carpet would be my first priority.

As it is, I have other problems to occupy me. I am still trying to get my head around my new job. I'm a human rights lawyer who specializes in the rights of women and children in conflict settings. I was drawn to a career in law as a way to combat injustice, but I cut my legal teeth in a big corporate firm. Working on cases in which business partners fought ferociously over financial losses taught me the perils of coveting money. Accounting for my work time in six-minute intervals taught me to work quickly, efficiently and transparently. These were all useful skills for my career in human rights. There is never enough money in this sector, so I need to be able to do a lot with a little, produce the same amount of work in a week that others might produce in a month and, always, be above reproach when it comes to accounting for how funds are spent.

My first job in Kabul involved researching national human rights problems and lobbying the international community to take action. So I'm used to focusing on the big picture. In this new role, however, a big chunk of my daily work involves responding to and documenting individual cases of human rights violations. I receive a complaint from someone about police brutality or being illegally detained and it is my job to decide whether there is enough evidence to support the allegation. If there is, I raise the case with the responsible Afghan officials.

Pursuing one case after another in this way seems a Sisyphean task, especially in the face of the large-scale injustices that keep vulnerable

Afghan people from getting out of poverty and fear. I knew when I took the job that I would be dealing with individual cases, and I do believe it is worth doing anything we can for each individual complainant. But in practice it is proving harder than I expected to maintain a sense of hope and usefulness. It is easy to get lost in the endless parade of human suffering and never feel any closer to making a difference. Only a month in, I'm having doubts about the effectiveness of my work in this new role.

The office was understaffed before my arrival, and my colleagues were forced to postpone their much needed occasional recovery break while they waited for reinforcements. Now I've arrived, they are desperate to get out of here.

A few days before Eid, the holiday that marks the end of the holy month of Ramadan, my boss calls me into his office. "I have a request," he says.

"Yes," I reply, already nervous. "What is it?"

"I'm supposed to be going on leave for Eid. I've booked a flight home to Spain to see my parents." He pauses. "I've already canceled two previous trips home because there was no one to cover the office…" He trails off and looks at me pointedly. I begin to squirm, but try to keep a poker face. I nod for him to continue.

"Now it seems I'll have to cancel this trip as well. All of the other senior staff are also due for a break and if I can't find anyone to cover as officer in charge I won't be able to go…"

"Mmm hmm," I mumble noncommittally.

"So I want to ask if you will cover for me. I know you are new here, but you were in Kabul for six months so it's not like you just stepped off the plane. I'll only be gone a week and it will be the Eid holiday for most of that time so our office will be closed. There won't be much for you to do." My first instinct in response to any request is to say yes. This desire to please everyone gets me into trouble, but it persists. So the fact that I now hesitate shows just how uncertain I am about my readiness for the responsibility of running the entire office.

"I'd love to be able to help you," I say, "but I'm not sure I can do the job. I don't know any of the local officials yet, I barely know what's going on in the region and I wouldn't know where to start if something went wrong."

"You wouldn't be alone," he reminds me. "Even though the international staff will mostly be gone, our senior Afghan staff will still be here. They'll help you with anything you need to know."

I am losing my resolve. He is clearly exhausted and needs the break. Maybe he is right. He will only be away a week, and of that time our office will be closed for four days for the Eid break. I only have to hold the fort for three days. Surely I can manage that.

"Okay," I relent, "I'll do it. Tell me everything I need to know. What is going on right now and what could possibly go wrong?"

With a relieved smile, he begins to brief me on the major political tensions in the region. There are many, but the name on everybody's lips this week is Amanullah Khan.

Amanullah Khan is the leader of a branch of the Noorzai tribe based in the Zir Koh valley to the south of Herat city. I haven't yet visited Zir Koh but I know that it is in Shindand district, a couple of hours' drive south of Herat. Like most of the land south of Herat the valley is mostly dry and arid, and the only arable land is found along the river, which is where most of the small villages are clustered.

The Zir Koh valley–based Noorzai tribe is only one small part of a much larger clan, one well-known member of which is Arif Khan Noorzai, deputy speaker of the Afghan parliament. Members of Amanullah Khan's local branch of the Noorzai tribe are believed to be responsible for the death of an elder from the Barakzai tribe, a neighboring tribe in the Zir Koh valley. This happened just a week ago.

While my boss is briefing me on these tribes, I am furiously scribbling notes and hoping that I will be able to remember all these new names. I wonder again if I am signing on for more than I can manage.

I don't entirely understand the origins of the conflict between the Noorzai and Barakzai tribes. Like many tribal conflicts in Afghanistan, it has been going on so long that it seems no one in my office remembers its original source. What is clear is that the most recent killing has rekindled tensions and there is a high risk of escalating violence.

Our office has been encouraging peaceful resolution of the ongoing dispute for years and, more recently, has been talking to each of the two tribes to encourage them to find a nonviolent way to resolve the murder of the Barakzai elder. It is highly unlikely the elders will be willing to entrust the case to the formal justice system, which is seen by many ordinary Afghans to be slow, expensive and highly corruptible. Instead, our office has been encouraging both groups to consider traditional conflict resolution methods such as *jirga* or tribal councils. These councils are groups of respected tribal elders who are trusted by their community to make decisions about matters such as who committed a crime and what compensation they should make to their victims.

I haven't been involved in any of this. This kind of diplomacy is the responsibility of my colleagues in the political team and isn't part of my human rights work. I am only learning about it now so that I can report intelligently on progress in my boss's absence.

On the day of my boss's departure, my confidence flags. I am not sure I am ready for this responsibility. I need to double-check with him.

"I'm not backing out on you," I say, "but I'm having doubts about my ability to do this."

"You'll be fine, Marianne," he reassures me. "As long as no one kills Amanullah Khan, you'll be fine."

At 9:00 a.m. on Sunday, October 22, 2006, he leaves me in charge of the UN mission in western Afghanistan.

3
Worst-Case Scenario

Sunday, October 22, 2006: Herat, Afghanistan

*I*t's almost lunchtime on my first day in charge. My boss left this morning and so far things are going according to plan. I'm in my office working on the weekly report. I find this both tedious and harrowing given the grim tally of deaths and maimings. In my boss's absence I have to prepare the report for the entire office, as well as for my own human rights team. Just before midday, Asif, one of our senior Afghan staff members, comes in to talk to me.

"Amanullah Khan has been killed," he says.

For an instant I wonder whether he's joking but the look on his face and the tone of his voice are unmistakable. "What happened?" I ask.

"He was traveling in a convoy with some of his supporters when a rocket hit his vehicle. He was killed instantly. His son may have been in the vehicle with him and might also be dead, although we aren't sure about that yet." He stops for a moment and stares at me, as if to gauge my reaction. "They will seek revenge for this," Asif continues, "and it could escalate very quickly. We need to do everything we can to contain this situation or many people could be killed."

My disbelief is already giving way to fear. I feel it in my belly first, and my stomach clenches as though I can keep this disaster at bay with my abdominal muscles.

"Yes," I say, redundantly, "we need to do everything we can." What I'm not clear on yet is what that "everything" might be, but I know my first responsibility is to manage the office, where news of the assassination is already spreading in a wave of barely contained panic. People are huddling together around their desks listening with wide eyes.

In the initial hours after the attack I struggle to make sense of the confusing and sometimes conflicting reports that flood in. Every time the phone rings the news gets worse. Asif's sources in Zir Koh say Amanullah Khan's men are descending on villages of the Barakzai tribe—who they believe are responsible for his assassination. They are making their way from house to house executing adult men and any boys they deem old enough to fight. The reports claim men are being killed in front of their children, boys in front of their mothers.

As Asif and I try to confirm this from other sources, the phone rings again; it's a journalist from Reuters. Word of Amanullah Khan's murder and the reprisal attacks is spreading. "How many dead?" he asks. "We're hearing anything from forty to a hundred and forty."

No one seems to know, least of all me. Almost everyone agrees on one thing: Amanullah Khan's murder was a revenge attack in response to his men killing a Barakzai elder a week ago. Our efforts to broker a peaceful solution failed. Now the question is whether we can prevent things getting worse. I spend the afternoon in my boss's office while Asif comes and goes with new information and advice. The phone rings frequently as people from our head office in Kabul call to ask for more information and to give me advice about how we should intervene. I'm supposed to promote a peaceful solution to the fighting. I don't understand why they think I would have more luck now when my boss and his superiors were unsuccessful up to this point. But I'm hardly in a position to refuse.

If I had been asked to envisage a worst-case scenario for my first day in charge of the office, this would be it. In truth, there is very little that the civilian component of a United Nations mission can do once fighting has broken out. In these early hours of the fighting, the first response will come from the Afghan security forces, possibly with the support or assistance of their international military counterparts. My job, initially at least, is simply to try to form an accurate picture of what is actually happening. And that is proving to be much harder than it sounds.

Compounding the difficulties, I learn, is the extraordinary power of the Afghan rumor mill. Distance and security concerns prevent us from getting to the place where the crisis is unfolding, and limited mobile phone coverage means that we have to rely on information from a small number of informants. So we work on the basis of secondhand accounts. I'm not sure what to believe. The potential cost of getting the facts wrong is so high that I won't pretend to be able to handle this situation alone. I call Asif into my office again and tell him, regretfully, that I need him to work with me through the Eid holiday. He doesn't hesitate to agree. He himself is Pashtun and knows the people at the heart of this conflict well.

For the next thirty minutes he tells me everything he knows about the men likely to have stepped into the breach left by Amanullah Khan's murder, the men most likely to be giving orders to the fighters who have descended on the Barakzai villages, and who will be making decisions on how to respond to this conflict. As I listen to him, furiously scribbling notes on all the key players, I start feeling slightly less panicked. His calmness is rubbing off on me and my legal training is kicking in. The more information he gives me, the more comfortable I feel. I might be a complete novice to this local conflict, but processing lots of information quickly is familiar territory to me. If all I have to do is get my head around the conflict and write articulate, intelligent reports about it, I'll be okay. The problem is that people are dying as I sit in my office getting my head around it all. I need to take action now.

First order of business, Asif advises, is to set up meetings with the relevant local authorities. Each province in Afghanistan has a governor and a provincial council. The president appoints the governor, and the council members are elected in local elections. The governor holds more executive power in the running of the province, but the council generally has a lot of influence with the population. So I need to talk to them both. The commanders of the police and the army also need to be consulted, along with tribal and religious leaders.

Asif starts calling the various players, starting with the governor, and discovers that the governor has already convened an emergency security *shura*, or council, to discuss the situation. I am invited to join them. Our office's role, in this kind of situation, is to advise and assist the government of Afghanistan in order to promote peaceful resolution of the conflict.

The meeting is at 4:00 p.m. I have time to go home and get changed. I came to work this morning in an embroidered orange *shalwar kameez*—a cotton suit made up of a long tunic and loose pants that cover my arms and legs, as is respectful—and a large headscarf. This occasion, however, calls for something more formal. Once home, I change into a loose-fitting black business suit with a long skirt and a sober black headscarf. I look at myself in the mirror: with my dark hair, hazel eyes and olive skin I blend in well here. I'm not confident of much else today, but I am confident that I look the part.

My shoulders and chest are tight with fear and I feel the weight of all that could go wrong at this meeting, heavy and low in my pelvis. If I had more time, or a little more clarity, I would probably roll out my yoga mat and do some sun salutes. As it is, I sit down at my kitchen table to drink some tea—my response to any situation that seems beyond me—and think things through.

I am about to meet the governor, the chair of the provincial council, the head of the Afghan National Army and the chief of police. I feel a heavy sense of responsibility. If I mess up because I don't know who is who, or what political games they might be playing at the expense of the lives of people in the Zir Koh valley, those lives will be on my head.

One of the things I've learned in my career so far is to always, *always*, call on local expertise when you are out of your depth. So I call Asif again, for the third time today, and ask him if he can come to my house to brief me on each of the men who will be at the meeting. I need to know their ethnic, tribal, and political allegiances. He agrees to come in twenty minutes. I use the time to call a colleague. Talatbek is not exactly local—he's originally from Tajikistan—but he has been in Afghanistan for almost twenty years. He's the head of the United Nations Assistance Mission in Afghanistan (UNAMA) office in the troubled southern province of Kandahar. Although Herat is far to the west of Kandahar, the tribes involved in this particular conflict are subgroups of larger tribes based in Kandahar and I'm hoping Talatbek will know something about them.

Although I have never met him in person, I'm sure Talatbek has handled many situations just like the one I am facing. If anyone can help me right now, it will be him. I call him at his office and explain quickly what I know about the conflict, asking for his advice about my next moves. In response he is calm and kind.

"Do you want me to call my contacts in the Zir Koh branches of the Noorzai and Barakzai tribes?" he asks. "I think I can probably talk them into holding fire while you and the governor pull together a peacemaking delegation from Kabul."

"Yes please, Talatbek." I like that idea very much. By the end of our conversation I am breathing a little easier. I thank Talatbek and assure him I'll call again if I need more advice.

As I get off the phone with Talatbek, Asif arrives. Over yet another cup of green tea, he fills me in on the political affiliations of each of the men who will be in the room that afternoon. We don't have long, but it is enough to alert me to the agendas that might be playing out in our discussions. What is making Asif particularly nervous is the possibility that this conflict is bigger than Zir Koh valley.

"The real problem," he explains, "is that behind the tensions between Noorzai and Barakzai tribes lies a much bigger battle, the battle for power between Amanullah Khan and Ismail Khan."

Asif refers to Ismail Khan as IK, which is initially a bit weird for me because it's what my sisters and I call our father (Ian Kennedy Elliott). It is always a little unsettling when details of my life in New Zealand appear without warning here in Afghanistan. It seems incredible to me that life in New Zealand could carry on as usual, unaffected by the devastation that surrounds me in Afghanistan, so I've come to imagine the two places as existing in different, parallel, universes.

I already know a little of Ismail Khan's history. He first came to international attention when he led a local garrison in Herat into an uprising against the Soviet government in 1979. This uprising was defeated but Khan went on to become a powerful commander during the Soviet war in Afghanistan. He was also a key member of the Northern Alliance, a group of commanders from the north of Afghanistan who, in 2001, formed an alliance with the United States to topple the Taliban.

Once the Soviets had been ousted, Ismail Khan became the governor of Herat province, successfully defending the province against the Taliban in 1995. Yet he was no liberal himself. Before I even moved to Herat I had heard stories about how he opposed women's participation in higher education and the workforce. He was renowned for his repression of journalists and the press.

Asif explains to me that, despite his reputation for repressive policies and brutal policing, Ismail Khan still has many supporters in Herat.

"After the fall of the Taliban, despite efforts to reestablish a national government in Afghanistan, IK continued to rule Herat as though it was his personal emirate," Asif explains. "He collected taxes and customs duties himself and refused to pay them into the central purse in Kabul. Instead he used them, or at least some of them, to rebuild Herat city."

I can see how this diversion of public money would have made IK popular here in Herat. While Kabul, the capital, waited for the slow trickle of international aid, Herat's roads, bridges and schools were being rebuilt. I remember being surprised, when I first arrived in Herat after living in Kabul, to discover that the sewerage system seemed to be largely intact and functional, putting Herat well ahead of the capital.

As I listen to Asif, I think that President Karzai might have tolerated Ismail Khan's independent streak were it not for two factors. Firstly there was the problem of access to funds. Herat province borders Iran, so the customs duties collected in Herat constitute a large proportion of national revenue. The government can't afford to allow Ismail Khan to keep those funds in Herat province.

Secondly, Khan works closely with Iran. The United States is caught up in an increasingly tense standoff with Iran. Over the past few years George Bush's administration has been moving U.S. forces into position in western Afghanistan, where they could theoretically launch an air attack on Iran. It seems unlikely to me that President Karzai's main supporters, the Americans, could have been happy about Khan's cozy relations with Iran. In 2004, at the urging of the United States, President Karzai agreed to send Afghan National Army units to Herat to remove Ismail Khan from power.

Asif informs me that in the clashes that ensued Khan's son was killed. As a conciliatory gesture, the president offered him an especially lucrative ministerial post, that of minister for energy. Khan accepted.

"Although Ismail Khan no longer holds any official positions in the government of Herat province," Asif explains, "I have no doubt as to his ongoing political power and influence. Whenever IK comes 'home' to Herat we know that something big is going down. He still sends his thugs out to catch and punish anyone who dares to break the fast of Eid," Asif goes on. "He is also the 'godfather' of a local mafia that controls all construction projects in the city and"—Asif drops his voice—"is rumored to be siphoning large amounts of public money into their private investments."

The image Asif is drawing of IK as a mafia don reminds me of the first time I saw Ismail Khan in person. I was surprised at his modest stature; his reputation is so gigantic that it was hard to reconcile it with the small, round man with a long white beard whom I watched descending from a private plane at Herat airport. However the caliber, and political stripes, of the supporters who had shown up to welcome him home had tipped me off to the identity and importance of the man on the tarmac. I couldn't help staring. Here before me was a character of legendary proportions in Afghanistan and he looked so ordinary.

"Amanullah Khan," Asif carries on, "was probably the only person in western Afghanistan who had the courage and the backing to openly challenge Ismail Khan. Rare among men in the western region, he didn't seem to be afraid of Ismail Khan."

"I've heard rumors," I tell Asif, "that Amanullah Khan has received clandestine support from the central government to mount a campaign against IK."

"I've heard them too," he agrees, "but it's impossible to know whether they are true."

Either way, Amanullah Khan had already shown himself to be willing to rattle Ismail Khan's cage. Eighteen months ago, for instance, a showdown between Amanullah Khan and Ismail Khan resulted in tribal fighting in Shindand. I know about this because the members of my human rights team were left with the grisly task of taking stock of the dead and hearing the harrowing testimonies of the survivors.

"It's slightly more complicated," Asif continues. "Not only are there two powerful personalities at play, there is also an ethnic dimension to the tension. Amanullah Khan's tribe, the Noorzai, are Pashtun while Ismail Khan is Tajik."

Pashtun are the ethnic majority in Afghanistan. President Karzai himself is Pashtun. Tajik are the second-largest ethnic group in Afghanistan. To simplify, you could say that Pashtun leaders are more closely linked to Pakistan while Tajik leaders, who are Persian-speaking, are closer to Iran.

"As the removal of IK from his position of governor of Herat demonstrated," Asif explains, "the U.S. backers of Karzai's government have little tolerance for friendly relations between the powerful elite of Afghanistan and Iran. Iran, on the other hand, is very keen to make friends in Afghanistan and is happy to spend money to do so."

I've seen the figures and know that Iran spends large amounts of money on reconstruction efforts in Afghanistan. Most of these efforts are centered in Herat province, where Iranian money has paid not only for the construction and repair of *madrasas* (religious schools) and mosques, but also of orphanages, roads and hospitals. Different groups of Afghans view these efforts very differently. In our own office, for example, there are tensions evident between the Pashtun staff, who tend to be more suspicious of Iran and its influence, and the Tajik or Hazara staff, many of whom have themselves lived in Iran, often as refugees.

Asif explains that the relationship between Iran and the United States provides the backdrop to the relationship between IK and Amanullah Khan. Meanwhile, tensions between these two men have fueled the conflict between the Noorzai and Barakzai. Even the suggestion that Ismail Khan is behind the murder of Amanullah Khan increases the stakes of this conflict considerably.

I'm about to walk into a meeting of the key local officials, so I ask Asif whether each of them is likely to be more sympathetic to Ismail or Amanullah Khan. He tells me that while the chief of police and the chair of the council are generally assumed to be affiliates of Ismail Khan, the governor has a tense relationship with IK—which isn't surprising, as he was appointed to replace IK when he was deposed.

I thank Asif for the briefing and suggest that we head to the governor's office. That's when I find out that he's not coming with me. Apparently only I am invited. I argue that the invitation is actually to our office and so it would be fine for Asif to come with me. He's not convinced.

"It's important that you attend this meeting alone, Marianne," he says, "so these men begin to take you seriously as the acting head of office." I can't argue with that, so he goes home to his family while I steel myself to face the task ahead alone.

I'm not really alone, though; I may not have Asif with me, but one of the language assistants from the office, Abdul-Rahim, will come with me to interpret. The discussions will all be taking place in Dari and my Dari doesn't extend far beyond buying fruit and vegetables and giving simple driving directions. If only the answers to this afternoon's dilemmas were as simple.

4

Are We Doing Enough?

Sunday, October 22, 2006: Herat, Afghanistan

*T*he governor's office is not far from my house: I could walk, were it not for security rules that dictate I must travel everywhere in an official UN vehicle. I radio for a car and a driver, and ask them to collect Abdul-Rahim on the way.

Security at the governor's office is higher than at most other offices in Herat, which is a less fortified city than Kabul. The guards stop our car outside the gates and tell us we won't be able to drive inside. This is standard protocol in Kabul. Most offices here in Herat are more relaxed, but the governor needs to take more precautions. All the same, I don't like the idea of our driver waiting outside on the street, a sitting duck for any stray rocket, so I send him back to my guesthouse to wait. He's happy to drink tea with the security guards who sit in a small hut outside the gate of our house all day long. I tell him I will radio when our meeting is over.

Abdul-Rahim and I walk to the security checkpoint at the front door. The guards give us no more than a cursory glance before waving us through. The only place I've ever been thoroughly searched in Herat is at the airport, where there are female security guards. Everywhere else, the lack of female guards means I can walk into even the most fortified spaces without even a pat down. In any case, the guards here seem relaxed and confident I am not hiding a grenade beneath the folds of my conservative black suit.

The governor's office is out the back of the cavernous town hall. We enter through the back door and are shown to the waiting room. The building is simple, and clean, with brightly colored ornate furniture.

We wait at the governor's office for about half an hour, presumably while the local officials discuss whatever it is they are not willing to talk about in front of me. As we wait, I am struck by how incongruous my presence here is. It's one thing to have met with Afghan judges to talk about problems with trial proceedings or illegal detention; I'm a lawyer, after all, and can talk about Afghan criminal and procedural law with relative ease. But I'm about to meet the provincial commander of the Afghan National Army to discuss tactics for calming and stabilizing a district beset by tribal fighting.

Eventually I am called into the meeting. The governor's office is a large room with a grand-looking desk in one corner and four couches arranged in a square facing each other in the center of the room. The governor welcomes us by placing his right hand on his heart as he gestures toward the empty couch. His hand-on-heart gesture is warm and welcoming.

Before I move to sit down, I stand for a moment to acknowledge each of the men in the room. I look at each for a moment, placing my hand over my heart, bowing my head slightly and greeting them with *"Asalaam u aleikum."* The Afghan practice of making time to acknowledge and greet each person in any room strikes me as a particularly mindful way to make an entrance.

"U aleikum salaam," they each reply to my greeting, as they look with curiosity at this young woman who has turned up in place of the man with whom they are accustomed to dealing.

The army and police chiefs are dressed in their uniforms, khaki green for the former and dark gray for the latter. Learning to decipher and remember the rank of military officers is a challenge for me. I know the secret is on the lapels of each man's uniform, but I struggle to remember what the various stripes mean. Fortunately for me, the governor introduces these two men using their rank. The police chief is a colonel, and the army commander, impressively, is a general. Their seniority only serves to underscore just how serious this meeting is. I feel my stomach knot; what if I say something stupid and expose myself as a fraud? My own embarrassment would be one thing, but it would be much more serious to damage the reputation of our office. I remind myself that I am as well prepared for the meeting as I can be under the circumstances. I take a deep breath and exhale slowly to hold back the rising panic.

I wait for the governor to speak. He is dressed in a traditional shalwar kameez, with a gray woolen vest and a white and silver turban. He has a round, handsome face and a small, neatly trimmed beard. As I watch him, I mentally review the briefing I received on each of the men's ethnic and tribal affiliations.

As I understand it, my role is to provide some form of external accountability for the decisions they are about to make. From their point of view, however, I have probably been included in the meeting because only I can mobilize the resources of the international community. These men are all aware of the potential use that my office can be to them. I can ask the international military forces to consider joining with the Afghan forces in their efforts to stem the violence in Shindand. I can also call on my colleagues in the United Nations humanitarian agencies, UNICEF (the children's agency), UNHCR (the refugee agency) and others, to provide emergency humanitarian assistance to the families affected by the fighting. Perhaps most importantly, I can urge my own ultimate boss, the Special Representative of the UN Secretary General (SRSG) in Kabul, to try to influence President Karzai's response to this conflict. I am at this meeting either because they hope to convince me to take one or more of these actions, or because they plan to talk me out of taking them—I am not yet sure which.

The governor brings me up to date on their discussions. He tells me they have already decided to send a unit of soldiers from Herat to Zir Koh valley to end the fighting and secure the area.

This is not a good start. Their very first decision is one I discussed with Talatbek and I have concerns about it. Given the allegations flying in Shindand that Ismail Khan had a hand in Amanullah Khan's murder, an influx of soldiers or police officers from Herat could be inflammatory. The Herati police force is still widely seen to be under the influence of Ismail Khan who, after all, handpicked many of its senior officers. The army falls under the same suspicions.

"Have you considered," I venture, "using soldiers or police from another province?"

I don't want to start my relationship with these men off on the wrong foot, so I am not about to name Ismail Khan or to suggest that the local security forces are anything other than impeccably neutral. I trust the men in the room will understand my concern without the need to be explicit. To my relief, the general himself steps in to agree with me. It is almost as though he had been thinking the same thing, but the topic was too sensitive for him to broach. Once I broke the ice, perhaps, he felt able to chime in with support.

The men all agree to ask for soldiers from another province. If they had gone ahead and sent the soldiers and police from Herat into Zir Koh there was a good chance that the fighting would have escalated. It seems I have helped to avert that. So far, the meeting is going surprisingly well.

Next on my list is to get their support for my plan to undertake a verification mission to Zir Koh valley. This is part of my normal job as human rights officer; I meet victims in order to verify and document their account of the events. In particular, I want to find out if it is true that the fighters have killed children and unarmed adults.

"If the rumors are untrue," I argue, "and if they are allowed to persist without any independent verification, this will only continue to fuel the conflict. The best thing I can do to help you bring an end to the escalating cycle of violence would be to go down there myself and carry out an independent investigation."

As Abdul-Rahim translates my arguments, I watch the faces of the men who have the power to make it either easy or almost impossible for me to do my job. They are listening intently and as the governor responds in Dari the others are nodding. I feel hopeful. But when I hear the translation, it is not the response I was hoping for.

"Yes," Abdul-Rahim explains, "they all agree that an independent investigation should be carried out as soon as possible. But for now it is simply too dangerous."

Damn. I'm frustrated that I won't be able to get down there and do my job, my real job that is, as a human rights officer. Abdul-Rahim translates the governor's explanation.

"We are concerned about rumors circulating in Shindand alleging that the U.S. military were behind the assassination. The rumor is that the United States wanted to create a violent conflict between these two tribes so that they would have an excuse to send soldiers into their villages and conduct house searches."

Thanks to Asif, I know the background to these rumors: the U.S. Special Forces believe that the Noorzai in Zir Koh valley have relations with the Taliban. I don't know if that is true, but it makes sense that the Special Forces would make the most of any opportunity to get into these villages and have a good look around. Whether or not they would be willing to assassinate Amanullah Khan in order to create that opportunity is a matter that can only be speculated on.

Whether they are true or not, these rumors will be inflaming anti-U.S. sentiments in the valley. Although I am not American, I am a foreigner, and that makes it especially dangerous for me to travel there at the moment. As badly as I want to get to Shindand and into the Zir Koh valley, I understand it is not a good time for a foreigner in a large white 4x4 to turn up in the district. We agree to revisit plans for a verification mission later in the week.

The meeting ends with a review of our respective action plans. The governor is going to talk to the president about getting a high-level delegation of Noorzai and Barakzai leaders from Kabul to come to Shindand and talk to both sides. This is exactly the plan Talatbek proposed to me so I'm happy to support it. For my part, I will ask the SRSG to have a quiet word with President Karzai extolling the virtues of this approach. I am fairly confident that he will be happy to do this. I also agree to call a meeting of all the UN agencies that can help with a humanitarian response to the crisis. The biggest ones here in Herat are UNICEF and UNHCR. They have their own warehouses in Herat with emergency response kits containing everything from tents to cooking oil, baby blankets to plastic buckets, and are best placed for fast responses to local emergencies. The governor has received unverified reports that Barakzai families have fled the fighting in their villages without food, clothing, shelter or fuel. The UN agencies will need to verify these reports and then put together a plan to get emergency supplies to the families in need.

It is early evening by the time I get back to my guesthouse. First thing, I call the heads of all the UN agencies in Herat and invite them to an emergency response meeting at our compound in the morning. They all agree, readily, and I hang up the phone feeling satisfied I'm finally taking the kind of action that will help people affected by this fighting.

Because all my international colleagues are out of the country, the house is empty, dark and cold. Despite being happy with the outcome of the meeting, I am tense and jittery. Without realizing it, I've been holding my jaw, shoulders and belly tight all day. My instinctive response to the stress and adrenaline is to want to run it off.

I consider going over to the UNHCR guesthouse to use their treadmill. That would involve calling for a car and driver who would then have to sit in the UNHCR guardhouse drinking tea while I run. Even though I'm fully entitled to do so, I still feel weird about calling a driver for a personal errand; more so when tensions are running high in the city, meaning it may not be safe to be out. Instead I run on the spot and do jumping jacks in the hallway.

During my six months in Kabul I came to appreciate yoga much more; it has become a reliable way for me to release tension. So once my halfhearted aerobic efforts have warmed me up enough, I do a few yoga poses to stretch out the tight muscles in my back and shoulders, and even take a few deep breaths. By the time I'm done, my belly is no longer twisted from anxiety and I feel ready to eat.

I heat up some lentil soup for dinner and pour myself a glass of red wine. I want to celebrate this afternoon's small but significant success, and a glass of wine seems a suitable way to do so. Wine is not easy to come by in Herat; this bottle came from the Italian army base where it is possible to buy wine and salami *only* if your name is on a special list maintained by a rapidly rotating civilian–military liaison officer. My name is not yet on that list and my Italian housemate left this bottle for me before she went on holiday. I pour a glass, toast myself for surviving the day and think of Joel. I'd much rather be sharing this wine with him. If I could, I would call him, but he just finished his contract in Kabul and is in Alaska with his brother, out of cell phone coverage. So instead, I drink alone, determined to enjoy every mouthful.

The enjoyment doesn't last long, however. The more I think about the events of the day the more agitated I feel. I'm wondering what the point is of the enormous presence of the international community in

Afghanistan if we can't even prevent a fatal conflict between two local tribes. And our presence really is enormous. The civilians, like me, are only the tip of the iceberg. I'm really struggling to get my head around all the different kinds of international military forces in this country. What are they all doing and, for that matter, what good are they if they can't protect a village from this kind of attack?

The International Security Assistance Forces (ISAF) have tens of thousands of soldiers spread across Afghanistan. Many of them are based in units called Provincial Reconstruction Teams (PRTs), a controversial and experimental model used in Afghanistan to combine security-related activities (like patrolling) with reconstruction activities (like rebuilding bridges and schools). These soldiers are not UN peacekeepers. They each wear the uniform of their home country and, although they come under an overall ISAF command, each PRT is led by a commander from its own nation.

In 2006, a massive transition is taking place in Afghanistan. The previously separate Coalition Forces—a U.S.-led military "coalition of the willing" that entered Afghanistan in 2001 with the express intent to topple the Taliban and capture Osama bin Laden—are being brought into the ISAF fold. Unlike the Coalition Forces, the ISAF were invited into Afghanistan by the democratically elected government of Afghanistan and under a United Nations mandate. ISAF's job is to support the Afghan government to secure the country against the "insurgency"—a term used to describe a wide range of antigovernmental military and paramilitary activities ranging from rocket attacks on police stations to roadside bombs. These activities are by no means exclusively carried out by the Taliban, but the group is certainly one of the biggest players.

Even as the Coalition Forces come into the ISAF fold, U.S. Special Forces continue to operate in Afghanistan outside the ISAF mandate. The U.S. forces rumored to have been behind the murder of Amanullah

Khan, for example, have nothing to do with the ISAF forces based in Herat who are under a regional Italian command.

I'm getting confused just thinking about it all. I'd give up trying to make sense of it, if it weren't for the fact that part of my job is to monitor whether the international military forces in Afghanistan are acting in accordance with international humanitarian law, the rules of war. So I have to get my head around these different military configurations quickly.

At 11:00 p.m. I get a call from Chris, the head of the political wing of UNAMA. I know Chris fairly well from my days in Kabul because I was friends with his girlfriend. He's young—not much older than I am—and incredibly sharp, almost frighteningly so. I'm used to being able to keep up, mentally, with most people I meet, but I hold no illusions about being able to keep up with Chris.

Over the Eid holiday, while the SRSG is out of the country, Chris is the acting head of mission. Like me, he is covering for his boss. Unlike me, however, he is well prepared for his temporary additional responsibility and has a long list of questions for me about developments in the conflict. Chris seems able to keep vast quantities of complex information in his head and talks intelligently with me about the details and players in this local conflict, in spite of the fact that he is responsible for the whole country. His competence only serves to further highlight my inexperience.

I answer his questions as well as I can, repeating what I've learned from my colleagues that afternoon and adding in the new developments from my meeting with the governor. I tell him about the rumors of Ismail Khan's involvement and about the allegations that the U.S. military might be behind Amanullah Khan's murder. Chris is not surprised; much of the background to this conflict was already familiar to him. I tell him about my plans for the emergency meeting with all the UN agencies in the morning.

"The governor asked me to ask if you would speak to President Karzai about sending a delegation of Noorzai and Barakzai elders to Shindand," I say. "He thinks a traditional conflict resolution council could help. The chief of police and the army chief agree."

"Of course," he says, "I'm happy to talk to the president. You're doing a great job, Marianne."

"To be honest," I reply, "it doesn't feel like it. There are so many of us here, and still we couldn't prevent this fighting. Nothing I can do now feels like enough to make up for that. All this money is spent having us here, and yet we couldn't even save the lives of those children in Zir Koh. I don't know what more I should be doing, but I don't feel that I'm doing enough."

My exhaustion and frustration are showing and my voice quavers. I don't know what I expect him to say in response. Perhaps I think he will reassure me that I'm not alone in my sense of despair. Perhaps I hope he will tell me what more we can do.

"What you have to remember, Marianne," he says, "is that more people in Afghanistan are killed in tribal conflicts than in the insurgency. These men are fighters. They're warriors. They live by the sword and they die by the sword. It's been happening since long before we came here and there is very little we can do to change it."

I like and respect Chris, so his comments, which seem callous and cynical to me at the time, shock me. I don't say so, though, because even in my disappointment I can see he is trying to reassure me.

When I hang up the phone I pour myself another glass of wine. Unlike the first, this is not celebratory. I'm turning to wine in the hope it'll take the edge off my anxiety and help me unwind enough to sleep. This isn't unusual for aid workers—or office workers for that matter— but for someone as disciplined as me, it's a sign my usual coping tools are failing me.

I pull out my laptop and type as I drink, barely tasting the wine.

I finish the report well after midnight. I'm exhausted and expect to collapse into a deep sleep as soon as my head hits the pillow, but unsettling thoughts won't leave my mind. I'm beginning to question the worth of our mission. If we can't actually prevent fighting, if our only purpose is to show up after the event and document the fatalities, then can we really justify the expense of being here? When I took on this job I believed our presence could actually protect people. But within months of taking up my post I am having a crisis of faith in my role, which is also my life mission. Am I actually helping anyone, or am I nothing more than the ambulance at the bottom of the cliff?

Maybe the nature of the UN's work in Afghanistan is shifting. The mission was established to support and assist in the reconstruction of a democratic and peaceful Afghanistan. That was what I signed on for. But the fighting in Afghanistan is intensifying rather than lessening, which places our mandate under pressure. Our mandate calls on us to support peaceful resolution of conflicts. Yet one of the most senior members of the mission had just told me that there is little we can do to prevent violence. While my report sets out what I know about the events of the day, what seems more important to me now is what I no longer know. Is it even possible to build peace in Afghanistan? Can we offer any kind of protection to civilians?

These questions gnaw at me as I try to sleep. I wish, not for the first time, that I were not so utterly alone. I think again of Joel, but he's still out of reach in Alaska.

5
Joel

Joel arrived in Afghanistan two weeks after me. He was the new research intern at the organization I was working for in Kabul. He had recently graduated with a master's in conflict resolution from Portland State University in Oregon. I had an idea of the kind of man who would go to PSU to study conflict resolution. So when I went to the airport to meet Joel I knew what to look for: a slim, androgynous vegan with thick-rimmed glasses, a floppy fringe and an ironically retro T-shirt.

What I didn't know was that Joel's father was in the military and that Joel had come of age working on oil rigs off the coast of Alaska. When he emerged from the crowd milling around the airport exit he was tall and muscular, sporting a buzz cut, decidedly unhip Levi's 501s and workboots. Androgynous hipster he was not.

Joel and I were the only two non-Afghans at the office, and we spent all our days together, our desks pushed up against each other in the small room we shared with our four Afghan colleagues. We very quickly became close friends. Joel was the most constant presence in my life during those early, turbulent weeks in Kabul. Whenever I was nervous—and there were plenty of opportunities to be nervous—he was reassuring. When I lost confidence in my ability to do the job, Joel was my cheerleader. When I was frustrated he would make me laugh, and even when his teasing cut a little close to the bone I was grateful for the reminder not to take myself too seriously.

We spent most of our nonwork hours together as well. We lived in different guesthouses, but they were just around the corner from each other. After work most days we would have the office driver drop us off at a UN guesthouse where there was a small gym in the basement. Joel would pump iron while I ran on the treadmill. Once I had run far enough to feel the tension leave my body I'd go over to the yoga mats next to where Joel was working out, and as I stretched we'd talk over the day. Then we would walk home together. We weren't really supposed to walk at all but Joel would walk on the street side of the footpath, where there was a path, providing me with a reassuring sense of being protected. In retrospect I realize how vulnerable and afraid I felt much of the time during those early weeks in Kabul. With Joel, I felt less afraid.

Once we got back to my house, Joel would often stay and cook for us. Before coming to Afghanistan, I had been a keen cook and was known for hosting fabulous dinner parties. It was a novelty to have someone else cook for me, and I was happy to just sit in the kitchen and talk. After dinner we'd watch *The Daily Show* and *The Colbert Report*. Joel was a big fan and, though I didn't always understand what they were talking about, I promptly fell in love with Jon Stewart and Stephen Colbert. From where I was sitting, in Kabul, their lampoons of U.S. politics and foreign affairs seemed like the only sane thing on television.

The first week after his arrival in Afghanistan, Joel and I set off with our Afghan colleagues on a road trip to Gardez, in the southeast of Afghanistan. We were planning to do some field research on the right to education. As it turned out, we only made it as far as the mountain pass between Kabul and Gardez. It began snowing heavily and, despite the snowchains Joel and our driver attached to our wheels, we lost grip and slid off the road. It was dangerously cold, and one of our colleagues was eight months pregnant. Fortunately a truck stopped and helped to pull our vehicle back up onto the road.

We decided to turn back to Kabul. On the ride back Joel and I were squeezed together in the backseat and I was very aware of the heat that spread through my body where it touched his.

Despite the physical attraction, and though I was grateful for Joel's friendship and for the sense of security that his presence brought me, there was a toughness in him that I was instinctively wary of. As tender as he was capable of being with children, animals and me in my vulnerable moments, I saw the way he hardened against his own perceived weaknesses, and some part of me wondered whether he would eventually respond to me in the same way. But Afghanistan—and the isolation of life as an aid worker—has a way of shouting down our inner warning systems.

After we had been working together in Kabul for three months, Joel and I planned a trip to Pakistan together. We needed a holiday, a break from the constant tension that comes with living in Kabul. Before we left we made a trek to the U.S.-run hospital in Kabul to stock up on insulin for Joel, who is diabetic. We then headed off on our long weekend getaway in Islamabad to visit a friend of mine, Imogen, who was working there with the UN on the response to the big Pakistan earthquake of 2005.

Imogen and I had met in Gaza when we were both working for local human rights organizations. She was a fellow Kiwi, and in the years between Gaza and Islamabad we had spent short stretches of time in New Zealand together. She had become one of my dearest friends, and I was longing for her company after those challenging early months in Kabul.

Soon after we arrived in Islamabad, Joel got what seemed to be food poisoning. This was so common among foreigners in Kabul that we initially thought nothing of it. But after it had been going on for twenty-four hours, I began to wonder why he was vomiting but had no diarrhea, which generally comes with food poisoning. I suggested that we go to the doctor but Joel refused, insisting he would be fine. I trusted his judgment.

By the next morning, however, he was still sick and Imogen and I were both concerned. I looked up Joel's symptoms on the internet, and the first hit I got was for diabetic hypoglycemia, which, if left untreated, could be extremely dangerous and even fatal. I didn't need to look any further. It was clear the insulin we bought in Kabul wasn't working.

By now Joel was so weak that he stopped resisting our efforts to get him to a doctor. Imogen's landlords volunteered their car and their son drove us to the emergency doctor. The doctor took only a few moments to decide that Joel was indeed experiencing severe diabetic hypoglycemia. He called for an ambulance to get us to the hospital as quickly as possible. By the time we arrived at the ER, Joel was drifting in and out of consciousness. The hospital staff told us that he was in a state of advanced diabetic ketoacidosis and that his life was at risk. They needed to know what type of insulin Joel usually took. I didn't know and was terrified my ignorance might mean they couldn't help him. Joel roused himself out of his diabetic coma long enough to give them the details they needed before passing out again.

As the emergency room staff got to work, there was nothing more for me to do but pace anxiously. Imogen dragged me out onto the steps of the hospital to take a few deep breaths. Eventually she had to go home to sleep so that she could get back to work the next day.

After a few hours they moved Joel to the intensive care unit. Although he was now stable, his condition was still serious and they needed to keep him under close observation. But before they could move him they needed a family member to fill out all the required forms and asked me if I was related to Joel. If I said no, then presumably Joel wouldn't be admitted to the ICU.

"Yes, ma'am," I told the receptionist, "I am his wife." I hoped that, as Joel's fake wife, I would be allowed to stay close to him and the doctors would tell me what was going on.

That night I slept on the floor of the ICU waiting room. Well, I didn't exactly sleep—the fluorescent lights stayed on all night and the floor was cold and hard. But I rested, I breathed deeply and I ran through a body relaxation practice that I had learned at yoga. It helped keep my mind from racing away with the frightening possibilities that might yet befall Joel.

Joel was in the hospital for three days. I spent as much time as I could there with him. As his condition improved I told him about my fake wife status. To my relief he understood, and even found it funny.

Once Joel was well enough to take control of his own treatment, I stepped back, but the emotional impact of the experience didn't fade quickly. If it hadn't already seemed inevitable we would end up together, it certainly did now. I was still doing my best to ignore all the signs, but Imogen wasn't about to let me get away with that. The night before Joel and I were due to fly back to Kabul, she and I were lying together in the double bed we had been sharing throughout my visit.

"What's up with you and Joel?" she asked. Like many New Zealanders, Immy has a fabulously straightforward way of getting to the point. I did my best to divert her.

"We are great friends," I said. "He's my closest friend in Kabul."

"He's more than that," Immy said. "He obviously adores you. When you guys arrived my impression was that he was smitten, but you were only interested in being friends. But after watching you the past few days I'm not so sure anymore."

Damn girlfriends. They see too much.

"Well," I stalled, "there is chemistry between us. But I don't know. There's something keeping me back. Maybe it's because I'm officially his supervisor at work, so nothing can come of it. Anyway, I need his friendship. I have so few real friends in Kabul that I can't risk messing with this one. If we went for the romance and it didn't work out, then I'd be even more alone. I can't afford to lose him as a friend."

"Sweetheart"—Immy smiled at me—"I know how lonely it is. God help me, I know. But this 'friendship' is already changing whether you like it or not. That's what happens when you take two people who are attracted to each other and throw them together for twenty-four hours a day in the pressure cooker of a war zone. You two are going to end up in bed together one way or another. I think you should go and talk to Joel, now, about how and when you want that to happen."

"I will," I promised, hoping it would get her to shut up. "I'll talk to him tomorrow."

"No, not tomorrow. You need to talk to him now."

I knew she was right. If I didn't make use of the momentum of Immy's prodding, I might never gather up the courage to talk to Joel about this.

It was late and Joel was already in bed in the spare room. I knocked on the door, and he called for me to come in. I walked over and sat on his bed.

"I don't know how to start this conversation," I said, "but I think we have to talk about where things are going between us." I stopped, grateful that it was too dark to see Joel's reaction. I took a deep breath and went on. "I'm attracted to you, and I think maybe you feel the same way." I took another deep breath and willed my heart to slow down.

"Lie down," he said, patting the bed beside him.

I lay down beside him and he put his arm around my shoulders. A feeling of safety and ease came over me.

"I already know how I feel about you," Joel said. "I want to be with you."

I let out the breath I didn't realize I'd been holding, and felt a wave of relief relax my jaw and shoulders.

"But these have been a pretty intense few days," he continued, "and I think you should give yourself time to see how you feel. If it turns out that you really do want to be with me, I'll be very happy. But I want you to be sure it's not just a reaction to seeing me sick and taking care of me. Let's give it a week, get back to Kabul, settle back into our normal routines and then see how you feel."

I didn't know what to say. I was happy to know for sure that he wanted to be with me, but at the same time I felt let down, by his response. I would have preferred a great, passionate scene in which we declared our irresistible attraction to each other. It seemed wrong, somehow, that Joel was able to contain his feelings for me so well. Perhaps this was related to the toughness I'd sensed in him before, a way of controlling his emotions that made him seem almost cold. Then again, I do have a tendency to be impetuous. Joel was probably right. I agreed to wait.

A week later, true to his word, Joel took me out to a Chinese restaurant in Kabul for lunch and to talk about how I felt. I told him that my feelings hadn't changed. I was sure that I wanted to be with him. Both of our jobs were about to change so I would no longer be his direct supervisor. Nothing was standing in our way; we were free to leap into a romance in Kabul.

❖ ❖ ❖

Six months after I had arrived in Afghanistan, my contract in Kabul ended. By then I had fallen in love with Joel and with Afghanistan. Neither had been love at first sight; it had taken time for me to embrace both the country and the man. Once I did so, however, there was no going back. The life I had carefully laid out for myself to return to in

New Zealand no longer compelled me. I wanted to stay in Afghanistan and I wanted to stay with Joel.

I had an offer of a job in Kabul. It was a great job with a research organization doing really interesting work on human rights issues. I could have stayed on in Kabul with the friends I had made over the previous six months. It was the obvious and easy option.

My other offer was the job as human rights officer with the UN mission. Ever since I'd been old enough to understand what the United Nations was and what it did, I'd imagined myself working for the organization one day. As my human rights career had developed, I had started applying for positions in the UN. I must have applied for more than twenty different posts, only once ever getting an interview. Now, I found myself in Kabul with an offer to take up the position I'd wanted for so long.

I had high expectations for this job: it would be my chance to get out into the community. Human rights officers in the UN mission didn't just sit in their offices writing policy reports, they were out there in the prisons and police cells across Afghanistan documenting violations of human rights, and convincing police officers and prison officials not to torture their detainees. They helped monitor and document the activities of the international military forces in Afghanistan. They were the watchdogs who made sure that American planes didn't bomb civilian villages or, if they did, that they were held accountable for it. The UN mission had a level of power and influence that nongovernmental organizations (NGOs), like the ones I had worked for in the past, could only dream about. In a job like this, I would actually be able to make a difference to the lives of ordinary Afghans.

The only problem was that the UN couldn't tell me where I would be based until after I had accepted. I might be stationed in Kabul, but I could also be in any one of the other eight regional offices across Afghanistan.

Joel and I talked about the options. He understood how long and hard I had worked to get this offer. He encouraged me to take the UN job. "Once we know where you are going to be based," he said, "I can start applying for jobs in that region as well."

It sounded easy, but the truth was that it would depend a lot on where I was posted. If I were to be posted in Kabul, Joel would have no trouble getting work. But if I were posted in one of the smaller or more remote offices, there was no guarantee that he would be able to find a job. I would be taking the risk that we would be separated for a significant amount of time. We had only been together for a few months and I wasn't sure whether our fledgling relationship would survive a lengthy separation.

On the other hand, my romantic history to date had taught me to be wary of placing too much value on a relationship. My work had generally been a more reliable source of fulfillment and passion than my boyfriends. I decided to accept the UN job.

Then began the process of becoming a part of the massive administrative system that runs the UN peacekeeping missions around the world. A week before I was due to be deployed to my new position they announced my new duty station: Herat. This was a huge relief. After Kabul, Herat was one of the largest centers for international civilian workers in Afghanistan. Of all the places I could have been sent to outside Kabul, Herat offered perhaps the best chance for Joel to find work.

As I set off for Herat, Joel finished his contract in Kabul and headed home to the United States to begin his search for jobs in Herat. I was hopeful that he would be able to join me before too long.

Now, less than two months after arriving in Herat, the good news is that Joel has found a job here and should be on his way by the end of the week. The bad news is that, in the meantime, I won't be able to get hold of him. So I do what I have done for many years as a single woman: I get on with the job.

6
No Reinforcements

Monday, October 23, 2006: Herat, Afghanistan

I spend most of Monday morning meeting with the heads of the UN agencies in Herat to discuss delivery of emergency supplies into the affected area. We need to get food, shelter, fuel and water to the families that have fled the fighting. This might sound like a simple process. In reality, however, delivery of humanitarian aid after a disaster is always a complex affair, even more so when the disaster is man-made and the conflict is still simmering. For one thing, unscrupulous or desperate people can use the state of emergency to their own ends. Public officials may inflate numbers of people in need in order to attract additional assistance to their area. Local leaders may skew the numbers in favor of their own tribe or village. Knowing this, the UN agencies I work with are unwilling to release our supplies until we are able to confirm the numbers ourselves.

We hear reports that hundreds of people have fled the fighting, most of them making their way to Shindand district center. Some are injured and others are sick after walking for many hours through the cold night. Most have taken refuge with relatives, but even they are in no position to feed or house them for long. They have fled without bedding or blankets. In late October, winter is on its way and these families are suffering. Winters in Afghanistan are bitterly cold, with heavy snow and bone-chilling winds. In addition, Afghanistan is in the grip of a deadly food shortage and if we don't get emergency food supplies to Shindand soon, the host families might begin to suffer as well as those who were displaced.

I'm still trying to get clearance to visit Shindand myself. Apart from confirming how many people were displaced and what they urgently need, which would normally be the responsibility of my absent humanitarian affairs colleagues, I want to get on with my own human rights work. For now, though, the governor advises me that it is not yet safe to travel to Shindand. A misguided sense of bravery on my part could put my Afghan colleagues in danger, so I accept his advice and stay put. It seems the assessment of the need for emergency assistance will have to be done by local officials in the area.

This approach carries a higher risk that the numbers could be distorted, but a much lower risk of provoking further conflict or loss of life. I think it is a fair trade-off. All the UN agencies accept this solution for the short term, but it remains clear that we need to get UN staff into the area as soon as possible.

Apart from me, the only remaining international staff in our office are the military liaison officer and the security officer. This is fortunate because although I have some idea of what I should be doing about political, human rights and humanitarian efforts, I'm less sure when it comes to the military.

The rapid rotation of international military personnel in Afghanistan—and the effect this has on our ability to coordinate efficient responses to emergency situations like the one in Shindand—is currently the subject of considerable debate. In my opinion, rapid turnover makes sense for combat fighting but becomes problematic when the military chooses, as it does in Afghanistan, to get involved in relief, reconstruction and development work.

Staff turnover isn't the only problem with the military getting involved in reconstruction and development work. Another big concern is the blurring of the line between humanitarian and military personnel. Civilian humanitarian personnel in Afghanistan include people like myself, working with the United Nations, but also hundreds of people working with not-for-profit development and aid organizations. Traditionally, in a conflict zone, there has been a distinction between the kind of work civilians do, like building schools and running livelihood training projects, and the kind of work the military does, like security patrols and searching for "enemy" fighters.

The lines have probably always been a bit blurred, but in Afghanistan, increasing forays by the military into what were traditionally civilian activities are blurring them to a point that endangers civilian lives. When a group of fighters (in this case, usually, the Taliban) can't be clear about the difference between military and civilian activities, the risks increase considerably that civilian aid and development workers will be targeted.

In Afghanistan, humanitarian aid has been explicitly used by the international military as a tool of war—to "win the hearts and minds" of the local population in support of their troops. So it was inevitable that all humanitarian work is now suspected of being a tool in the hands of the international military. By straying into "our" humanitarian territory, the military has effectively tarred us all with the same brush in the eyes of the insurgents. The Taliban have already announced that they consider civilian aid workers legitimate targets because our work is "associated" with the military. Our status as humanitarian actors no longer affords us protection. There haven't yet been any proven direct attacks by the Taliban on UN targets but the consensus is that it's a matter of when, not if, this will happen. And Afghan aid workers are at much greater risk than internationals. They are being attacked and killed in Afghanistan at an alarming rate.

As concerned as I am to find out what is really going on for those fleeing the fighting, I will not place my colleagues at any kind of unnecessary risk. I resent the way that the international military presence in Afghanistan is making it more dangerous and difficult for international or Afghan civilians to help protect and serve those most directly affected by the fighting.

The ISAF in the western region of Afghanistan are under Italian command. We continue to receive reports of movements of armed men in Zir Koh valley. As long as the conflict is active, our office needs to be talking to the commander of the Italian forces every hour. Local Afghan security officials are calling on him to send international forces and aircraft into the Zir Koh. I'm not keen on the idea. Given the rumors flying in Zir Koh about an American hand in Amanullah Khan's murder, I worry that sending in international troops will further escalate the violence. So I am hoping to convince the Italian commander not to send his soldiers.

My contact point with the Italian base is through our own military liaison officer, a lieutenant colonel in the Uruguayan army. On Monday afternoon we travel together out to the Italian army base to talk about the fighting in Shindand. Much to my colleague's disgust, the commander doesn't meet us himself but instead sends several Italian officers who, while quite senior, are still well below our military liaison officer's rank. Although the lieutenant colonel never comes out and says it, from his snide remarks I deduce he is also less than thrilled about taking direction from me. I understand his discomfort. As a military man it must be galling to report to a civilian in the first place, let alone a young female civilian. I'm not exactly comfortable with it either. He is not only older than me and considerably more experienced in warfare, he is also willing to show his disdain for my lack of experience in front of our local colleagues. I feel more undermined by him than supported. But we are both part of a civilian UN mission and only a civilian can be the officer in charge. That means me.

✸ ✸ ✸

Monday ends and I decide I need to start the next day with some yoga. In Kabul I had found a group who practiced yoga together twice a week, and it became a lifeline for me. There is something about yoga that helped me find a place of calmness and stability even in the midst of the chaos of life in Afghanistan. So I roll out my mat beside my bed, ready for the morning. I set my alarm to be sure I have plenty of time.

Before the alarm sounds on Tuesday morning, I am woken by a phone call. It's Joel, calling from Alaska to say that there are problems with his medical clearance for his new job in Herat. If the clearance doesn't come through, we'll be back to square one: him looking for another job and me not knowing when he'll get here. I feel myself crumple at the thought.

For the past forty-eight hours, since Amanullah Khan's murder, I've been comforting myself with the knowledge that Joel will soon be joining me. I feel sure that once Joel is here, I will get through this crisis. Six months might seem a short time in which to form such a close connection, but we had both left our friends, family and all that was familiar to us behind when we came to Kabul. Joel had filled the void left by my entire social circle. I need him and he was meant to be on his way.

When I get off the phone, feeling sorry for myself, there is my yoga mat, where I put it the night before. I sit down on my mat. I really don't feel like doing yoga but I know it will help so I decide to start with some simple breathing exercises. After a few minutes of deep breathing and a few rounds of sun salutes I feel noticeably calmer and ready to start the day.

At the office I receive a report of violence in Herat. A group of families affiliated with Amanullah Khan fled Shindand and arrived in the outskirts of Herat, not far from our office. Apparently, Herat-based supporters of Ismail Khan are attacking them. If this is true, things are getting much worse. It means the crisis in Shindand is spreading to Herat and I'm in a heap of trouble. We all are.

Before I have time to find out whether the reports are true, I get a call from the chief of police. He is concerned and wants me to enlist the support of ISAF troops to help him stem the tide of violence. There is a part of me that is ready to panic—my fight or flight mechanism is kicking in. But I'm also beginning to understand that times of conflict give rise to countless rumors and the seed of a true story can rapidly grow into something unrecognizable. Before I do anything else, I need to find out what is really happening. I take a moment to breathe deeply and bring my body and mind back to calmness.

I call a meeting of everyone in the office. I ask our senior security adviser and the military liaison officer to find out everything they can about the reported fighting through their police and military contacts. In response, and in front of all the other staff, the Uruguayan lieutenant colonel tells me not to panic. I know he wouldn't have spoken that way if I were a man and I feel my pulse quicken in anger. I say nothing and continue with the meeting, asking each staff member to gather as much information as they can about the supposed fighting in Herat. As I close the meeting I ask to have a word with the military liaison officer. With some effort I keep my voice calm.

"Please don't speak to me that way again."

"What way?"

"It was inappropriate and condescending of you to tell me not to panic. Given the circumstances, I think I am doing a good job of staying calm. I'm not panicking; I'm gathering more information. So as well as being condescending your comment was redundant."

The satisfaction I derive from my eloquent response to his provocation lasts all of about three seconds.

"I don't understand these words," he responds. "What is 'condescending'? What is 'redundant'?"

By the time I explain what I mean, the point of the discussion is lost. I'm still furious but I'm ready to move on.

Reports start trickling in, and to my relief, it seems the fighting in our neighborhood is an unrelated and minor scuffle rather than a new phase of the Shindand conflict. I'm able to advise the Italian colonel that UNAMA doesn't think it will be necessary for him to send any troops in to support the Afghan security forces. I am able to tell our staff that it is safe for them to leave the compound and head home to their families to continue their celebrations of the Eid holiday. I can even head home myself.

After work I get dropped at the guesthouse of the UN refugee agency to use their treadmill. I run for about an hour, imagining myself running around the waterfront in Wellington. In my mind's eye I escape the gray concrete walls of the room and tread a familiar path past rugged, windswept beaches where hardy surfers brave the bracing waters of Wellington's south coast.

After my run I call another car and get dropped back at my house, where I shower and head into the kitchen to see what our cook, Parwaiz, has prepared for me. Although I would be happy to cook for myself, some of my housemates have never prepared their own meals. My Sudanese colleague tells me that he can, in fact, cook, but he's never had to because ever since leaving his parents' home he has lived either in a university hall of residence or a UN guesthouse. Even if we were all keen cooks, we wouldn't be encouraged, for security reasons, to do our own shopping at the market. Parwaiz does all our shopping and prepares a cooked meal every evening. I often return late from the office, so it's a luxury I have come to appreciate; and I'm always touched by the effort Parwaiz makes to prepare special dishes that suit my vegetarian diet.

While I have the house to myself during the Eid holiday, I prefer to eat my dinner up in my room where I can listen to my own music or watch a DVD on my laptop. The more frantic and stressful my day is, the more likely I am to want to watch mindless comedy. Fortunately I have a boxed set of the TV series *Scrubs* that fits the bill perfectly.

As I unwind with *Scrubs*, I remind myself that I've survived many crises before, and that things often turned out to not be as bad as first reports suggested. Just a few months ago, Joel and I survived big anti-foreigner riots in Kabul together. The riots were sparked after a foreign military convoy hit a local vehicle. Crowds of angry bystanders gathered around the convoy and the soldiers fired into the crowd, killing several people. The city erupted. Hundreds, maybe thousands, of young Afghan men stormed the streets, finding an outlet for the frustration and anger they must have felt at the constant presence of foreign military in their streets, and the failure of the international community to make any palpable difference to their lives. They targeted places where internationals were known to live or work.

At the time, Joel and I were housesitting for a friend who, though American, was born and raised in Afghanistan. Her close relationship with her neighbors may have saved us. We spent two tense days confined to the house, watching plumes of smoke rise up from buildings in our neighborhood and listening to gunfire. The mobile phone network was completely overloaded, so we couldn't call friends or colleagues to find out if they were okay, or even to find out what was going on.

Eventually, as we had feared, we heard the cries of a mob in our street. The shouting got closer and then we heard them pounding against our wooden gate. Someone obviously knew or guessed that there were foreigners living in the house. I was terrified. What if they got in? Would they kill us? Burn the house down?

Our gardener, a man in his sixties who had worked with our host's family for decades, was trying to hold the gate closed and yelling at the protestors to leave the house alone. He told them there were no foreigners in the house, only his own wife and children who were terrified by the mob. Fortunately for us, our neighbors came out of their homes to shout at the mob, insisting there were no foreigners in the house.

When the mob smashed a hole in the wooden gate, Murat, the gardener, yelled at us to hide in the back bedroom, telling Joel to open the window so we could escape out and over the back wall if we needed. But what would we find on the other side of the wall? More angry mobs? I hoped we wouldn't have to find out.

The house cleaner, who had also worked with the family for many years, came up with a plan to get me out safely. "You put on this burqa" she said holding out the blue covering that usually hung on a hook in the kitchen while she worked, "and once we get over the fence and into the street, you stay close to me and we will walk right through the mob to my house."

Her plan was reassuring, though I wasn't sure I'd be able to walk straight in a burqa. But the plan didn't account for Joel or the family dogs. I didn't want to leave them behind. Eventually, to my enormous relief, the pleas of our neighbors were heeded and the mob moved on.

It would be nice to have some company through this current crisis. But until Joel arrives, or my colleagues get back from their holiday, it's just me and the cast of *Scrubs*.

Somehow, with the help of *Scrubs*, some yoga, a giant box of chocolate and long runs on the treadmill, I make it through the rest of the week. I try repeatedly to get approval to undertake the human rights verification mission into Shindand. The situation remains unstable, however, and neither the Afghan security forces nor my superiors within the UN are willing to let me go yet. I'm still struggling with the feeling I failed the families affected by the fighting, especially the children I now know for sure were killed that day. I remain convinced that if I can only get there and talk to the women whose children were killed I will finally be doing something useful for them.

At 10:00 p.m. on Saturday I get a phone call about some demonstrations planned for Sunday in Badghis province, to the north of Herat. Tribal elders are protesting against the recent murders of government officials from their district. Like the situation in Shindand, this has the potential to explode into violence. I *really* don't want to be responsible for all of this anymore. I take a deep breath and remind myself that the boss is due back tomorrow morning and he will be able to take over again, leaving me to get on with my human rights work.

I should have known that fate wasn't going to let me off so lightly. The UN flight from Kabul to Heart on Sunday is canceled, so my boss can't return. Instead I have to deal with the ongoing fallout of the events in Shindand, as well as these new developments in Badghis. The tribal elders in Badghis are threatening that if the government doesn't take immediate action, they will take matters into their own hands "like they did in Shindand."

So I have to keep going. Initially I'm devastated by the news of my boss's canceled flight. I am exhausted by the week. And lonely. Still, there is nothing to be done but to get on with the job. To my surprise, some part of me is beginning to relish the challenge of extra responsibility. I'm enjoying the opportunity to learn so much, so quickly, about how our office and our mission operate. I would never have asked for this, yet I'm not sure I'd want it to be taken away now. I'm learning that I'm capable of more than I ever would have imagined.

Looking at the crises piling up before me, though, I wonder what the next day, the next week, will bring. I've signed on for at least six months of this. What on earth have I got myself into? Yes, part of me is thriving on the adrenaline, but a larger part is afraid I've overestimated myself. And now I wonder whether this job is about keeping peace and protecting civilians at all.

I end the week with a strange mixture of feelings: a growing sense of futility about the purpose and usefulness of my work, alongside a quiet excitement as I watch myself cope with challenges that only a week ago seemed well beyond me.

7
Get a Thicker Skin

November 10, 2006: Herat, Afghanistan

*T*wo weeks after Amanullah Khan was murdered, Joel finally gets his medical clearance and, soon after, arrives in Herat. When he lands, he is not met by the same optimistic, confident girlfriend he left in Kabul only two months earlier.

I held myself together under the pressure of those first few days after the assassination, but I'm not doing so well now. My fundamental beliefs and expectations about my job have been challenged and my own sense of confidence and purpose has been undermined. I'm no longer sure we are doing any good here. My colleagues have returned from their Eid holidays and when I confide to one of them that I'm having trouble letting go of the feeling that we failed to do enough to protect the children who died in the fighting in Shindand, she says the same things Raji said, all those years ago in Gaza.

"You need to get a thicker skin, Marianne. You can't let it get to you. We have a job to do and, yes, it's an important job, but you can't take it too seriously. Come drink Campari on the deck with me; forget about all that for the night."

If I knew how to get a thicker skin, believe me, I would. People have been telling me to since I was a child. The difference with Raji was that after our two years working together he decided my sensitivity was also my strength. Part of me believes that too, but another part believes I just need to toughen up, have a cocktail and get over myself.

It's easier said than done. Thoughts of those dead children stay with me and I feel deeply unsettled and constantly anxious. I'm having trouble sleeping. The less I sleep, the more anxious I feel. It's a downward spiral and I'm desperate to take hold of something solid. Joel is it.

Joel's boss, a young American woman, has come down from Kabul with him and will stay a couple of nights to help him settle. They have work to do, but she also knows Joel and I haven't seen each other for a while. When I arrive at Joel's new compound after work, she retreats to the spare room to give us time to catch up.

In Joel's bedroom, we talk about his new home. He is thrilled with his little cottage and assumes I'll move in with him immediately.

"I don't think I'll be able to move in here." It comes out before I think whether this is the right time. "It's UN security standards," I try to explain myself. "I have to live in a house with an armed guard and a safe room."

"But you can get around that," Joel says, unperturbed. We know plenty of UN staff in Kabul who live in houses that don't meet the minimum UN security standards.

"Herat is too small; we won't be able to get away with it here," I say. "But I have a nice room in the UNAMA guesthouse. You could move in with me."

"No way," he says, "I don't want to live in a shared guesthouse anymore. I finally have my own place for the first time in six months."

I feel tears coming. The safe place I had imagined would open up for me when Joel arrived is evaporating before my eyes. We won't be able to live together and suddenly that seems insurmountable.

I burst into tears.

"Don't cry," he says, "we can't solve this at the moment. I have my boss waiting for me. Let's just put this aside and agree to talk about it over the weekend."

I try to stop crying, but I can't. This is the first time I've cried since the day of Amanullah Khan's murder, and now that I've started I can't stop.

This is not how our reunion was supposed to go. Barely conscious of how much I've been relying on Joel's arrival to reassure *me*, I had planned to provide him with a warm and reassuring welcome to his new home. Instead, against my independent nature, I am clinging to Joel as though he is my life raft. He has barely put his own feet down in this new city, in his new job, and I'm asking him to be a solid place for me to stand. At the same time, I'm telling myself to get over it all. It seems unreasonable that this one incident in Shindand could have such a profound effect on me. Nobody else seems to be bothered. But I am. And now Joel is bearing the brunt of it.

"I don't know what's wrong with me," I say between sobs, "but it has been a tough couple of weeks. I'm sorry I'm such a mess. I haven't been sleeping much and I feel a bit desperate. It would help to have some kind of reassurance from you that I'm okay, that I'm not going crazy here."

Joel looks uncomfortable. His boss is still waiting in the other room. He also doesn't know what's wrong with me. We've had little contact over the past few weeks; he's been traveling and out of reach so I haven't told him much about what's been going on.

"We really need to go out there and have dinner," he says, looking a little pained. "Maybe we can talk more about this later."

"Okay," I agree reluctantly.

Although I'm desperate for a hug or a kind word, I recognize the careful control Joel maintains over his emotions and realize he is unwilling, perhaps even unable, to meet my messy confusion with empathy or warmth. We all have our own ways of dealing with the emotional challenges of this work. Joel's way seems to require that he never lose control of his feelings, so my unconstrained weeping must feel like dangerous territory. I send him out to talk with his boss while I take a few minutes to breathe deeply, and wash my face, slowly bringing myself back under control.

I do my best to appear professional over dinner with the boss, asking questions about their organization's child protection program, for which Joel is now responsible. I'm also responsible for child rights within our office, so at least Joel and I are going to be working together.

❖ ❖ ❖

A few days after Joel arrives, three weeks after Amanullah Khan's murder, I finally get clearance to travel to the town in Shindand where the women who fled the fighting are living with their surviving children. I'm worried about their well-being. As far as I know, they are without adequate shelter, food and medical care.

Together with my human rights assistant Amir and Mr. Popal, a colleague from the Afghan Independent Human Rights Commission, I travel to Shindand district center, about two hours from Herat city. The landscape is like much of the area surrounding Herat—long stretches of parched brown land broken by small villages of mud-brick compounds, located to take advantage of natural springs, rivers and wells. Each village is surrounded by a small ring of irrigated fields and trees and appears like an oasis in the otherwise arid land. Beyond the villages, the brown plains stretch for miles, dotted with green patches where villages seem to have grown out of the earth, their mud-brick structures so perfectly in harmony with the surrounding landscape.

Far away to the east, in the direction of Kabul, are the foothills of the great Hindu Kush mountain range. The lower reaches of the hills are also dotted with villages and I can just make out the trace of a road disappearing up into the mountains. Beyond the hills the Hindu Kush rise up out of the land, marking the beginning of an eight-hundred-kilometer mountain range stretching as far as northwestern Pakistan. I gaze at the mountains, and imagine following them all the way to the Himalayas, of which they are a subrange.

As we drive through the barren plains, far from any visible village, I see girls dressed in bright greens and reds taking their small herds of goats out to find food. Others are gathering up whatever greenery they can find, tying it up in huge bundles on the back of their donkeys and hauling it back to feed the animals at home. Women and children are gathering sticks and dried dung to use for fuel on their fires. A shortage of wood is driving them to pull out small desert shrubs by the roots, and their desperation is putting the precarious environmental balance into even greater jeopardy.

The town of Shindand is the administrative center for the district; it is much larger than any of the other villages we have passed on the way from Herat, but like them, it blends easily into the surrounding landscape. Unlike Herat or Kabul, the buildings in this provincial town are all made of mud-brick, and the roads are unpaved.

We enter through a main dirt road surrounded on either side by residential areas. A high mud wall surrounds each house, providing privacy and security to the family within. Each wall has a metal gate, often decorated with swirls or lattices of wrought metal, and painted in contrasting bright colors. These gates add a splash of color to a scene that is otherwise entirely dominated by the brown of the earth from which the road, homes and walls are constructed, and the mud that cakes the shoes and hems of the people walking in the street.

We pull up in front of the municipal offices, a modest building near the center of the town. We send our police escort away to the local police station for some tea and conversation, and make our way into the building where the district governor welcomes us and, unusually for Afghanistan, gets straight down to business.

The governor presents me with a list he has compiled of the people killed in the fighting. We will double-check the names and ages as part of our own investigation, but I have the impression he has done a thorough job. I scan the page quickly, reading down the column that lists the ages of those killed. It looks like twenty children were killed on the day of the clash. The thought of these murdered children has been haunting me for weeks. Now my ghosts have names.

On another page the governor has compiled the claims he has received for property damaged in the conflict. These families live on the very edge of survival. Most of them have no income at all and rely on their subsistence farming to feed themselves. If their wheat crop fails they will starve. Not only will they have no flour to make the naan bread that is their staple diet, they might also be without the seeds they need to plant next year's crop. For these families, getting compensation for a destroyed home or motorbike might be more urgent than seeking justice for the death of a husband or son.

"What will be the process for prosecuting those responsible for killing these children," I ask the governor, "and for getting compensation for the families that have lost their property?"

"The elders of the two tribes will probably agree on compensation as part of some kind of peace-building process," he explains. "Prosecution is more difficult. Any attempt to prosecute the gunmen for murder will interfere with the conciliation process."

I know, as a human rights lawyer, I am biased toward seeking "justice" through the formal legal system, and I am open to the possibility that this might not be what the victims here actually want. Before I'll agree to back off my investigation, however, I want to speak with the displaced mothers. This has become my focus in the weeks since the killings. I hope that by hearing from these women, by championing their cause, I can redeem and release myself from some of the guilt I feel over the deaths of their children.

This guilt isn't based on anything I've done. I didn't kill those boys. I didn't kill Amanullah Khan, beginning the chain of events that led to their deaths. The guilt isn't even really based on anything I have failed to do. I wasn't in a position to prevent the fighting and although I feel that other people in my office might have failed in their mission to keep peace in the area, I can't blame them for the deaths, either.

The guilt is almost existential. It's as though I feel guilty for being alive, when others are dead. I feel guilty for having a warm, safe home to return to every night while these women remain homeless. I feel guilty for what I cannot do, and for what I cannot *undo*, despite having no real personal influence over the situation. It is an irrational guilt, but that doesn't make it any less powerful. If I am completely honest with myself, I hope that this trip will give me a chance to redeem myself in my own eyes and ease the guilt that is keeping me awake at night.

One of the Barakzai elders comes to the governor's office and offers to take me to meet the women. He is a smallish man, shorter than me. He has chosen not to dye his beard and I admire its snowy whiteness. He wears a white shalwar kameez, covered by a gray polyester cardigan and a woolen waistcoat. His turban is white with gray stripes. This outfit, which is replicated in various tones of white, gray, brown and black on every man in the town, is as effortlessly elegant as it is practical and comfortable.

Given the ongoing security risk in the area, we have to be back in Herat before sunset so we need to complete all the interviews that day. I'm impatient to get started. Together with Amir and Mr. Popal, we set off to meet the first family.

8
Women of Shindand

November 14, 2006: Shindand, Afghanistan

After driving through Shindand's market—a depressing collection of half-empty stalls set up in salvaged shipping containers—we turn off the main street into a narrow mud alley and pull up alongside a green metal gate. When our guide, the elder, opens the metal gate, I expect to see a house. Instead, the courtyard is empty, apart from one small tree. The ground is thick with mud. In the center of the courtyard, squatting under the tree, is a small group of women and children.

One of the women stands up and walks over to us, acknowledging and welcoming her elder. As he presents us to her, she glances at me. Under her gaze I am suddenly painfully aware of my thick, padded coat and winter boots. In contrast, she is dressed in layers of thin cotton, with rubber clogs on her bare feet. I place my hand on my heart and greet her.

There are three women living in this courtyard, together with their fifteen children. All their clothes are covered in mud. There are no bathing facilities and the effort required to haul water from the nearest well makes it too precious to be wasted on baths. They fled the fighting in Zir Koh with only the clothes on their backs, so they haven't even been able to remove and clean their clothes.

The elder leads me over to the tree, where I squat down with the women to talk. The children hover around their mothers, watching me warily and listening to our conversation. One little girl, who can't be more than four or five years old, catches my attention with her striking head of spiky red hair. She stares back at me quizzically, one eyebrow shooting toward the sky. A small boy, perhaps three years old, decides I make a good audience and begins clowning around, dancing for me and pulling on the clothes and hair of the bigger children. Everyone laughs at his antics, including me, and the atmosphere relaxes considerably.

What we have to talk about, however, is not lighthearted. All three of these women's husbands were killed on the day of Amanullah Khan's assassination. Terrified, the women fled through the night with their children to seek safety in this muddy backyard.

They sleep here with their children in unsealed storage spaces built into the exterior walls of the compound. These small rooms were designed for storing food or fuel. In the weeks to come, winter will arrive in full force in Shindand. Temperatures will drop well below freezing and these families will need to find somewhere warmer to sleep before the snow arrives.

These women are young, probably still in their twenties, and their children are all too young to have been targeted as potential fighters. They have lost their husbands but not their sons. That is, however, small comfort to women who have no way to earn the money they need to feed and care for their children.

They each tell their stories, and Amir translates for me, describing how the Noorzai gunmen came to their village. Their husbands went out to defend the village. They were shot and killed while out fighting, not at home in front of their wives and children. Again, it was a small mercy, but one that makes a difference to my investigation. If you are actively engaged in fighting then you are not a civilian under humanitarian law and your death, though no less tragic for your family, is probably not a breach of international law. It is my job as a human rights lawyer to make the legal distinction in my report. It is plain, though, that these legalities are irrelevant in this muddy courtyard.

A part of me is in lawyer mode, asking increasingly detailed questions to ascertain exactly where and how their husbands were killed. Another part of me sees how much these women have suffered, and I start to feel uncomfortable with the job I am here to do. The questions I need to ask seem intrusive and unsympathetic in the face of their vulnerability and pain. Is this interrogation worth it? Whether their husbands were combatants or not makes no difference at all to these women's current plight. What they need now is practical help and the best I can do for them is to make a note of their immediate needs— food, fuel, blankets and tarpaulin—and make sure that humanitarian supplies reach them as soon as possible. At least I have something useful to offer these women. My lofty ideas about justice, human rights and accountability of perpetrators seem hollow in this empty courtyard.

We next visit a woman who has found refuge with relatives. At the urging of the tribal elder she comes out into the front yard to talk to me but shrinks away from my questions, looking to him to answer in her place. Several times I explain that I really need to hear her account of the events directly. The elder keeps encouraging her to speak to me. She looks away from me as she speaks and answers in a low, uncertain voice.

Her husband was killed. But he was not fighting. Gunmen came to their home. They found her husband inside, dragged him outside and shot him dead. She was in the house the whole time, begging for his life and terrified for her own. The men who killed her husband then set fire to their shed, burning the motorbike that was stored inside and destroying their seed crop for the coming spring. She fled with her three small children, running through the night to her uncle's home.

She wants compensation for the motorbike and the seeds. I ask

her about her husband's murder. What does she want to have happen
about that?

She shrugs. "There is no justice here," she says. "They kill us whenever they want to. The government can do nothing to stop them."

As Chris told me the night the fighting broke out, these men live
by the rule of the gun. The men whose deaths I am investigating could
just as easily, if events had unfurled differently, have been the perpetrators of attacks on a Noorzai village. What strikes me—what always
strikes me—is that women and children have the least control over
tribal conflict, yet they are inevitably the ones left to suffer its terrible
consequences. This injustice is a large part of the motivation behind
my quest to gather the stories of these women. In this effort, I am
encouraged by the enthusiasm of my guide, the Barakzai elder.

I have often been told that in Pashtunwali, the traditional code of
Pashtun society, there is no place for women in the public decision-
making processes of the tribe. Yet this Pashtun elder clearly believes that
these women have important stories to tell, and that they should be
heard by the visiting foreigner. He coaxes the women to tell their stories
and insists that I need to hear their views rather than his. It seems to me
that I am not the only one who sees value in their unique perspectives.

The final house we visit belongs to relatives of the Barakzai leader
whose death set off this whole sequence of events. The widow of his
brother, who was also killed in the fighting, is staying in this house with
her children. I have heard that her husband was shot despite being paralyzed from the waist down and confined to a chair. I want to speak to her.

She is waiting for me in one of the rooms, surrounded by her nine
surviving children. She sits on the floor, looking very small, wrapped
in her large black shawl. I find it hard to guess the age of most Afghan
women because their harsh lives age them so quickly, but her hands
and face are marked by deep lines that suggest to me she is in her mid-
to-late forties, despite the infant she is nursing.

She introduces me to her eldest daughter, who stands against the wall nursing her right arm, wrapped in a makeshift sling. "She is twenty years old," her mother tells me, as Amir translates. "A very good girl. She helps me with the other children and I couldn't manage without her. She was shot while she tried to protect her father from the gunmen. I'm worried about her arm and I think she needs to see a doctor. But it is too dangerous for us to go into town. The men who killed her father and brothers are still looking for us. Can you send a doctor for her?"

I promise to ask a doctor to come to see her daughter, but I'm not sure whether anyone will agree to come to this house. If she is right, and the Noorzai gunmen are still hunting her family, then this house is hardly a safe place for a doctor to visit. For that matter, it is hardly a safe place for me to visit. I suddenly imagine myself crouching here with this woman as Noorzai gunmen burst through the door of the compound. The image sends a wave of fear through my body and it takes a moment to recover my composure.

The woman tells me she is thirty-four years old. We are the same age. I am shocked. It is not the first time I realize how my privileged life has protected me from the aging process. Once, in a salon in Kabul, a beautician quizzed me for an hour about my secrets to youthfulness after she learned my age. I didn't know how to tell her that my secret was to have all the food and drink I have ever needed, free health care and protection from the environment in the form of a warm, dry home and gallons of sunblock. Apart from the sunblock, they weren't exactly things I could bring back from New Zealand for her in a bottle.

What strikes me now is not just how much older the woman looks than me; I'm used to that. It is the contrast between our lives. She has been a mother for twenty years. For the past five years she has also taken care of her husband, paralyzed in an earlier battle. She is now widowed and her eldest sons, who should take over responsibility for providing for her family, are also dead. She fled her home in the middle of the night, knowing that the men who killed her husband and sons may be pursuing her with the aim of killing more of her children.

When I finish this interview I will return to my warm, comfortable room in Herat. She will still be here, trying to find ways to feed her children and to get treatment for her daughter. I really don't know why I've enjoyed so much privilege while she has experienced so much pain. My yoga teacher might say it's karma: the effect of our respective actions and conduct. But I can't see what I've done to deserve the good things in my life, and I certainly don't believe this woman has earned the suffering in hers. The church I grew up in might say it is God's will, or the result of sin in the world—neither of which explain the disparity between my life and hers. There doesn't seem to be anyway to make sense of it. It's the injustice of this that drew me to this work in the first place. My work—taking concrete actions to reduce that injustice—has been the only meaningful response I've been able to find to these questions. And now I'm not sure my work means anything either.

I continue my interview. She tells me that the Noorzai gunmen killed her husband in her house, in front of her and the children. The two older boys were killed outside, trying to protect their family. She relays this information with no sign of emotion although she holds my gaze as she talks. There is no nervous glancing away as with the previous woman. Her lack of apparent emotion is unsettling. She might be in shock. I wish I knew enough about trauma to be of more practical help to her.

Instead I do the job I know how to do. I ask her for more details about the night of the killings. Can she identify the men who killed her husband and sons? Had she seen them before? Were her sons armed at the time of the killing?

Already I'm regretting this interview. It represents all that is wrong with our legalistic approach to human rights in Afghanistan. As human rights officers we are supposed to ask direct and detailed questions. Our job is to reconstruct, with as much detail and clarity as possible, the facts of the case so that we can form a legal opinion on whether international human rights or humanitarian law have been breached.

Trauma and shock, however, don't generally lend themselves to directness, detail or clarity. Sometimes trauma stories will be revealed indirectly, answers will be confusing or circular, dates and times will not match. More importantly in this instance, the fine points of international humanitarian law can't bring a husband or son back to life. They can't even feed or heal the children who survived.

For weeks I have been looking forward to this day. I've been frustrated by all the men sitting around in Herat and Kabul presuming to know what was best for these women. I was determined to hear them speak for themselves, and to do the best I could to make sure their voices were heard. This is why I came to Afghanistan, because I believe these women are intelligent and competent agents of their own future. I believe that if they are given the space to be heard they will help find a way to save their country. This is what I have been impatiently anticipating since the day the fighting broke out, a chance to use my position to give voice to the most marginalized people in the conflict. I hoped that this trip would begin to renew my confidence in the usefulness of our office, of my work.

Instead, the most useful thing I do all day is to connect the women with the humanitarian agencies that are distributing food, fuel and medical supplies. I have always believed that by promoting and protecting human rights we can reduce conflict and prevent suffering before it happens, rather than waiting to respond when things have already gone wrong. For now, though, the simple act of providing a mother with food to feed her children is the best I can do.

The plight of this woman hits me hard. I can't imagine ever forgetting her face, her story, her pain. Maybe it is because she is the same age as me, though our lives are as different as any two women's could possibly be, and because of the questions that brings up for me about the inherent unfairness of life. Perhaps it is because I feel I have wronged her. I questioned her when she needed care, not interrogation. After all the trauma that she had been through, I came with my clunky interview process and, with all the best intentions in the world, may have subjected her to even more trauma.

This I cannot undo.

9

Into the Fog

November 2006: Herat, Afghanistan

*I*n the weeks following the killing in Shindand, I spend much of my time lost in a thick fog from which I begin to think I will never emerge. My heart aches for the stories the women in Shindand told me in quiet understatement and without tears. I am filled with a great sadness that feels like a deep bowl of water balanced precariously within me. When I tip too far from center it begins to pour over the edges and the sadness floods me, drowning any feeling of hope or certainty. In an effort not to be overwhelmed, I try to hold myself very carefully, to avoid tipping the bowl. But life in Afghanistan is bumpy and there are inevitable spills.

I don't really understand where the sadness is coming from. I have dealt with human suffering before, so why am I so affected now? Worse, I have no idea how to make it go away. At times it feels like a bottomless well. Will I ever feel anything other than sadness again?

Along with the sadness, I am filled with guilt. I feel terrible guilt that I have failed the mothers in Shindand. There is the irrational, yet persistent, guilt that we were unable to protect their sons in the first place. On top of that, I now also fear that my interviews have not achieved enough good to justify the pain they might have caused the women. I have written up my report and submitted it to my boss, together with an impassioned plea that the views of these women, and all the women affected by the fighting, be taken into account in our office's efforts to help resolve the conflict. But the perfunctory responses I receive to my efforts make me doubt anyone is actually paying attention. Have I, in my naïvety, subjected these women to unnecessary suffering?

This is not the first time in my career I have had questions about the effectiveness of this kind of work. In Gaza I wrote lengthy reports based on interviews with people whose homes had been destroyed and saw no real change as a result. What's different now?

For one thing I expected more of this role. In Gaza I worked for a small NGO and never expected our reports to have a direct impact on official UN policy. In this role I thought I'd have more influence, which was part of the reason I took it. For another thing, I'm not sleeping much, which leaves me vulnerable to the kind of obsessive thoughts that take hold in the wee hours. And maybe as I get older I am getting more, rather than less, sensitive. Perhaps it is now easier for me to empathize with the suffering of a woman whose husband or child has just been killed.

One thing is clear: working face-to-face with the individuals affected by human rights violations leaves less space for rationalization than working on national-level policy. It may be true, as Chris said, that there is little we can do to prevent that kind of fighting. But when it is your job to meet and interview the mothers of the boys killed it is hard to forget them, or to let go of the feeling that you should, *surely*, have been able to do more to protect their children.

Guilt is a consuming emotion. In the weeks after my trip it eats away at me. I get up every day and go to the office, but I feel as though I am sleepwalking through my own life. Between guilt, sadness and fatigue from insomnia, I begin to feel numb. I try to rouse myself from my own despair but most of the time I am distracted and lethargic.

I struggle to concentrate on the reports I'm writing about the seemingly endless parade of human suffering that comes across my desk. I've always prided myself on my work; being a competent, dedicated human rights advocate is a deeply ingrained part of my identity. Watching even that slip away from me gives me a profound sense of dislocation. I don't recognize myself. I am no longer sure I am the competent, resilient, independent person I always imagined myself to be.

At home I am fighting with Joel. I hope he will make me feel better about myself but, of course, he never can. In Kabul, Joel was always able to help me see things from a new perspective and, most importantly, make me laugh. Now I feel like he is withholding something from me, some magic tonic that will make everything better but which, for some cruel reason, he refuses to give me.

My guesthouse is only two hundred meters down the road from Joel's home and office, but for security reasons neither of us is officially allowed to walk in the street. I alternate between sneaking along the road in the hope I won't be noticed and obediently calling for a car and driver. Sometimes I wait thirty minutes to get a driver to take me a distance that I can cover on foot in less than five.

I am also officially prohibited from staying the night at his place. He works for an NGO that has a gun-free policy, so its compound is guarded by unarmed men. The UN policy in Afghanistan is that all staff must sleep in compounds that meet the official "minimum operating security standards." Those standards require armed guards at the gate.

I chafe at these standards, partly because I don't believe that having men with guns at my front gate makes me safer, especially not when they seem to be a bit vague much of the time. One of my housemates suspects them of smoking hashish, which would certainly explain the vacant grins they give me as I come and go each day. I also resent the inconsistent way in which the standards are applied. When I go on road missions, I am allowed to sleep in gun-free NGO houses, or in police stations. But in Herat city, which is considerably safer than some of the remote areas into which I travel on a regular basis, I am prohibited from staying in Joel's secure compound. Admittedly, when I travel on mission we move in convoy with two cars filled with Afghan police officers, all of whom are armed. But at night they generally sleep at the local police station, even if I sleep at an unguarded NGO house.

In any case, I do stay over at Joel's place often, mostly because he doesn't like to stay at my place. Our house is large, cold and uninviting. Joel's house is cozy, warm and private. So, more often than not, after work I get dropped off at home and wait until there is nobody around in the foyer or yard. Wrapping myself in my darkest, longest scarf and coat, I scurry along the road to Joel's compound. We spend the evening together and I stay the night. Every night I have to make a radio check, calling in on my handheld radio to the control room to confirm that I am safe at home by my curfew. Many nights I make these calls from Joel's front porch. It could be funny, sneaking around like a teenager, but these days I'm too sad to see the humor in it. In the morning I wake very early so that I can cover myself and scurry back along the road again.

I don't have a key to my own front door. If I followed the security rules I would be driven in an official UN vehicle whenever I left the house, so there would be no need for me to have a key. As it is, when I return early in the morning I have to press the buzzer and hope that Parwaiz is the first to hear the bell and open the door for me. He never comments on my surreptitious early morning arrivals. Instead he greets me as though it were perfectly normal to be arriving home at six in the morning, and I scoot upstairs for my morning rituals before heading into work.

Parwaiz has taken a shine to me, and I to him. He is a thin man with dark skin and hair and huge brown eyes that reveal a mixture of affection and anxiety when he approaches me. He always seems fearful that I won't be satisfied with what he has cooked for me. I wonder about the responses he must have received from UN workers he has cooked for in the past, so visibly nervous is he about my reaction to his obviously heartfelt efforts to please me. At a time in my life when I myself am feeling so uncertain, so fragile, Parwaiz's vulnerability only endears him to me further and we become gentle allies in the harsh world in which we both live.

Parwaiz speaks a little English from his years cooking for foreigners, but his vocabulary centers mostly on cooking so we switch to my halting Dari to find out more about each other's lives outside this house. He's about forty years old, a married father of four. He lives at home with his family and comes to our house to cook six days a week. I live with my boss and several of my colleagues; together we hail from Sudan, Kenya, Japan, India, Italy and New Zealand. Parwaiz's recipes are mostly Afghan but the influence of Carolina, my Italian housemate, shows. She has taught him to make gnocchi, risotto, fresh pesto and pizza.

If I'm not with Joel I spend most of my time with Carolina, the only other woman in the house. After work we visit the UNHCR treadmill together and later, while the men lounge around the living room watching satellite television, she and I sit out on the balcony so she can smoke her herbal cigarettes while we drink tea and talk over the day.

Parwaiz also does the shopping for us. I'm not vegan, but I have never liked milk, so one of the treats that I miss in Afghanistan is my morning soy latte. When Parwaiz realizes that I am going without coffee in the morning because I lack soy milk, he takes it upon himself to find me some. There is a small grocery in Herat that caters to foreigners and Afghans who have lived abroad. They mostly stock American junk food, but they also import Iranian food for the many Afghans who have lived in Iran and miss Iranian cheese and sweets. After two months searching fruitlessly for soy milk in Herat, Parwaiz convinces the owner of this store to import some from Iran.

The morning I open the fridge to find soy milk on the shelf I am filled with a now unfamiliar joy. Even as winter approaches, I'm still enjoying my breakfast in the sun every morning. This morning I sit out on the veranda with my bowl of cereal and drink an enormous soy latte. It is pure bliss.

Parwaiz, in turn, is thrilled that he can make me so happy so easily. "For the remainder of our life together," he declares in an endearing and decidedly Afghan fashion, "I will dedicate myself to making sure you have coffee with soy milk every morning."

If it wouldn't be scandalous, I would hug him for his kindness.

Parwaiz arrives at the house early every morning. I am usually the first person awake in the house, so Parwaiz starts his day by preparing a small stove-top espresso pot of coffee and warming up soy milk for me. I insist many times that I can prepare my own coffee but he refuses to let me. I wake at six and pad quietly down the stairs to the kitchen where he greets me with a lovingly prepared soy latte. It is perhaps the sweetest moment of my day, every day.

Together with our cleaner, a motherly type who takes offense if I so much as gather my own laundry from the drying room, Parwaiz watches my life with some concern. When Carolina is away, if I don't eat at Joel's house, I take my food up to my room and eat on the roof. To Afghans, my solo meals signify a dreadful kind of solitude.

"It must be hard for you to live so far away from your father and mother," Parwaiz says to me one day. I haven't lived with my parents for more than seventeen years, but even with my basic grasp of Dari I understand what he is asking. He must wonder if I am lonely. He might also be wondering if I feel safe. In Afghanistan I am without family and, for a single woman, being without family means being without protection.

I might not have the protection of my father or brothers-in-law, but I do have the protection of my office. I'm not really expected to comply with the social norms that constrain the behavior of Afghan women. The fact that I live in a mixed house with men and women, although it is completely beyond the bounds of Afghan social norms, is tolerated if not understood by my Afghan colleagues. My reputation, unlike the reputation of any Afghan woman who would dare do anything as radical, is not ruined by my circumstances.

After Parwaiz and I exchange our morning greetings every day, he pours my coffee and I tiptoe back up the stairs past the rooms of my sleeping housemates. Back in the sanctuary of my rooftop room, I set down my coffee, with the saucer over the cup to keep the coffee warm, and go through my morning yoga practice.

In New Zealand yoga was a way to keep my muscles limber after all my running. In Afghanistan, it is becoming a refuge. Though life remains foggy and confusing, I can roll out my mat and find a rhythm in my breath that is becoming familiar to me. Yoga is helping me little by little to trust my breath and my body, and to loosen my tight grip on control. I am starting to get glimpses of what yoga might be able to teach me, but I am still a long way from really being able to experience the kind of deep release that yoga invites.

Ever since Amanullah Khan's assassination I have had trouble sleeping. Some nights I lie awake all night. My body knows that it is time to sleep, but my mind seems to be in a different time zone and I don't feel sleepy at all. After four or five consecutive nights of insomnia, my addled mind is running in ragged circles. I visit a local pharmacy and, using a combination of rudimentary Dari and mime, ask the pharmacist for something to help me sleep. He doesn't seem to be in the least surprised by my request. Perhaps sleeplessness is a common problem in Afghanistan. He slides about five different boxes onto the counter and begins to explain the differences between them. After a few minutes of instructions that I don't really understand, he hands me three different boxes of pills and sends me on my way.

When I get home I look up the names of the pills on the internet and realize that he hasn't given me sleeping pills. These are Lexotan, which is a kind of bromazepam, derived from benzodiazepine. This is antianxiety medication, used for the treatment of "anxiety, insomnia, agitation, seizures, muscle spasms and alcohol withdrawal." In New Zealand these would be available only by prescription from a doctor. In Afghanistan I have bought them over the counter from a pharmacist who obviously had no trouble understanding my body language. I probably should be concerned about the ease with which I obtained these drugs, which Wikipedia tells me have potentially serious side effects including dependency and withdrawal problems. Instead, I feel only relief.

I start out carefully, taking the minimum recommended dosage. Almost immediately I am able to sleep a little. Sure, I wake up feeling woozy and the ground moves beneath my feet like a boat, but I'm sleeping. By this stage, wooziness seems a small price to pay. My anxiety levels seem to ease back a little. After about a week I decide to take a break from the drugs. I am, after all, wary of becoming dependent.

Without the antianxiety medication, my self-doubt rushes to the surface again and one night I leave work consumed by doubts about the worthiness of anything I have ever done. My mind seems to be stuck in a wretched cycle, feeding my own worst fears. Am I going mad? I decide to go directly from the office to Joel's house to get some reassurance of my own sanity and worth.

By the time I get to his place, Joel has already had a long day at his own demanding job. He spent his day out at the Afghanistan/Iran border interviewing children there. These children live and work in dangerous conditions. They are vulnerable to child trafficking and prostitution rings as well as the obvious physical dangers of their work, siphoning petrol from trucks and carting freight across the border. Joel and I worked together to design the survey he is now carrying out, so if I'd stopped to think about it I would have guessed he was probably exhausted after his day.

But I don't stop. When I arrive at his house I don't even ask him how his day has been. My entire body is a taut bundle of nervous energy, the numbness of the previous weeks replaced by a jangling, panicky feeling. I feel as though I may be teetering on the edge of a precipice below which lies the dark and shadowy realm of madness. What I want most of all is for someone to look me in the eye and tell me that I am not, in fact, mad. I want someone to tell me that I am okay, that I am still a good person. I want Joel to tell me that he still sees the good in me and still loves me.

I have no idea how to get him to tell me these things, so I just launch into it. "I'm not sure what's wrong with me," I say, "but I feel terrible. All day long I feel as though I'm going to burst into tears at any moment. At night I lie awake. If I'm not anxious, I'm numb. I don't even care about my work anymore; it all seems pointless and futile. I don't like myself, I don't like who I've become." I can hear the pleading in my voice.

"You'll get through this," he says, "but you have to stop dwelling on it. You need to focus on the positive things."

His words, though well intentioned, are not what I need to hear. The implication, in my mind, is that if I just tried a little harder I could make this all go away. I feel overwhelmed and completely misunderstood. I had been so sure Joel would be able to make me feel better, as he always did in Kabul, that the disappointment brings me to tears. As I begin to cry, the fear within me rises up to the surface and I hear myself pleading with Joel.

"I just need you to reassure me," I beg, "to tell me that I'm okay, that you still think I'm a good person, that you still love me."

I don't see it clearly, but I'm dealing with a psychological and emotional triple whammy. First, the sustained insomnia is sliding toward the doldrums of depression. Second, I'm exhibiting some of the symptoms of chronic anxiety associated with posttraumatic stress disorder (PTSD) and adjustment disorder: lack of sleep, difficulty concentrating or completing tasks, feeling detached or estranged from other people and uncharacteristic outbursts of emotion. To top it off, I'm in the midst of an identity crisis.

Like everyone who gets into this line of work, my compulsion to save the world has been fueled by my own private fears and insecurities as much as by my compassion and commitment to justice. In my case, it's mostly a fear of not being good enough, and a need to prove my worth in the world. These less admirable motivations were easy to ignore as long as I believed I was actually doing some good. But now that I'm harboring doubts about whether I am doing any good at all, a bright light is being shone on the darker corners of my psyche and I don't like what I'm seeing.

When I ask Joel to tell me that he still loves me, I am really asking him to tell me that I am okay. That I'm good enough. My desperation makes me insistent. When Joel takes a moment to absorb my tears and pleas, I interpret his hesitation as a refusal to give me what I so desperately need and what seems, to me, to be so easy for him to give. I don't realize how hard it is for Joel to get past his own fear that I might actually be going crazy. Just as he is my only friend in Herat, I'm also his only friend. Joel is afraid that he is losing the only person he can rely on. The more desperate I appear, the more his own fears are triggered.

"Can't you see I'm desperate here?" I plead. "When I look at myself at the moment I hate what I see. All I'm asking for is some reassurance that you can still see the good in me, that you can still love me. I need something to hang on to here."

"I'm sorry." He is silent for a long while. "I really am. But you seem hysterical and I just don't want to feed into that hysteria. It feels completely wrong for me to say that I love you right now. It's as though you are manipulating me with your tears, your hysterical pleading."

"I'm not in any state to be manipulating anyone," I yell. Joel's response has loosened any grasp I had on my emotions. "Yes, I am desperate and emotional. I was hoping that you could see past that and help me see past it as well. I need you to help me see that what remains in me is…lovable."

Fear and shame have contracted so tightly around my chest that I am in physical pain; it is difficult even to breathe. A part of me is aware that I need to step away from the confrontation, breathe deeply and find some kind of stable ground within myself, but I feel unable to do so. I make one last plea for Joel's reassurance. I am beyond yelling now; I struggle to speak through the tight squeeze of fear around my throat.

"Please," I beg, "all I want is some reassurance. Can't you look me in the eyes and tell me that you see someone lovable?"

But he shakes his head. "No," he says. "I can't do this. I've been here before with someone else, and I know where it leads. Whatever is going on for you right now, you need to find a way to calm yourself down and then we can talk about it. I can't talk to you like this and I won't be pushed into saying what you want to hear."

Even in my state, I can see the impossible situation Joel is in and I'm furious with myself for putting him there. As unreasonable as it may seem, I also think I should be able to resolve this for myself; no one else can fix this for me. But I feel so fragile that his words are like rocks shattering whatever remains of my hope.

I leave his house humiliated by my vulnerability and devastated by Joel's response. As I walk the short distance back to my house, I weep tears of shame, remorse and self-pity. The night guard lets me in and I sneak up the back stairs to my rooftop room so that I won't be seen by any of my housemates. Back in my room I want nothing more than to sleep. I am exhausted by my own emotion and just want a rest from it all. I pull out the Lexotan and decide to take the highest dosage recommended on the box. I wash three pills down with a glass of wine and put on some soothing music.

The next morning I wake up feeling more woozy than usual. I forgo my morning sun salutes because the floor of my room is rocking. I have, however, slept solidly for more than eight hours and the relief of being free from my own thoughts for such a long period of time has brought a new sense of hope to my morning.

It isn't until I get to work and see an email from Joel that I realize that he called me last night. Concerned, he phoned not long after I left his house. I must have woken from my drug-assisted slumber to take the call. According to him, I thought he was in the room with me as we talked. He thinks I was hallucinating. When we spoke I must have told him I had taken sleeping pills, because he tells me how concerned he is by my "self-destructive" behavior. He tells me in no uncertain terms that I cannot carry on like this.

His email wakes me up. It is time to sort my shit out or risk losing my sanity, my boyfriend, or both.

The problem with sorting my shit out is that I am drowning in it. It is going to be hard to pull myself together in Afghanistan where the pressure is constantly on at work and where my only real friend is a boyfriend who, to protect himself, is wary of getting entangled in my drama.

Fortunately, the end of November brings a trip home to New Zealand to attend my sister's wedding. It's a time of celebration for my family, so I decide to keep my desperate state to myself. But I also realize that it is time to take better care of myself. I consider booking myself in to see a doctor, but I've been disappointed by the medical profession before. I'm also worried that a doctor could label me with something, such as PTSD, that might stand in the way of me returning to my work. On top of that, I suspect a diagnosis of a psychological dis-order could prevent me from getting humanitarian work in the future. Instead I turn to my new love—yoga—and book myself in for four days of personal sessions with a yoga teacher after the wedding.

10
Coming Home to Afghanistan

November 24 to December 4, 2006: New Zealand

*M*y trip home is a stark contrast to my life in Afghanistan. Over three days my family celebrates my sister's marriage at a vineyard on Waiheke Island just off the coast of Auckland. I'm nourished by the warmth and generosity of my extended family, and at the same time overwhelmed by the incredible privilege we enjoy in contrast to my friends and colleagues in Afghanistan.

It's not just the food, the wine or even the beautiful setting that creates the stark contrast. Most of all, I realize, it's the sense of safety and freedom we enjoy in New Zealand. I'm reminded of the sense I had when I first landed in Afghanistan that such suffering couldn't possibly exist on the same planet as the ease and comfort that my family enjoys in New Zealand. I know there are plenty of people suffering in New Zealand, but on this island it really does feel like I've slipped into an alternate reality. Dancing with my cousins and siblings, I'm reassured of my own capacity to laugh and to feel something other than sadness. Yet, even in the midst of all this, I feel lonely. There is a part of the person I have become that I can no longer share with anyone here.

After the wedding, the exhaustion of the past few months catches up with me and I spend a few days in bed, not sure whether I am really physically ill or just emotionally spent. I drag myself out of bed for my yoga sessions, at which the teacher, Jude, insists on me doing gentle, restorative yoga rather than the more vigorous practice I expected. It's not what I asked for, but in the weeks and months to come in Afghanistan it may well prove to be exactly what I need.

At the end of my visit, I go to say good-bye to my younger sister. As we hug, I am caught off guard by my own emotion. I cling to her for a little longer than normal and I whisper something that I haven't dared to admit till then.

"I don't know if I am ready to go back," I confess.

I've never been afraid to go back before. Not to Afghanistan, not to the Gaza Strip, not to Timor-Leste. I've been angry, excited, maybe even nervous, but never afraid. Not like this. And it's not the bombs or the Taliban kidnappers I'm afraid of. I'm not scared of war zones, riots or rocket-propelled grenades. I am scared that I am not in control of my life or the world around me. I am scared that I am not doing any good in the world. I'm scared of this sense of uncertainty that challenges the very foundations on which I have built my life. And, perhaps most of all, I am scared of my own sadness; a sadness I found among those mothers in Shindand and that I still haven't learned how to set down.

"You did it, Marianne," my sister responds kindly. "You got your dream job, and you did your best. It's turned out to be too much, but that's nothing to be ashamed of. There aren't many people who could handle what you've put yourself through. Why don't you just complete your six-month contract, and then come home?"

What she says makes sense. It seems unlikely that a war-torn and grief-stricken country like Afghanistan will be the best place to recover from the persistent sadness that fills up all the spaces of my life. Here in New Zealand, surrounded by my happy, healthy family and friends, the pervasiveness of my sadness is even more apparent. The buzz of the wedding reception had barely worn off before I was laid out in bed again.

But I am reluctant to leave Afghanistan just yet. Why? Because what brought me to Afghanistan in the first place was my belief in the possibility of a safer, fairer world, and in my ability to play a role in bringing that world about. Somewhere in that muddy courtyard in Shindand, or in the weeks of sadness that followed, I lost that belief in myself and in the possibility of a better world. I want to recover it. I need to. I'm not willing to leave Afghanistan until I have. I'm determined to find a way to be of real service in Afghanistan, despite the challenges of the past weeks.

So I board the plane. I leave my family behind once again. By the time the plane stops over in Melbourne three hours later I have stopped crying. Fifteen hours later, when I land in Dubai, I am ready to do whatever it takes to find my way out of this sadness and back to the work I came to Afghanistan to do. As I board the plane to Kabul, in the special terminal reserved for flights into Afghanistan and Iraq, I look around me at the mix of ex-soldiers, diplomats and aid workers and wonder how many of them are searching for the same sense of hope as I am.

As I land in Kabul, I feel a strange sense of coming home. I have come back to Afghanistan to find some answers. Can I transcend my personal sadness and be of service to the people of Afghanistan? Is there still reason to believe in a better world? Is it still possible to believe in peace?

11

Buffy and Badghis

December 2006: Herat and Badghis, Afghanistan

W hen I finally get back to Herat it is the beginning of December.
More than a month has passed since Amanullah Khan's assassination and, although my report on the women affected by the fighting seems to have disappeared into the bureaucratic quicksand of the
UN system, my colleagues are still talking regularly with the elders on
each side of the conflict. I'm convinced that nothing will really change,
in this or the larger conflicts playing out in Afghanistan, until everyone
affected by the fighting is able to take part in the discussions. So, as
long as the women are left on the sideline, I hold out little hope.

There is plenty of other work to keep me busy, though. My Afghan
colleague Ahmed and I are working on a national project to document
illegal detentions in Afghanistan. Our job is to carry out inspections
of all the provincial prisons in our region, and several district jails in
each province. While I was away he visited the prison in Herat city,
and now it's time for us to head north to Badghis province to visit the
prisons there.

I only have one day in Herat before I leave for Badghis. This is one
of the reasons Joel and I are taking so long to confront the growing
problems in our relationship. We both travel a lot within Afghanistan

for our work and we have very little time together. Even when we are both in Herat, our jobs are demanding and tiring, so it isn't really surprising that we often spend what little time we do have together collapsed on the floor watching DVDs. Joel has introduced me to *Buffy the Vampire Slayer*. *Buffy* may be the perfect escape for someone who has lost her world-saving mojo. Watching *Buffy*, I can indulge in the fantasy of a world in which all it takes to kick evil ass is a great pair of boots and a bit of karate. And as long as Joel and I are watching DVDs, we aren't fighting.

When I get back from New Zealand there isn't even time for us to share a *Buffy* marathon. The day after I return to Herat, I pack up my yoga mat, determined to put into practice what I learned from Jude in New Zealand, and set out for Qala-e-Naw, the provincial capital of Badghis.

The road to Qala-e-Naw is risky in some places. Not long before I arrived in Herat, armed men attacked a UNICEF vehicle on this road. The driver was killed. His brother works at our office as a security officer and the murder has understandably made everyone in the office more wary about our road trips to Badghis. On this trip, two police vehicles will accompany us throughout the journey, one at the front and one at the rear of the convoy. Each police jeep carries four armed officers, in addition to the driver. As our security director briefs the police escort, another colleague translates for my benefit.

"It is your job to protect this convoy. This means you must stay close. You must remain in radio contact with the two UN vehicles. Miss Marianne, here, is in charge of the mission. You will stop when she says stop. You will go when she says go. You will not create problems in the villages that you pass through. If you encounter trouble then you must not run away like you did when the UNICEF convoy was attacked. You are not here to run away. You are here to protect our staff."

It is not the most reassuring security briefing I have heard but the trip passes without incident and we make it to Qala-e-Naw safely.

Qala-e-Naw, the center of Badghis province, is a smallish town with dirt roads lined with makeshift stores made out of shipping containers. The stores are filled with dusty piles of cheap plastic goods, tinned food and motorcycle parts. Along the edge of the street, planks of wood form a precarious-looking footpath. In December, the dirt roads have turned into rivers and only the planks save us all from disappearing into the mud.

When we arrive in town, everyone is talking about the arrest of two men accused of kidnapping the son of a local merchant for ransom. I ask our local staff what they know about it, and they tell me they've heard the men have been beaten during the investigation. This fact alone might not have generated much interest—or gossip—were the men not Pashtun and from Farah province, south of Herat. There are long-standing ethnic tensions between the Pashtun minority and the Tajik majority in Badghis province. The fact that these detainees are Pashtun is threatening to reignite those tensions, as the local Pashtun minority accuse the police of beating them because of their ethnicity.

Eager to get to the prison to see these two men, I speed through my courtesy visits to the governor and the chief of police. My colleagues tell me this governor is deeply corrupt—too busy lining his own pockets and spending time in Kabul lobbying for a transfer to a more appealing post, he is not very interested in getting anything done for the province.

When I meet him, the tea his aide serves me smells rancid. I have to reach for a sweet to cover the taste. And it isn't only his tea that is off. Everything about this man screams foul to me. His manners are exaggerated and oily and he speaks about the province with a thinly veiled contempt. It is obvious that this man, an urbanite from Kabul, resents being posted to this remote and, in his words, "backward" province full of "peasants and uneducated people." For the province's sake, if not for his, I hope he gets his transfer and that Badghis gets a new governor who actually cares about this place and its people.

I rein in my distaste just long enough to ask about reported food shortages in the province. I was asked by my colleagues in Herat to find out if it is true that the dry summer has led to massive crop failures in Badghis. The governor confirms that there are significant food shortages across the province and promises to send a message to the Department of Agriculture asking them to prepare some data for me to collect tomorrow.

The provincial chief of police is quite a different sort of a man. He welcomes us into his office with a stern nod and seems uninterested in charming me. Once he starts talking, I understand his no-nonsense approach. The security situation in Badghis is not looking good. Last week there was a rocket attack on one of the district police stations in the province. He also has reports from the northern part of the province of "night letters" being delivered, written warnings telling teachers and students to stop attending school or risk death. There have been many of these "night letters" in the southern provinces of Afghanistan. Mostly they are attributed to the Taliban, but other conservative, antigovernment groups also use them. The goal is to inspire terror in the community and, from what I have heard, they often work. They are a new phenomenon here in the north and the police chief, understandably, isn't happy about this development. I'm worried too. This may be a sign that support for the Taliban has spread to northern Badghis. My office will want to know more about this so I make a note to ask around town about the letters tomorrow.

Before I leave I ask the chief of police about the two Pashtun detainees I heard about last night.

"I'm worried that rumors about mistreatment of these men are stirring up ethnic tensions in Qala-e-Naw," I say. "My office is very keen to do all we can to help avoid more of the kind of violence that took place here in 2005."

I'm referring to fatally violent clashes between the Pashtun minority and the predominantly Tajik population in the town. They resulted from the escalation of a very similar ethnic tension. As my colleague translates my words, I see that the chief is nodding in agreement, so I continue.

"If I could visit these men as an independent UN investigator," I begin, "then we can get to the bottom of the case and put an end to the rumors."

Once again he is nodding in agreement, so I ask for his support to get access to the detainees. He agrees and assures me that I will be welcome at the prison anytime I want to visit the detainees.

The meeting closes with as little ceremony as it started, leaving me with the impression that this is a man with more pressing concerns than a visit from a UN human rights investigator. If his officers have indeed been beating the two Pashtun detainees, he doesn't seem to be very concerned about the possibility of me uncovering that fact. I suppose that doesn't necessarily mean he has nothing to hide; it may simply be that he sees no reason to hide it from me. I'm not sure whether to feel pleased he has acknowledged the potential usefulness of my role, or concerned that he doesn't seem to care what I see.

In any case, I ask Ahmed to take me straight to the prison. While the police chief doesn't seem to be worried about hiding anything from me, it still makes sense to get there before he can instruct the prison director to hide evidence or to coach or threaten any witnesses.

12
A New Mission

December 2006: Badghis, Afghanistan

*T*he provincial prison in Qala-e-Naw is the first prison I visit in Afghanistan and I am not sure exactly what to expect. But I have seen Afghan homes that make New Zealand prisons look lavish so I am not expecting any kind of luxury.

We arrive at the entrance to the prison and Ahmed leads me to the office of the prison director. Having already made the effort to get here as quickly as possible, I now want to get through the introductory meeting with the director quickly as well. I would rather not give him time to have guards sent to bully the detainees into saying only what he wants us to hear. I move as quickly as I can through the initial interview, but I do take time to make sure that Ahmed has the complete register of detainees. That way we can check that we don't miss anyone as we make our rounds. I'm making some of this up as I go along, but we do have a checklist from the national project on places of detention, and it specifically mentions counting the prisoners off against the register.

The prison building, like most of the buildings in Qala-e-Naw, is made of mud-bricks. It is a single-story structure with a corridor down the center and four cells off to each side. I ask the director to open the door to the first cell. As I enter the room, where about ten men sit on thin mattresses on a concrete floor, the director begins to follow me. The checklist is very clear about talking to the prisoners without any staff present. I'm not sure how he's going to take this, but I explain to him that I need to talk to the men in private and ask if he'll wait outside. To my relief, he agrees and walks back out into the corridor.

Ahmed translates while I explain to the men who we are and why we are here. Our goal is to find out if they are being detained legally, treated fairly and accorded their rights under Afghan law. I list some of those rights for them, realizing that many of them will have little idea what I am talking about. I explain that we will speak to each of them separately and that we will sit in a far corner of the room so that they can speak without being overheard by each other or by the director, who I suspect is hovering at the door.

I don't explain, although this experience will teach me to do so in the future, that I am not a defense attorney. That seems to be the impression that I have given the men. As far as I can tell, none of them has ever been represented by any kind of lawyer. I spend half my time with each detainee explaining that I cannot, unfortunately, represent them in their trials.

I wish I could promise them that I will get some legal aid lawyers to visit them but, unlike Kabul and Herat, Badghis has no legal aid projects. Instead I make a vow to myself that I will do everything I can to convince the legal aid organizations I know in Herat to expand their services to Badghis. In the meantime I listen to these men's sorry tales. The checklist is clear—if I find someone illegally detained then I should raise the matter with the prosecutors; otherwise there is little I can do.

A disturbing number of the men in the cell are being detained because they failed to pay their debts. It seems immoral to me to imprison a man for being poor. But their detention is lawful and, as much as they break my heart, they don't meet the checklist criteria. Still, I can't resist trying something to help them. I decide to ask the prosecutor's office to show me their charge sheets in the hope that I find some kind of technical problem. In other words I will do what their defense lawyer would have done, if they had one. So much for sticking to my checklist.

Two of the men are being detained because their relatives are alleged to have committed serious crimes and the police haven't been able to find them. The idea seems to be that the wanted relatives will hand themselves in, or be handed over by their families, in order to liberate these innocent men. In these cases I can do something. Under Afghan law, you cannot detain someone just because a member of their family may have committed a crime. I promise these men I will raise their cases with the police and the prosecutors. I can't guarantee that they will be released, but at least I have a legal leg to stand on. I feel good that I can actually do something for a change.

All of the men want to talk with us so it takes us several hours to make our way through them all. By the time we emerge into the corridor the director has gone, leaving us under the watchful eye of one of his guards. The guard sends one of the detainees to call for the director and within a few minutes he is back. In the meantime, I ask Ahmed to check the names of the men we have just interviewed against the names in the prison register.

There are only two other detainees in the register, and they are the alleged kidnappers. Each is being held in a separate cell, which concerns me. You only have to spend a few days alone in a room to know that it can be a fast track to madness. If, on top of that, you have just been arrested in a place far from home and are being held in solitary confinement in an Afghan prison, things could get pretty grim pretty quickly. I am worried about these two men before I even step into their cells. I'm also nervous about how I'm going to handle what I might be about to find. If the reports are true then they may both have been badly beaten and traumatized. I plan to tread very gently.

The director leaves us alone with the first detainee. Unlike the men in the first cell, he has no mattress or blankets, cooking equipment or food. As we step into his cell he is sitting on the dirt floor in the corner farthest from the door. The room is dark but I can see his face clearly in the light from the open door behind me. He is thin, with hollow cheeks above his dark beard. He looks up at us with an expression of such terror that I feel a pang of guilt for being yet another strange and fearful arrival into his day. I feel clumsy and alien and am flooded with a sudden wave of gratitude that Ahmed is with me. Ahmed is Pashtun so he can speak with this prisoner in his mother tongue. The pris-oner appears so distressed that I suggest Ahmed approaches him alone, while I stay by the door, to explain who we are and why we have come.

As I watch, Ahmed approaches the man gently, speaking in a low tone. Within a few minutes he has his arm around the man's shoulder and as he speaks I see the prisoner look up at me questioningly. It seems Ahmed is able to convince him that I can be trusted because a moment later he summons me over to them. Ahmed explains the man is very afraid of the director and that he says he has been beaten and abused since his arrest. Ahmed keeps his voice low and gentle, presumably so as not to frighten the prisoner, but I see a flash of fiery anger in his eyes.

I ask Ahmed to check if the man is willing to answer a few questions for me. When I see his nod of assent I begin to gently ask about the events leading up to the arrest. He admits that he was involved in the kidnapping and describes being caught by the police and brought to the police jail for initial questioning.

"Then they beat me on my back, my chest and my arms," he says in a shaky voice. "They yelled at me and called me bad names."

He shows me bruises on his arms, back and chest and I curse myself for coming to the prison without a camera. We have only one in our office, which someone else was using when I left for Qala-e-Naw, but now I wish I had brought my own.

What strikes me more than the physical marks on the man's body, however, is the fear in his eyes. It is easy to imagine that an Afghan kidnapper would be immune to the kind of fears that I myself might experience if I was locked up in an Afghan prison. But this "kidnapper" is just an ordinary man who, in the hope of making some money, resorted to desperate measures and he is clearly petrified.

Most of all, he says, he is afraid that he will be sentenced to death because of the strong anti-Pashtun feeling in the town. He wants to be transferred to a prison in his home province of Farah. In Farah, he believes, he will not be beaten just for being Pashtun and might have a better chance of getting a fair trial. I tell him I'll be strongly recommending to the local authorities that he be transferred to Farah, but I'm not confident of our chances. People in this town are angry about the kidnapping and they'll want to see "justice" done here on their soil.

I am worried that any report from me about his condition could lead to the prison director punishing him, without bringing about any meaningful result. I tell him my concern. He says he understands the risk but he's willing to take it and gives me his permission to raise his case with anyone who I think can help. He also asks me if I can help contact his family in Farah who, he believes, have no idea where he is and must be worried about him. I feel a rush of relief because this request, unlike all the others I've received today, is easy to fulfill. Ahmed writes down the satellite phone number the man gives us for his relatives. I tell him I will also report his case to the AIHRC staff, who I know will be visiting Badghis in about a week. I will ask them to visit him and see whether things have improved.

By now we have been in the cells for hours and we still haven't spoken to his companion. It is time to move on, but it isn't easy to leave this frightened man alone in his cell. I tell him we will do all that we can for him. Ahmed embraces him, whispering words of prayer in Arabic, and exhorts him to place his hope in Allah. Reluctantly, we head back out into the corridor.

We repeat the process with the other Pashtun detainee, getting a very similar story from him and further physical evidence of mistreatment. In his case, however, there is the added complication that he claims to be unwell. He's thin and has a persistent cough so I assure him that we will do all we can to get a doctor to visit him as soon as possible. Given that the hospital is right next door to the prison, it seems to me this shouldn't be too difficult.

Once again we reluctantly leave him in his cell, Ahmed clasping his hands together and praying with him, and me silently offering up my own prayer for his safety. The director meets us in the corridor.

As we follow the director back to his office I run over in my head the things I want to say to him. I am wary of making things worse for the detainees by letting on that they have complained about him. On the other hand, it seems to defeat the whole purpose of my visit if I say nothing at all about their complaints and leave him with the impression that everything is just fine.

I decide to start with the positive—the conditions of the men in the main cell—and move on to the concerning but not particularly controversial issue of the legality of the detention of some of the men in the first cell. I step carefully through my concerns about the condition of the two Pashtun detainees, and finish up with more warm words about the conditions of the main group of prisoners.

It seems to go fairly well. I think I have managed to raise my concerns about the Pashtun detainees without letting on that they complained specifically about him. He even promises to get a doctor in to check on the second of the Pashtun men. Ahmed says he will come back tomorrow morning to see what the doctor says. As we leave I wonder whether I have been too diplomatic.

My first imperative is to "do no harm" and if the director is as violent as the two men claim, then it seems quite possible that he could punish them for speaking out of turn. On the other hand, I am left feeling I may have compromised too much. It's a difficult balance and I'm still feeling my way. The real challenge, as always, is in the application of the guidelines in the UN training manual to real life, in which nothing is ever as clear as a textbook hypothetical.

Most of all, I am exhausted. We have been at the prison for nearly five hours. Night is falling and I am ready for yoga and then bed. First, however, I pull out my satellite phone so that Ahmed can call the relatives of the two detained men. It takes a few attempts but in the end he gets hold of an uncle of one of the men. Their families didn't even know that they had been arrested. Once Ahmed has relayed the bad news, the uncle assures him that he will come to Qala-e-Naw as soon as possible. Satisfied that we have achieved at least one useful thing with our day, I go to my room and roll out my yoga mat.

Tonight is the perfect opportunity to put into practice something Jude taught me as I was going through the yoga sequences for her on our first day.

"When I watch you practice," she said, "I notice a lot of strength and determination. You are a very strong woman and you've made a lot happen in your life by working hard, right?"

"I guess so," I replied, thinking about all the places I've lived and worked and all the projects I've bullheadedly pushed through to completion, sometimes long after everyone else had given up.

"Well, sometimes working harder and doing more isn't what is needed," Jude continued. "Sometimes what is needed is for us to learn how to do less, how to let go of the need to be in control for a little while. Sometimes we need to accept that we can't do everything and just take a rest."

I think about her words tonight, and decide that after a long day in an Afghan prison it might be time for a restorative yoga practice. This basically means lying around in really comfortable poses for a while. It doesn't look or feel like I'm *doing* anything, but Jude insisted that it is "real" yoga, and I suspect that I could benefit from a bit more lying around and a bit less doing.

The next day begins as planned. I start by meeting the director of the Department of Agriculture to discuss the food shortage. I'm able to pull together enough data to support the claims of food shortages for my colleagues in Herat. I check that item off my list.

Next I go to meet a teacher from one of the more remote districts. The teacher claims to have received one of the threatening night letters mentioned by the chief of police. When we meet he shows me the letter. From what I've seen, it looks a lot like the letters that have been distributed by the Taliban in southern Afghanistan. My colleagues in the security department are going to want to see this. He allows me to take the letter to the Spanish army base to make a copy for my colleagues in Herat. Another check.

Meanwhile, Ahmed has been to the prison to confirm that the doctor has indeed visited the sick prisoner. He's being transferred to the hospital until he improves. A third check. The day is going surprisingly well.

Finally, Ahmed and I go to meet the local prosecutors to go over the case files of the men we interviewed in prison. We get through the main meeting without too many surprises. The prosecutor agrees that there are problems with the detention of some of the men in the prison and promises me that he'll follow up on their cases. After our meeting one of the prosecutors approaches Ahmed and me.

"I want to talk to you about one of my cases," he says.

"Of course," I reply, thrilled that he is interested in talking to me. "Tell me about it."

"A young woman in a small village near Qala-e-Naw ran away from home with her boyfriend. They tried to escape on a motorbike, but the neighbors saw them and caught them."

"Uh-huh." I nod.

"They were both arrested for *zinna*."

Zinna is the crime of adultery, and it requires some kind of sexual contact. I assume that I am about to have a technical discussion about whether it was possible to arrest the girl for adultery without proof that she had sex with the boy. Instead, the story continues.

"The local police didn't have any separate jail for women so they sent the girl home to her family. Her father beat her and locked her in the house. A few days later she tried to kill herself by setting herself on fire."

I gasp. I have heard of young women setting themselves on fire in Herat, but I didn't realize that the practice had spread to Badghis.

"She survived the fire," he says. "But she is badly burned. She is now here in the hospital in Qala-e-Naw."

"Oh, I'm so sorry," I say, rather lamely.

"What I want to know," he continues, "is whether I should still prosecute her for zinna. The reason I ask is because I don't think it would be safe for her to go back home to her father's house. It is probably better for her to be sentenced to prison and transferred to the women's prison in Herat than to be sent back to her family."

I don't know what to say. I have wondered the same thing myself before. It is easy enough to make the legal argument that this young woman should *not* be prosecuted in the absence of reliable evidence that she had sex with her boyfriend (evidence that almost certainly does not exist). But where will that leave her? Better off? Or worse?

I want to talk to the girl, to find out what she wants. I will visit her in the hospital. I know that seeing her may be almost more than I can bear, but if this young woman has to live with the unimaginable pain of her burns and the fear of an uncertain future then, I reason, the least I can do is to go and talk to her about what she may want.

As Ahmed and I approach the hospital I steel myself against the suffering that I know awaits me inside. My resolve to remain professionally detached, however, dissolves as soon as I see her. Her head, face and arms are wrapped in gauze but through it I can see the red, swollen mess that is left of her face. As I move toward her, softly saying her name, she looks at me with an expression of such hopelessness that tears begin to fall silently down my cheeks before we have even spoken.

She is unable to say very much. Her mouth is badly burned and it obviously causes her pain to try to talk. But now that we are here I ask Ahmed to tell her who I am and to ask her what I can do to help her. She tries to respond, but it is impossible to understand what she is saying.

Ahmed takes over, asking her to simply blink her eyes to signal "yes" when he suggests something that she likes. I send a quick prayer of thanks to Allah for the man's gentle wisdom, and watch as she blinks to indicate that she wants to be moved to the hospital in Herat. This is something that we can help with. I know women's organizations in Herat that specialize in the care and rehabilitation of women who have burned themselves. I promise her that we will do all we can to get her into their care.

Before I leave the hospital I talk to some other women in the ward. It turns out she is not the first case of self-burning in Badghis. One of the other women I meet tells me she went to the police to complain about the violence she had been suffering at home, but they did nothing to protect her. In desperation, she tried to kill herself. I decide on the spot, this is where I need to pour my energy. I need to do anything I can to help these women. There is little I can personally do to change the underlying social problems that are leading to family violence in Badghis. But I can work with the police and the prosecutors to help make sure any women who approach them get the best help available.

This becomes my new mission. I have been asked several times by local police and prosecutors to help get them more training. Now I know how I am going to do that. I will organize a training workshop in Badghis on the rights of women under Afghan criminal law. I've been at similar workshops in Herat and Kabul and I wonder, why not here? Why shouldn't women in Badghis benefit from a little bit of the money pouring into this country for police training?

13

Headstrong Women

December 2006: Herat, Afghanistan

$\mathcal{E}$very day in Afghanistan I deal with deeply entrenched social and cultural attitudes about the place and role of women. When my young female Afghan assistant faces sexual harassment from local colleagues, I find little enthusiasm among my international male colleagues for my efforts to make sure our office is a safe place for women to work. One of the men appears to have no qualms about taking the work of his female colleagues (including mine) and presenting it to our mission leaders in Kabul as his own.

One day I get an anonymous email telling me that if I don't stop teaching Afghan women to behave immodestly, I will be personally responsible when the unnamed author beats his wife for following my bad example. Although this email sends a shiver of horror through me, I'm unwavering in my commitment to support Afghan women. I'm not even entirely sure what the email is about. All the women's rights work I do, I do in collaboration with local women's groups or with the Afghan Independent Human Rights Commission. I'm not a renegade foreign feminist. I'm working with Afghan women—and men.

Nonetheless, for every honorable, respectful Afghan man I work with, I meet five men (American, Kenyan, Uruguayan, Australian or Afghan) whose explicitly sexist attitudes make my days just that little bit more exhausting. In the midst of all this, a more subtle form of sexism is having a corrosive effect on my self-esteem and my relationship with Joel.

In the world of humanitarian and development workers in which I live in Herat, there is a strong value placed on emotional detachment, the ability to remain coolheaded under any circumstance. I am often perplexed by how emotionally untouched the people I live and work with seem to be by the tragedy that is playing out all around us. Whenever I begin a conversation about the emotional impact of what we see each day, it goes along the same lines. "Doesn't it ever get to you?" I ask them. "All this terrible suffering and so little we seem to be able to do to prevent it?" Most people acknowledge that it is hard. But, they say, you have to stay a little bit detached from it. You have to retain your professional distance, keep a sense of perspective.

I understand what they are saying, but some part of me resists this idea of detachment. This part of me remains convinced that being able to really feel the sadness of all that we see is essential to my humanity. The pressure to appear emotionally detached feels like denying what drew me to this work in the first place.

The other thing is that "staying a bit detached" doesn't really seem to be working for my colleagues either. Some of them show signs of chronic anxiety, like facial tics or insomnia. Others get blindingly drunk once a week to "clear all the crap out," as one of them put it. One of my housemates retreats into his bedroom as soon as we get home from work and doesn't emerge until the following morning. Apparently, he's playing computer games. All of this may be more socially acceptable in our community than my bursts of crying, but I am not sure it's necessarily what "coping well" looks like.

This reminds me of another of the things that Jude explained to me about my yoga practice. I was doing a cobra pose, lying on my belly on the ground and lifting my chest, head and shoulders up.

"Do you notice," asked Jude, "how you lead into this pose with your head instead of your heart?"

I stopped to notice what I was doing. She had instructed me to draw my heart forward, to lengthen through the spine. Instead I was thrusting my head up and back.

"Headstrong women are great," she said. "I'm one too. We get things done, we make things happen. The world needs us. But sometimes we need to take a break from all that striving and simply allow ourselves to be led by our heart. There is a softer, intuitive wisdom in the heart that helps us to see what we really need.

"In someone as determined as you, Marianne, yoga can easily become yet another opportunity to drive yourself hard. But if you allow your heart to guide you in your practice you will find a kinder path."

Back in Afghanistan, I've been applying Jude's insights to my yoga practice, allowing myself to soften more into the poses rather than trying to force my body to do what I want. And I'm beginning to realize that this is just as relevant off the mat. I'm learning to trust the softer, intuitive wisdom of my heart in my work, and on some deep level I feel confident that this is the right way for me. But I still wrestle with the idea that I should be tougher, have a thicker skin.

This internal conflict sits alongside the ongoing tension in my relationship with Joel. During those first weeks after his arrival in Herat, Joel struggled with my outbursts of sadness and my emotional instability. One evening he confessed to me, "I am afraid of 'crazy.' I trust you enough to believe you aren't crazy. But the way you are acting looks a lot like what I've seen before in someone who really was mentally unstable."

As the months pass and my emotional state remains wobbly—I often find myself bursting into tears in the midst of even the mildest argument—Joel is losing patience. His response, increasingly, is to suggest I will feel better if I am less emotional about it all. He simply can't see what I am so upset about. On several occasions he refuses to even talk to me until I calm down. The problem is that I can't always work out how to calm myself.

The truth is that I still don't really understand where my sudden bursts of overwhelming sadness are coming from, and I'm very sensitive to the suggestion that I am overreacting. On some level his reprimands echo the messages I heard from my family throughout my childhood: "Don't be so sensitive, Marianne, you are overreacting." I've absorbed those messages so well that I now spend much of my own mental energy telling myself that I am overreacting and have no right, or reason, to be so sad.

I don't register that there is a gender dimension to what is going on between Joel and me. Joel is responding to me with the same discomfort that popular culture tells us men feel in the presence of strong emotions: he withdraws. The more I pursue Joel, seeking reassurance that he isn't abandoning me, the more he beats his retreat.

I'm resistant to the idea that men and women are doomed to act out these gender stereotypes. I believe that men can be and are emotionally intelligent, sensitive and communicative. I believe that women can be and are logical, levelheaded and pragmatic. But somehow, in Afghanistan of all places, I find myself caught up in the oldest relationship cliché in the book. As I watch myself pursuing Joel, I see a needy and insecure woman who has taken possession of my body. I want to know what she has done with my independence and confidence. I want my old self back.

Fortunately, even though my relationship seems to be stuck in a tortuous repeat cycle, I'm feeling a shift in my sense of confidence at work. My plans for the gender justice workshop in Badghis, in particular, are giving me a sense of purpose. I'm determined to do all I can to make it happen.

My first challenge is the devastating lack of resources in Qala-e-Naw, where we'll be holding the workshop. There may be billions of dollars of international "assistance" being poured into Afghanistan, but most of that is being spent on the military. The smaller pool of money that is available for initiatives like this is mostly spent in Kabul. Some of it makes its way to the other large urban centers like Herat, but Badghis is far off the radar and lacks even the most basic public resources.

The chief judge in Badghis doesn't even have any chambers. When I meet with him to talk about my plan to organize training for police and prosecutors in the province, we sit on the floor of his grubby, barely furnished bedroom. His nephew serves us tea. The judge has no personal staff, so his family sent the boy from Herat to live with and support his uncle. I am shocked, but I know that things can get worse than even the poverty I see in Badghis. In Ghor, for example, in the mountains to the east of Herat, I also met the chief judge in his bedroom—which was smaller and even more sparsely furnished than the judge's room in Badghis—and he served us the tea himself.

Because of the desperate lack of resources and the pathetically low salaries of officials in Badghis and Ghor, it is hard for me to be critical of them. For every time I visit the local officials with complaints about conditions for prisoners or court delays, I make two visits to their superiors in Herat, lobbying for the officials in Badghis and Ghor to be properly equipped, paid, trained and supported. Occasionally I have some success. For example, I earn the gratitude of the entire justice sector in Badghis and Ghor by finally procuring them copies of the laws of Afghanistan. These poor prosecutors and judges have, until now, been trying to work without even a copy of their own laws.

The other common request I get is for training. When I complain to the police about their heavy-handed interrogation techniques, they ask me to get them some mentoring on less violent ways to gather evidence. When I ask the prosecutors why they have taken no action against a man accused of beating his wife they ask me for a workshop on the Afghan laws relevant to domestic violence.

These requests are partly a diversionary tactic. Even if they don't have full forensic investigation skills, the police already know that they are not allowed to beat their suspects until they coerce a confession. As it stands, though, they are undertrained and I still have sympathy for them and their requests.

The workshop on women's rights for the police and prosecutors in Badghis is going to be my first serious attempt to respond to this need. I just have to figure out how to make it happen. In my job, I'm supposed to be coordinating, supporting and monitoring the training provided by other organizations rather than running workshops myself. The problem is that there are no other organizations working in Badghis. So I decide to bend the rules a little and make something happen.

There is already a prosecutor-training project in place in Herat so that seems like the obvious place to start. The project is being run by the Justice Sector Support Program (JSSP), which is funded and managed by the U.S. Department of State. I think perhaps they will be willing to extend their offering to Badghis. Eventually, I hope, I can get them to extend it to Ghor and Farah as well. With this in mind, I arrange a meeting with the American prosecutors who run JSSP in Herat.

14

Rambo and the Cowboy

*T*he American prosecutors show up at my office for the meeting with a Rambo-style "close protection officer," or bodyguard, in tow. He's one of the many private security contractors in Afghanistan, but unlike other bodyguards I've seen, most of whom keep their pistols in a discreet holster under their jackets, this guy is openly carrying a big gun. He holds his gun at the ready, stalking along the corridor as though there might be a Talib fighter hiding in our UN offices.

As soon as I see him, I rush to shoo him away, explaining to my visitors that our office is a gun-free zone and that their Rambo-for-hire is freaking out my colleagues. Rambo is not pleased about being dismissed, but the intelligent-looking woman who appears to be in charge of the group tells him to go and wait in the car while we talk. He reluctantly retreats. I wonder how he got the gun past our gate guards. They must have been intimidated, or impressed, by the American visitors, of whom we have very few.

The woman's name is Marie and she is indeed in charge and as smart as she first appeared. She gives us a rundown on their program, which will involve training and direct mentoring of prosecutors in Herat city.

It sounds like exactly the sort of thing the local prosecutors have been telling me they desperately need.

When Marie is done, she opens the floor to the two American men who have come with her. Her first sidekick, who is wearing cowboy boots with his suit, asks in a thick Southern drawl, "Is it true that there are Hezbollah terrorists in this region?"

It is such an unexpected question that I am struck dumb for a moment. Either this guy is way off track or I have somehow over-looked what would surely have been the most surprising political news of the year. Could I have missed hearing about the infiltration into Afghanistan of the infamous militant Lebanese group? I know that Hezbollah has strong connections with Iran, which is only a hop, a skip and a jump from where we are sitting. We could be at the border in less than two hours by car. So although it seems extremely unlikely, I'm not confident enough to dismiss his question out of hand.

"I haven't heard anything about a Hezbollah presence in Herat province," I say. "I'd be extremely surprised if that were the case. Are you sure you didn't hear about reports of increasing Taliban presence in the region?"

He shrugs. Perhaps they all sound the same to him, these "Arab" terrorist organizations. I am always shocked to discover how many people in the West think that Afghans are Arabs, so he might just be confused. Afghanistan is in central Asia—not the "Middle East"—and its population is made up largely of people of Pashtun, Tajik, Hazara, Uzbek and Turkmen ethnicity—none of whom are Arab. This kind of confusion is perfectly understandable in someone who has never studied about or traveled to Afghanistan. It's less excusable in someone working here. Still, I want to give him the benefit of the doubt. I know that these guys, as staff of the U.S. Department of Justice, live under even stricter security rules than I do. They have very little freedom to move about outside the military base where they live and work. It makes sense that they might be disconnected from even the most basic local knowledge.

I ask if they will consider running training courses in Badghis, Ghor and Farah.

The cowboy responds. "I don't think we'll be able to expand our program into those provinces in the next year or so," he says, "but maybe we could invite prosecutors from Badghis and Ghor to join our training in Herat."

"That's one possibility," I acknowledge, "but the challenge is there are so few prosecutors in each of those provinces that the chief prosecutor would find it very difficult to release any of them to come to Herat for the three months of the training."

"I see," he responds. "Well, then maybe the prosecutors could remain in their home provinces and just commute to the training course in Herat. The classes are only for one day a week; the rest of the time they could be at work."

I appreciate his willingness to find a solution for my friends in Badghis and Ghor, but the capital of Ghor is two days' drive from Herat. If one of the prosecutors were to try to commute to one class per week he would spend the rest of the week driving. This guy obviously has little idea about even the basic geographic layout of the region in which he is working.

Rather than complain about yet another American working in Afghanistan without the first clue about the place, since I was pretty clueless myself when I arrived a year ago, I decide to do something about it. I offer to visit them regularly out at the military base to keep them up to date with developments in the region that they might otherwise miss due to their relative isolation.

A few days after our meeting, while they are driving from the base into the city to meet the chief prosecutor, the JSSP prosecutors' car hits a roadside bomb. The consensus among our security analysts is that they were deliberately targeted because of their close association to the U.S. government and military. Although they all survive, Marie requests a transfer to Kabul. The cowboy stays on in Herat but his movements become even more restricted. My plan to visit him and keep him up to date with developments in the region becomes all the more important and, potentially, dangerous.

After a few meetings, the arrangement seems to be going well. I always take one of my local colleagues along. We pull out the map and go over the main tribal, political and social groups in each district. The cowboy always has lots of questions and generally we are able to answer them. He seems genuinely interested in rectifying the ignorance caused by his forced isolation.

I'm still hoping that by educating him on the profound challenges facing police and prosecutors in Badghis, Farah and Ghor, I'll convince him to expand the training there. But my good intentions backfire. I hear from friends in Kabul that the cowboy has been telling people I have a crush on him. I'm horrified! Here I was, thinking I was doing a good deed by helping a clueless cowboy find his feet in Afghanistan; meanwhile, he thinks I have the hots for him. I have no idea why he would say such things unless he actually believed them, so my helpfulness seems to have been misinterpreted as flirtation. From then on I am less helpful.

After all that, he says JSSP is not going to be able to offer any training to the prosecutors outside Herat city. I'm not ready to give up, so I approach my friend Kate, who works for the International Development Law Organization (IDLO), the other big NGO that runs training for prosecutors in Kabul, to see if they can help.

IDLO is an Italian/Canadian collaboration, and although they do excellent work they don't benefit from the kind of "preferred provider" status that JSSP (their American counterpart) has with the Afghan government. You'd have to be naïve to imagine that acquiring preferred provider status in a context like Afghanistan is all about providing the best-quality work at the best price. As always, politics are at play. The U.S. Department of Justice representative in Afghanistan is Afghan

Attorney General Abdul Jabar Sabet's biggest supporter. Sabet needs all the support he can get as he launches what is known as his "war on corruption" across Afghanistan. So Sabet is happy to reward his American benefactor for his support by giving all the good contracts for prosecutor training to the U.S. provider, JSSP. The other factor at play in situations like this is that the country giving the funding for the program may require that its own agencies carry out the work. So American "aid" money, for example, may in fact be used to pay the inflated (because you get paid more to work in Afghanistan, even if you think it's in the Middle East) salaries of U.S. prosecutors, and their expensive bodyguards. It's not a corrupt practice, per se, but neither is it necessarily the most cost effective way to get the work done.

Despite these politics, I know that the Canadian IDLO is doing great work. I see no reason not to approach them, especially since JSSP told me they can't do anything for prosecutors in the remote parts of the western region.

Kate is a whip-sharp lawyer and a great teacher. She is also an expert on sharia (Islamic law) and has developed a specialized curriculum for prosecutors on women and criminal justice. She is the perfect person to work with me on getting some training for the police and prosecutors in Badghis and Ghor. I tell her my plan to run a five-day training in gender and criminal justice for police, judges and prosecutors in Badghis. She immediately agrees to help me; we just have to get our respective bosses on board. This proves to be a little trickier than it should be, due to the politics of the justice sector in Kabul. Kate and I are not easily dissuaded, however, and between her diplomatic skills and my persistence, we eventually get approval for our plan.

Kate will teach the course. I will be responsible for getting the local police, judiciary and prosecutors on board and for arranging the logistics. I slide quickly into project-planning mode, which is a happy place for me. Reunited with my beloved to-do list, I feel better than I have in months.

Within a few weeks it is all settled. I have secured the support of the Spanish development agency in Badghis, who will supply cooked meals for the participants each day. We can use a meeting room at the hospital for the training. The chief of police and the provincial prosecutor have both responded with enthusiasm, assuring me they will send along their officers. My bright young human rights assistant, Amir, is busy working with Kate to finalize the curriculum. Kate will teach and Amir will translate, adding his own insights wherever possible.

Kate's boss agrees to release her from her Kabul work for the week. My boss agrees to fly her out to Herat on the UN plane and then approves her place in our road mission to Badghis. Things are coming together and I am remembering what it is like to feel enthusiastic and competent.

By the time Christmas arrives I am so caught up in my work that I don't mind being asked to stay in the office while most of my international colleagues head home to see their families. Just before Christmas, my closest colleague, Carolina, receives a temporary assignment at the UN in New York. Though this is great for her, it leaves me with one less person on whom I can rely at work and, more significantly, one less person in Herat whom I consider to be a friend. On the bright side, she leaves me the Christmas package her mother already sent: boxes of Italian chocolate, panettone, and brightly colored hand-knitted socks.

Joel is staying in Herat for Christmas as well, so we decide to host a Christmas Eve party for anyone who is stuck in Herat for the holidays. For several days before the party, we spend all our evenings in Joel's little kitchen preparing food. Working alongside each other, we rediscover the humor and playfulness that have always been the hallmarks of our friendship.

Without me knowing, Joel calls my sisters in New Zealand to ask what kind of special traditions we have at Christmas. My younger sister tells him we always have pancakes on Christmas morning. My older sister tells him about our family's traditional present game, in which we all buy five-dollar presents and then exchange them in a game involving lots of swapping, stealing, selling and screaming with laughter.

At the Christmas Eve party, a lovely, ragtag collection of people from all over the world gather to play—much to my delight—my family's traditional present game. As is always the case with my family, it results in loud shrieking, raucous laughter and general silliness. I'm in heaven, and I have Joel to thank for it.

On Christmas morning I wake up in Joel's little house to a decorated Christmas tree, a red stocking stuffed with gifts, and the smell of coffee and pancakes. Joel sewed the stocking himself and filled it with treasures that he found all over Herat, including some beautiful turquoise earrings. I am deeply touched by his thoughtfulness, and remember why I fell in love with him in the first place. He might not always know what to say to me, but when it comes to doing kind things, he is a master.

15
Back to Badghis

January 2007: Badghis, Afghanistan

*T*he snows arrive with Christmas. This delights me because in
New Zealand Christmas falls in midsummer. It also means that
the road to Badghis will soon be impassable for the rest of the winter.
As soon as we have all the pieces in place, come New Year, Kate flies to
Herat. We pack our supplies and head off for a week in Badghis. I am
excited to finally be on the road.

The drive to Badghis is even more spectacular than usual now the
landscape is snow-covered. We stop at the Sabzek Pass, which fortunately is still open, for a photo. The view from the top of the pass
is strikingly beautiful; Kate observes we could be in the Canadian
Rockies—as long as we overlook the armed Afghan police officers
spread around our vehicles.

Kate takes photos out the window of a constant parade of men
returning home to their villages after the emergency food distribution
in the valley. Their donkeys are laden with sacks of nutrient-enriched
flour and they carry large cans of oil. I'm thrilled to see them, because
this food delivery happened in response, partly, to the report I brought
back with me from my earlier mission to Badghis. After the heaviness
of months of despair, I am beginning to see that it is possible to get

things done. I just have to find my own way to do so; and I have to be willing to bend the rules a little when my own common sense dictates.

It is wonderful to be traveling with Kate. She brings me a sense of companionship, of being understood. We talk about her relationship in Kabul, mine with Joel, and our respective struggles with anxiety and sleep. I realize I am not alone. Next to Kate, I feel normal again. And I realize how badly in need I am of the company of a girlfriend.

Kate and I are staying at the new UNAMA compound in Badghis. It only opened in December so some things, like the kitchen and bathrooms, are not finished. In the grand scheme of opening a new UN compound in Afghanistan, these are apparently minor details compared with the really important things, like the barbed-wire-topped fence and security gate, which are reassuringly in place.

The accommodation building has two separate wings, so Kate and I claim one wing for ourselves and leave the other to the men. This way we can sleep, dress and bathe without causing too much embarrassment or discomfort to our Afghan colleagues. We even have a spare room in our wing that we use to practice yoga together in the evening. I have been pretty consistent with my yoga practice lately. It helps with my anxiety and seems to be helping me sleep as well.

Over coffee the next morning Kate and I discuss final arrangements for the workshop and I reflect on the significance of this event. I've been impressed by the cooperation I've received from all the men who have helped make this happen. The chief of police has been a great supporter from the outset, as has the head prosecutor and the chief judge. Over the past month I've been in constant contact with all these men, as well as with the Spanish police mentors from the PRT, and I've been struck by how much it's been possible to do in a short amount of time, with so few resources. I had no budget for this workshop and the entire thing has been made possible through collaboration and as a result of the relationships I've been building since I arrived in Herat.

By the time we get to the venue, people are already arriving. All thirty participants, including police officers and prosecutors from the most remote districts of Badghis, arrive on time. There are so few training opportunities in Badghis, in contrast to the frenzy of workshops in Kabul, that our event probably has novelty value despite the controversial subject matter.

I recognize the senior police officers and several of the prosecutors, and I introduce them to Kate. They are all very respectful and welcome her warmly to the province. This is one of the many ways in which Afghanistan defies Western stereotypes. Although I encounter sexist attitudes throughout the United Nations hierarchy and in the international military, most Afghan men treat me with the utmost respect. I'm not suggesting there is no sexism in Afghanistan, far from it, but in my professional dealings I very rarely have the impression that I am not being taken seriously because I'm a woman.

The participants take their seats around the long table that fills the small room. I step up to the head of the table to formally open the meeting. As I look up and down the rows of men, I see a mix of police uniforms and traditional turbans, white beards and clean-shaven faces. Near the back of the room sit three women, all staff of the local Department of Women's Affairs. They are often the first point of contact for women who are looking for help with domestic violence, accusations of adultery or threats of forced marriages. I invited them to take part in the training because most of them have little, if any, legal training and yet they are expected to play the role of lay advocates for the women who seek their help.

I smile broadly at everyone, thanking them all for coming. I don't want to take too much time away from Kate's teaching, but I do want everyone to know how much I respect and admire them for the difficult work they do, and how grateful I am for the opportunity to support them in any way.

When I'm done, Kate takes the floor. She is a pleasure to watch. Within minutes this pint-sized Canadian woman has a room full of Afghan criminal investigators and prosecutors hanging on her every word. To start with, she addresses the group in Dari. I don't know how many foreigners have shown up in Badghis speaking Dari before, but from the reaction Kate gets, I suspect she is one of very few. After a few minutes she explains that she'll switch to English for most of the workshop, to be sure that technical points are clear, and introduces Amir who will be assisting and translating.

Her opening remarks are on the rule of law, which provides, among other things, that officers of the law must act in accordance with the law. This may seem obvious, but in Afghanistan, where police and prosecutors often don't even have a copy of the law, it's not so straightforward. As she speaks, Kate recites entire clauses of the Afghan Constitution and Penal Code from memory, in Dari. I'm sure I see several jaws drop, but their beards make it hard to be certain. I feel deep pride for my friend, and for my own achievement in getting her out to this remote spot.

Kate moves quickly through her introductory talk and very soon has the participants engaged in the first of many interactive exercises. She worked with Amir and me to develop these hypothetical cases, so they reflect the kind of cases that we come across most often in the province. The facts of the first case study are thus very familiar to me.

A fifteen-year-old girl from a remote district of Badghis province is told by her father that she is to be engaged and then married to a local landowner. The landowner is fifty years old and the girl does not want to marry him. She is secretly in love with a local boy and so she convinces this boy to help her run away. He secures the assistance of a local taxi driver who takes both of the young people to Herat city. The taxi driver is with them throughout the journey and delivers the girl to the home of an uncle and the boy to the home of his aunt. The young couple tell their families that they want to get married but her father calls the police, asking them to arrest the girl and the boy and charge them both.

This first case study is supposed to illustrate the aspect of the rule of law that requires any criminal charges against a person to be based in an actual provision of the criminal law. In other words, the police and prosecutors need to be able to cite the actual section of the Penal Code under which they are charging someone.

"Would you lay a charge in this case, and if so against whom and under which section of the Penal Code?" Kate asks.

She divides the participants up into small groups and asks them to decide who will play the parts of the prosecutors and the defense lawyers. The "prosecutors" then have to decide who should be charged and under which law. The "defense lawyers" will then defend their "clients" against charges based on the facts we've been given.

I watch, intrigued, as a buzz spreads through the room. The participants embrace the exercise wholeheartedly and I hear voices rise in friendly debate. I wish that more people could see the Afghanistan that I am seeing. This is such a contrast to the version of this country shown in the Western media: images of a country filled with ruthless terrorists, corrupt leaders and helpless victims. Instead, here is a room filled with public servants enthusiastic about learning all they can to do their best for their country and for the people they serve.

I've heard lots of complaints about the Afghan police. According to many people they are corrupt, lazy and incompetent. And certainly some of them are. But I have also seen many committed police officers enduring inhumane working conditions and doing their best. They are paid less than a pittance. They often find themselves on the frontline of a war that they are ill equipped to fight. They bear the brunt of the public's resentment of the Afghan government's corruption and self-interest. To top it all off, they have foreign lawyers like me coming to inspect their lockups, complaining about mistreatment of detainees and miscarriage of justice. These men have every reason to resent Kate and me, and I would have understood completely if they had resisted the very premise of this training. Instead here they are, enthusiastically discussing the case study and arguing about who will play the role of the defense attorney. I am deeply impressed by them, and deeply encouraged. With people like this around, surely there is hope for Afghanistan's future.

As Kate has the groups report back on the outcomes of their discussions, it emerges that most of the prosecutors would bring charges against the girl and the boy. The girl would be charged with the crime of running away from home. The boy would be charged with assisting her to do so. Some prosecutors also suggest they should both be charged with zinna, which is a crime under Afghan law and can apply to any sexual relations between a man and a woman who are not married to each other.

The defense attorneys generally argue that there is no evidence that zinna has been committed, since the two young people were never alone together. But none of them argue against the charge of running away.

Kate then asks each prosecutor to cite the provision of the Penal Code that establishes "running away" to be a crime in Afghan law. Several cite the provision related to zinna and others claim they can't remember.

The truth is that there is no such provision. Despite widespread belief to the contrary, including among justice officials, it is *not* a crime under Afghan law to run away from home. If there has been no zinna, there has been no crime. When Kate proposes this to the participants, a lively debate ensues. Many of the participants are quite convinced that running away from home is a crime. But none of them can point to any provision in Afghan law that says so.

One of the older prosecutors seems to solve the problem by explaining that, although it might not be in the Penal Code, running away from home is a crime under customary law. In response Kate slowly but surely walks the group through her introductory lesson on Afghan constitutional law again. A prosecutor can only lay criminal charges if there is evidence that a crime has been committed. Crimes are defined, exclusively, in the Afghan Penal Code. It's a point I've made previously to several of the men in the room but I've never managed to speak with the clarity or authority that Kate is now demonstrating. An offense against custom, which running away from home might be, is not a legal crime unless the Penal Code says so. In the end, everyone seems to accept the point.

This is huge. Even in the few months that I've been working in Badghis I've seen many cases of girls being arrested and prosecuted for running away from home. If Kate has convinced these men that there is no legal basis for such prosecutions, then we really might be making a difference to the lives of girls in this province.

The workshop continues in this vein for five days. On the third day Pablo, a forensic nurse from the Spanish Cooperation Agency, comes in to talk about the role of physical evidence in prosecuting crimes against women. He has a slide show with photos of patterns of bruising that indicate strangulation. He then talks about gathering physical evidence of rape. It is heavy going for Amir, the young translator. I watch with my heart in my mouth as Amir translates Pablo's explanation of the signs of vaginal abrasions. But he seems very composed. I am impressed.

I'm not certain, but my strong suspicion is that we are traveling in previously uncharted territory. Everyone seems to be handling it well, even the older men from the remote and more traditional districts.

Following Pablo's presentation, an important discussion emerges about the burden of proof. Kate explains that the prosecutors have to prove *mens rea*, the intention to commit the crime. This means that if they decide to bring the charge of zinna against a woman who claims to have been raped, then it is not enough to provide evidence that she had sex. If she raises the defense of rape, then the prosecutors also need to provide evidence that the sex was voluntary. In other words, to make out the crime of adultery, the prosecutor has to prove she *intended* to have sex.

This is a desperately important point, as I know from several cases I have worked on in recent months. Kate and I have talked at some length about this section of the workshop. We want very much to get the point across clearly, because it has the potential to help women who have already survived rape and who are at risk of being further victimized, arrested, prosecuted and imprisoned. I want so badly for this discussion to go well that I find myself sitting on the edge of my seat, my whole body alive with nerves and excitement.

Kate asks the group to consider cases that they have encountered where circumstances might lead to a presumption that the sex was not consensual. I give the example of a case I documented in which a young woman claimed to have been raped in the street by three soldiers. The local prosecutor on that case tried to charge the woman with adultery and required her to prove that the sex was nonconsensual. I argue that the burden of proof in this case should have been the reverse. It is the prosecutor's responsibility to prove that the woman intended to have sex.

I argue that the very fact that there were three men involved makes it much less likely that the sex was voluntary, as does the fact that they were soldiers and that the attack took place in a dark alley in Kabul. This was clearly not a romantic rendezvous. The defense of duress therefore protects this woman from prosecution for zinna. The men, however, should be charged with rape (which is a form of zinna). The problem is that the law is so often misinterpreted, misapplied or simply ignored.

As the prosecutors respond to my argument I consider the unlikely picture we must make: two Western women in a remote corner of Afghanistan in deep conversation with a roomful of Afghan men about the likelihood that a woman would voluntarily have sex with three soldiers in a dark street. This kind of thing might happen every day in Kabul, where the majority of the aid money sent to Afghanistan is spent, but here in Badghis it's almost certainly a first.

For one thing, I'm surprised at how frank the discussions are. Kate told me that the young prosecutors who attend her lectures in Kabul are very open to discussing, in the context of their professional development, socially taboo subjects like rape. They are even willing to discuss explicit details of the kinds of physical evidence a prosecutor can use to prove that a woman sustained injuries in the course of sexual intercourse. I never doubted this was true among the sophisticated young urbanites of the capital city, but I wasn't sure we would have the same freedom in Qala-e-Naw, which is a very long way from Kabul. It seems I have underestimated the justice officials of Badghis. Perhaps this kind of conversation is common among these men, although Amir's nervousness about translating for this section of the workshop suggests otherwise.

As our discussions continue, it becomes clear to me that one of the younger prosecutors is also one of the most respected. He is the man who approached me about the case of the young girl who burned herself in Badghis. He is clearly intelligent and, unlike many of the police officers and even some of the other prosecutors, has a law degree from the University of Kabul. From the outset he asks the most challenging, and the most interesting, questions. Over dinner on the first night, Kate and I agree that winning him over is going to be the key to the success of the workshop. If he decides Kate is worth listening to then, we guess, the rest of the group will follow him.

The critical test comes during a discussion about the case of the young woman who burned herself. Sadly, she didn't survive her terrible burns. Before I was able to arrange a transfer for her to Herat, she died in the hospital in Badghis. Perhaps it was a mercy given the severity of her injuries, but I hope this workshop will help protect other women from the same kind of suffering.

Because she died, the prosecutor asks Kate whether she thinks he can prosecute the father for murder. The father repeatedly beat his daughter before she tried to run away and then, finally, kill herself. Although she died as a direct result of her own action, the young prosecutor wonders whether the father can be held indirectly responsible. It is a fascinating line of argument and I myself don't know the answer under Afghan law.

Kate does, however, and she is able to lead him to it. She passes him her copy of the Penal Code and asks him to look up a specific clause. "Read it out," she says, "and then tell me whether you think it applies in this case."

"If any person commits an act," he reads, "which is itself a crime under this law, that leads directly or indirectly to the death of another person, then they may be charged with manslaughter."

"So what do you think that means? Do you think it might apply to your scenario?" Kate asks him.

"It means," he says, "that if the father committed the crime of assault against the girl and that assault led to her death, directly or indirectly, then he can be charged with manslaughter."

"And do you think that you could establish that the assault led to the death of the girl?"

"Well, not directly. She didn't die as a result of injuries from the repeated assaults. But indirectly, yes. She attempted to kill herself because of the ongoing assaults and violence. I think I could try to make that case."

I am astounded. For one thing, my respect for Kate has just gone through the roof. The woman knows her Afghan law. More importantly, as a teacher she understood that it was better for her to give this man the material he needed to come to his own conclusions, rather than telling him what she thinks.

But what strikes me most is that this young prosecutor just demonstrated a willingness to interpret Afghan law in a sophisticated and controversial manner in order to hold a man accountable for beating his daughter. If I needed reminding that Afghanistan doesn't need people like me to ride in on our white horses to save the day, here it is. The future of Afghanistan lies in the hands of young people like this prosecutor.

After this workshop, whenever we receive a report of a woman being raped or committing suicide after prolonged physical or sexual abuse, I will call this prosecutor directly. I know that he understands the law and if anyone in Badghis can make a prosecution stick against a rapist or wifebeater, it will be him.

This is only one of the tangible outcomes of the workshop. A month later I am also able to report back, to both Kate's boss and mine, improved rates of prosecution of crimes against women in Badghis. This is so encouraging that Kate and I decide to try to repeat the workshop in Ghor. This will be more complicated, given how isolated Ghor is, but with a couple of months to organize things I'm confident we can do it. A workshop is manageable. What I'm less confident about is how to run my personal life.

16

A Resilient Woman

February–March 2007: Herat, Afghanistan

*D*espite successes at work, and moments of deep peace on my yoga mat, my self-image is still taking a battering at home. In the past few months I've watched myself transform from confident and independent to clinging and needy. I barely recognize myself and wonder whether I'll ever return to my old self. Joel is no doubt wondering the same thing.

One morning I'm getting ready for a meeting with Herat's chief prosecutor, Maria Bashir, the first female to hold the role in Afghanistan. I'm not particularly nervous about the meeting, but these days even the smallest amount of stress seems to be more than I can handle.

I get up early to do yoga. When I finish my practice, I put on a pot of coffee and hop on Joel's laptop to open an email I sent myself from the office last night with my notes for the meeting with Maria. I want to jot down the key points before I go to the meeting. Joel is woken, as usual, by the smell of the coffee. He also has a meeting this morning and, apparently, has overslept. He rushes to get showered and dressed.

"You'll have to hurry up," he calls from the other room. "I need to take that laptop with me to the office."

I rush to finish writing my notes but I'm not fast enough. Joel comes into the living room, ready to leave for work.

"Seriously, Marianne," he says, exasperated now. "I need you to get off that machine. I have to go. Now!"

It's no big deal, really. He's in a rush and I'm holding him up. Under "normal" circumstances I might have asked him to give me just five more minutes to get my notes done. Or I might have accepted that I should have printed out my notes the night before and handed over the laptop. No drama.

These are not normal circumstances. Joel's raised voice is the straw that breaks the delicate balance of my mood. My mind races off into worst-case scenarios. I'm a terrible person! Joel hates me! He is tired of the sight of me and just wants me out of his house! Before I can stop the runaway horse that is my mind, I'm in tears.

"No way!" he protests. "You are not going to cry about this! I just need my laptop to get to work. I've had enough of this drama. I'm not going to be manipulated by you. Just get off the computer and let me go to work."

I don't want to be this person anymore. I don't want to cry at the drop of a hat, to create drama out of the smallest issue. I'm sick of myself. I shut up the computer, without my notes for the meeting with Maria, and hand it over to Joel. I am, however, unable to stop myself from crying. I try for a while to explain myself to Joel, but I'm only making things worse. The angrier he becomes with me the more I feel myself crumple. I give up and tell him to go to work.

When he leaves I sit on some cushions on the floor. I'm still crying. My appointment with Maria is in half an hour, so I need to pull myself together. I take a deep breath. I exhale slowly. I take another deep breath and exhale even more slowly. In a few minutes I feel much calmer. I wonder where all that drama came from, so quickly, and how I can keep it from happening again. I wash my face, call a driver and head out to meet Maria.

Maria is just thirty-six years old. Even before this historic appointment, she had the reputation of being one of the smartest and most effective prosecutors in Herat. My colleagues and I were thrilled that such a worthy candidate had smashed the glass ceiling of the Afghan justice system. But not everyone was happy about her appointment.

Soon after the announcement, small groups of people gathered in the street outside her office, shouting protests. My local colleagues suggested that these protests were staged, that Maria's opponents had paid the protesters. Ismail Khan was one of those opponents. His conservative stance on the place of women prevented Herat's finest women doctors from working in the public hospital during his reign over the city. He still wields plenty of power and influence in the city and it seems feasible that he could be behind the protests. But Maria has other enemies, including the men who were passed over when she was appointed.

I've also heard reports that Maria has received anonymous threats against her family and life. When I ask her about the reports, Maria seems more weary than frightened.

"People have called me at home telling me that, for my own sake, I would be wiser to give up the job." She pauses, looking suddenly exhausted. When she continues it is in the same matter-of-fact tone. "Someone threw a brick through my window at home, with a note telling me to quit the job or risk putting my family in danger." Maria and her husband live in an apartment near my guesthouse with their two young daughters.

She is so matter-of-fact about these threats that I wonder how many times she has been subjected to this kind of harassment. It seems unlikely that she made it this far in her career without encountering resistance and opposition. It is precisely this kind of resilience that makes me feel so disappointed by my own emotional fragility. What right have I to be crumbling in tears over nothing, when women like Maria are holding up under so much greater pressure?

I'm officially visiting Maria to talk about Attorney General Sabet's "war on corruption." Not surprisingly, given widespread public frustration at official corruption in Afghanistan, this new "war" is capturing the attention of the media and the public alike. Sabet has publicly declared that the days of special treatment for the powerful are over. His prosecutors will be treating everyone equally under the law, no matter how powerful they or their friends might be. Prosecutors across the country have been instructed by Sabet to pursue prosecutions against warlords, drug lords and the reigning elite. It would have been hard enough at anytime to be the first female provincial chief prosecutor in Afghanistan, but at this particular moment it is going to be treacherous.

Maria assures me she is undeterred by the ongoing threats she receives. In response she has requested increased security protection in the form of an armored car and a few bodyguards, but she is not going to shy away from the controversial cases that need to be prosecuted.

In the weeks that follow, I visit Maria frequently as she navigates the dangerous waters of waging war on corruption in Herat. I spend many hours in her office hearing the latest developments in her work and discussing what, if anything, UNAMA could be doing to support her.

Around this time, in early 2007, Sabet sends some senior prosecutors from Kabul to make an audit of all the cases on file in Herat. At the end of their stay they present Maria with a list of outstanding cases of alleged corruption that need to be concluded as soon as possible. Included on the list is the name of the former mayor of Herat, who is alleged to have misappropriated public funds into a hotel development project that was being managed by one of his relatives. The ex-mayor is a close associate of Ismail Khan, and when he is included in the list of cases to be prosecuted as soon as possible, Khan takes action.

Initially the response is relatively discreet, by Afghan standards. There are more protests outside Maria Bashir's office and more phone threats. But she isn't budging. When it comes down to it, if she is unable or unwilling to carry out his orders, Attorney General Sabet will find someone to replace her. Maria is caught in the middle of a battle between two of the most powerful men in Afghanistan: Ismail Khan and Abdul Jabar Sabet.

As I spend many hours with Maria and gain insight into the challenges of her professional life, I come to think of her as a friend. When we bump into each other at social events, we embrace and chat in my very basic Dari. I am aware of the careful line I need to tread, given my responsibility to monitor her work. It's my job to investigate and report any activity by Maria or her office that might amount to a violation of human rights. But it is almost impossible to maintain a professional distance. Maria is a similar age to me. We are both lawyers. She is bright and ambitious. She is resilient and doggedly optimistic. She is committed to the cause of providing justice for the people of Herat. It is impossible not to like and respect her.

Above all, I want to trust Maria. I want to believe that she is genuinely committed to doing the best job she can. I want to reclaim my own dogged optimism and resilience. As I work with Maria I feel the return of my hope for a better tomorrow for the people of Afghanistan. I also see in her something of the strong, resilient woman I myself once was.

17
A Matter of Trust

March 2007: Herat, Afghanistan

Around this time, in March 2007, I get a call from two female police mentors from the United States. They have been working with the Family Response Unit in Herat. The Family Response Unit is a national experiment in making police stations more accessible and safe for women. One forward-thinking police commander in Kabul championed the idea of having special police units staffed by women officers and the idea is slowly being rolled out across the country. These units are supposed to provide a more friendly entry point for women who need the police's help or protection.

As a rule, the women who make police complaints are supported and accompanied by a male relative: a father, brother, or brother-in-law. Women without this kind of support go instead, if they go anywhere at all, to the Department of Women's Affairs, which is predominantly staffed by women. They do their best to support the women who come to them but my regular visits to Department of Women's Affairs offices in the four provinces of western Afghanistan reveal that they often are at a loss.

The Family Response Units are an attempt to fill this gap. I recently met Roya, the head of the experimental Family Response Unit in

Herat, at an exhibition of photographic portraits of women of significance in the city.

The exhibition was a great opportunity to meet with and celebrate
Afghan women I might not meet in my line of work. In one of the portraits a young Afghan woman wearing a neatly tucked black headscarf
and a long-sleeved white T-shirt with red stripes down the arms smiled
directly at the camera. She was the local Herati player on the national
Afghan women's soccer team. Another portrait caught my attention
because of the gathering of floral arrangements placed on the ground
below it. It was a photograph of a young Herati poet who had recently
been killed by her husband after she defied his wishes and attended a
poetry reading at Herat University. There were portraits of painters,
engineers, scientists, and lawyers—including Maria Bashir. Most of the
women in the photos were present at the exhibition, together with the
rest of the artistic, academic and political sisterhood of Herat.

Roya stood out. She had bleached her hair peroxide blond and was
wearing towering wedge-heeled sequinned sandals with her police
uniform. She had applied her makeup with enthusiasm and her finely
plucked eyebrows arched above sparkling blue eyelids and carefully
painted red lips. She was quite a vision in a room of the elegantly
but conservatively dressed matrons of Herat. I took a liking to her
immediately.

So when the U.S. police mentors come to visit me, all I know about
Roya is that she runs an experimental project to provide better access
for women to justice and that she has an audacious personal style.

The mentors are both police officers in the United States, special-
izing in family and domestic violence, who have been working with
Roya and the new Family Response Unit for almost six months. They
tell me that Roya has been arrested. For corruption. They've come to
see me because they think Maria Bashir, by ordering and pursuing
Roya's prosecution, is being unfairly harsh.

As they talk my heart sinks. It's alleged that Roya asked a female complainant to bring her a top-up card for her mobile phone so that she could make calls about the complainant's case. The woman returned with the requested card and a second one, for good measure. Roya accepted both cards, putting one in her desk and using the other to make the promised call. As soon as she was finished, one of Maria's prosecutors entered her office and announced that Roya was under investigation for corruption.

"How unfair!" I think to myself, fuming. Why has Roya been singled out for investigation when I hear reliable reports of much more significant corruption in the police force every day? Some of Roya's superiors are reported to have released serious criminals in exchange for a sufficiently generous bribe. It looks like Roya has been set up and made into a scapegoat, the softest target in an office overrun with corruption.

Outwardly, though, I maintain the neutral demeanor appropriate to my office. I may feel outraged for Roya, but I also understand the seriousness of these allegations. Many women in Afghanistan have little or no access to cash so even the smallest bribe can pose an insurmountable barrier. I'm troubled by the idea that a woman might have summoned up the courage to approach the police only to be told that her complaint couldn't be taken further until she provided a ten-dollar phone card. I am sure this troubles Maria Bashir as well.

The American policewomen want me to take the matter up with Maria. They have already spoken to their own counterpart, the U.S. mentor assigned to Maria's office. I know this guy well. Yes, he's the same cowboy who spread rumors in Kabul that I fancied him. In this case, he refuses to speak to Maria about Roya's case on the grounds that it could be seen to be interference in an active investigation of corruption.

I'm furious for Roya. Even if she wasn't set up—which I suspect she may have been—she is being singled out for prosecution when others are getting away with murder—sometimes literally. I want to be able to help her, but I realize that the cowboy is probably right. If I go to talk to Maria about this it will be seen as an attempt by the UN to interfere in the investigation. Admitting that the cowboy might be right about something only frustrates me more.

I also trust Maria. Or, I think I do. It has only been five months since Amanullah Khan's murder led to tribal fighting in Shindand and I lost all confidence in my own judgment. Suddenly I find myself caught between trusting Maria and trusting Roya. I know Maria much better, and I can see the pressure she must be under from her own superiors to single out a woman like Roya for punishment. I am not sure whom to trust or believe, so I decide to draw on the wisdom of Suraya Pakzad, the woman I trust and respect most in Herat.

18
Moving On

March 2007: Herat, Afghanistan

S uraya Pakzad is the founder and director of Voice of Women, a not-for-profit organization dedicated to providing legal, social and health services to vulnerable women in Herat. She runs Herat's only shelter for women, which is no small feat in a city that was until recently under the control of a conservative mujahedeen. The shelter and the legal and psychosocial services they provide enable numerous women to leave violent homes. This is not well received by the men perpetrating that violence. Suraya and her staff walk the gauntlet of public disapproval and personal threats every day.

Of all the inspiring women I befriend in Afghanistan, Suraya is one of the most impressive. In this country it takes a seriously strong and determined woman to get a women's shelter up and running. At the same time, Suraya is extremely professional, thoughtful and competent. Over the six months I've been in Herat, I have watched the care and expertise with which she runs her organization. She is very mindful of the risks that the women face when they make the giant leap of leaving their homes and seeking shelter with Voice of Women. She is precise and vigilant about professional standards for her staff, standards designed to protect both the staff and their clients. I know that. I can trust her judgment, so I talk to her about Roya.

I take one of my human rights assistants, Asiyah, with me to meet Suraya. Asiyah has been monitoring cases that come to Roya's Family Response Unit. On the way to Suraya's office, Asiyah tells me there are rumors that Roya forces young women who come to the Family Response Unit to sleep with her sons and with other men. The rumors seem to have sprouted from the fact that Roya takes some of these young women back to her own home when there is nowhere else safe for them to go.

Asiyah thinks Roya, because of those rumors and the "loose morals" they imply, has brought the corruption charges on herself. Therefore she doesn't deserve the support of our office. I have a big problem with Asiyah's attitude. For one thing, Asiyah herself has been the victim of rumors. Small-minded men who thought she shouldn't be working with me spread rumors around our office that Asiyah was having an affair with a married man. I ferociously defended Asiyah against the rumors because I believed them to be untrue, and because I knew how terribly damaging they could be. So I am disturbed to hear Asiyah repeat equally damaging rumors about Roya.

"Surely you, of all people, understand how easy it is for people to make up outrageous lies about women who are successful. You've been targeted yourself by men who just wanted to destroy your career. I don't understand how you can so easily believe the same kind of rumors about Roya?"

"Roya is different," she responds. "She doesn't dress modestly. She is divorced and she has men in her home who are not related to her. Her reputation is not good. So when she takes these young women back to her home it is easy for people to believe that she is doing something immoral with them."

"Easy for other people to believe," I say, "small-minded people who don't care about the difference between rumor and truth. But I expected more from you. I expected you to understand how easy it is for a woman, especially if she stands out from the crowd, to be attacked unfairly."

"Marianne, you don't understand our culture. For us, reputation is everything. When people tried to spread rumors about me I knew that I didn't have to worry. My reputation is good. But Roya's reputation is not so good. She has not been careful."

I understand what Asiyah is saying, but the reasoning seems circular to me. How is a woman supposed to maintain the reputation she needs to protect herself from false rumors when that very reputation can be undermined by false rumor? I decide to suspend my judgment until I hear what Suraya has to say on the matter.

There is no need to tell Suraya what I heard from the police mentors; news of Roya's arrest has already spread. Voice of Women works closely with the Family Response Unit, so Suraya probably knew long before I did. I ask her what she makes of it all.

Suraya speaks to me in English. She chooses her words carefully, aware, perhaps, of the weight that I will give to them.

"Roya did some very good work at the Family Response Unit," she starts, "but she was not always as careful as she needed to be.

"Our work demands great care. Women who have been abused or violated may be placing themselves in danger by coming to us. Here at Voice of Women we have very strict practice guidelines. Before a client can meet privately with any of our therapists or advisers, for example, she must leave her money and valuables in secure care. We cannot allow any opportunity for corruption or even the appearance of corruption."

Suraya pauses to make sure I understand, and then continues.

"We also have very strict guidelines to ensure the safety of the women who come to us. There are rules to determine who, among our staff, may meet privately with these women and under what circumstances. If we are having a family meeting then we have another set of rules to make sure that the family members who attend the meeting cannot threaten or intimidate the woman. Roya's police unit doesn't have these kinds of rules in place."

Again she pauses. I have to concede, nodding, that this is the case.

"It might have been well intentioned, but when she took women home with her, she placed their reputations in question. She lives with her two unmarried adult sons. You and I may not believe the rumors but many people will. Women who had already been victimized are now being subjected to further shame and risk. A woman in Afghanistan who loses her honor and reputation becomes a woman without protection."

Suraya herself has gone to great lengths to ensure that her own reputation cannot be challenged. From what I know of her, and her extraordinary spirit, I imagine that she must sometimes be tempted to break out of the constraints of what is considered to be appropriate behavior for a woman in Afghanistan. But instead, because of her commitment to the women she serves through Voice of Women, she toes the line. In other words, she dresses and behaves moderately.

Today she is wearing a loose-fitting brown suit jacket with a long navy blue skirt and matching headscarf. Her face may be radiant, but her clothing does everything possible to avoid drawing attention to her beauty. Suraya does not take women home to houses where there are unmarried men. She is meticulous about not accepting bribes or gifts. Despite her extraordinary strength and conviction, she speaks and moves without drawing unnecessary attention to herself. Nobody can accuse her of having loose morals and, as a result, her organization is above reproach despite its controversial work.

"What matters," she explains, "is that we can offer a refuge to women who have nowhere else to go. We may not agree with all the social rules that constrain women in my culture, but we follow them anyway. Not for our own sake, but for the sake of the women we serve."

I can't argue with Suraya's logic. She is right. I even have to admit that Asiyah is right.

Still, I'm finding it hard to let go of my desire to defend or support Roya in some way. I understand that she has made mistakes, but there is something of a self-made woman and a rebel in her that endears her to me. It is hard—in a sea of navy and black—not to be delighted by Roya's peroxide hair and sparkly pink sandals.

I'm also impressed by Roya's determination. According to her mentors, Roya is self-taught; she has never had any formal schooling. It was only after her divorce that Roya embarked upon a career at all. When she began her police training she was still teaching herself to read. Her mentors told me that she passed every test and every assignment of the police training despite her educational disadvantages. They painted a picture of a fiercely determined and hardworking woman with a strong sense of humor.

I wonder whether class is playing a role in Roya's current predicament; whether the female elite of this city are leaving this brassy, self-made, working-class woman out in the cold. My trust in Suraya's integrity, however, convinces me it is more than prejudice that is standing in the way of her supporting Roya.

I'm not under the same constraints as Suraya and Asiyah. My reputation is relevant to my work. It is important that I am seen to be a person of integrity and that people know they can trust me to keep my word and their confidence. But I'm not expected to behave as though I am an Afghan woman. I'm only expected to behave in a way that respects local cultural norms, to do my job as well as I can and to refrain from leading my young staff astray. I can get away with things that Suraya and others in her position can't, including speaking up on controversial topics. So perhaps I can still do something for Roya.

It is a fine line I am learning to walk. There are occasions when there is nothing useful for me to say or do. There are times when it is best for me to step quietly back into the shadows and let the people whose country or community is at stake do the talking. In some situations, my voice, my views, even my mere presence can exacerbate irritation and entrench prejudices. But there are also times—and my Afghan friends and colleagues often point them out to me—when only I can say what needs to be said; when it is too dangerous for anyone else to say it. Sometimes I am the only person in the room without a tribal or ethnic bias, real or assumed, on the matter. Sometimes it takes a "dumb foreigner" to ask the question on everyone's minds.

I want to talk to Roya about her case. I want to know whether there is anything I can do to support her. I want to ensure the ongoing survival of the Family Response Unit. I arrange to meet with her, and ask a colleague to come with me to help with language. My Dari is improving quickly and I can now understand a lot, but I'm not confident enough to go without help. Usually Asiyah would help me with translation, but I know her views on Roya and want someone with me who hasn't already decided she is guilty.

When we meet, Roya manages to surprise me yet again. I ask what I can do to help her. She tells me that I don't need to do anything.

"Everything will be fine," she assures me. "I have everything under control."

As soon as she says it, it seems obvious. A woman who survived a divorce, taught herself to read and made it through Afghan police training to become one of the few female police officers in the country is not going to be easily defeated. Roya is more resourceful and resilient than I ever imagined. Of course she doesn't need my help!

Although the case is still in progress, Roya seems to know what the outcome is likely to be. She doesn't come out and tell me in so many words, but she lets me know that although she won't be returning to the Family Response Unit, she will stay with the police in another role. If she is saddened at leaving behind the unit that she played such a central role in establishing, she shows no sign of it. I get the impression she is a woman who has learned to recover from knocks and move on to new opportunities with little time for indulging in regret or blame.

As I am driven back to my guesthouse, I realize that Roya has just given me a swift kick up the rear end. Six long months have passed since the killings in Shindand and I am still beating myself up for how I handled the situation and its aftermath. Life is too precious to waste in regret or blame, even self-blame. It is time to move on. The only question is how.

19
Sitting Still

March 2007: Herat, Afghanistan

$\mathcal{E}$ ven after the success of the workshop in Badghis and several months of growing confidence in my work, I've been having trouble sleeping again, and I'm still feeling unsettled by the lack of control I seem to have over my emotions and my mind. Perhaps most cruelly of all, I feel bad about feeling bad. All my colleagues seem to cope with the tragedies unfolding around us with so much less drama than I do. Joel wants to know when I am going to get over myself and move on. Harshest of all is the voice in my own head, telling me I have no reason to be depressed or anxious: I have a warm home and more than enough food to eat, my family is safe from war and I have a good job. I have no right to feel bad.

The voice is so insistent that I immediately back away from any examination, or even acknowledgment, of my darker feelings. I learn to avoid the silence in which they would arise. I distract myself. I work. I watch *Buffy*.

But the quiet moments still creep up on me, when I'm practicing yoga or trying to sleep at night. My mind rushes to fill the silence with thoughts about what I've done wrong in my relationship with Joel, and how I could do better in my work. I may have stepped back from the precipice of depression I was hovering on in November, but I am far from making peace with myself. I'm no closer to fully embracing Raji's celebration of my sensitivity as a strength. I am more troubled than ever by the voices in my head that tell me to stop being such a drama queen, such a crybaby.

I decide to try meditation. I have this idea that meditation will teach me to quiet the voices in my head, that I will rise above my own dramas and find some kind of peaceful transcendent state. I have a tape of a guided meditation my cousin gave me before I came to Afghanistan. I start listening to it as part of my morning routine. On a good day, I make it to about fifteen minutes before I get antsy or distracted. I persevere, convincing myself that in time either it will get easier or I will get more disciplined.

In fact, in the short term at least, neither is true. My mind is as disciplined as a frisky puppy. No matter how many times I grab it by the scruff of the neck, or coax it more gently, and return it to the object of my meditation, it always runs off again. I begin to suspect meditation simply isn't for me.

Out of desperation, I dig out some CDs that Jude gave me. They are recordings of a Buddhist nun, Pema Chödrön, reading a book she wrote about meditation called *The Places That Scare You*. As I listen to the CD, Pema speaks directly to me. She describes my feelings and fears so accurately that you would have thought she wrote the entire book just for the benefit of one depressed, confused human rights officer in Afghanistan.

Pema says the purpose of meditation is not to make us feel better. If we expect that, she explains, we'll end up thinking we are doing it wrong most of the time. Well, yes, exactly. That's certainly been my experience.

Instead, she explains, meditation takes us just as we are, with all our confusion. It is not a process of self-improvement, she insists, but a process of self-acceptance. This is a radical thought for me. I hadn't realized how deeply wedded I am to the idea of improving myself. As Jude had recognized, even my yoga practice had very quickly become another territory in which to improve myself. Sitting with myself exactly as I am—tears and confusion and all—is revolutionary.

I listen to Pema whenever I can. I transfer the CDs onto my iPod so I can listen to her while I am driven through the beautiful, brutalized landscape of Afghanistan. I even tuck my iPod headphones inside the large, padded headset we have to wear in the helicopter and listen to Pema while I fly over the foothills of the Hindu Kush and up into the mountains of Ghor. I listen to her in the morning as I get dressed for the day. I even listen to her at work, sneaking out into the yard at lunchtime to sit in the sun or walk laps around the compound. She tells me I can learn to sit with my discomfort instead of moving away or distracting myself.

I'm coming to see that there is no value in turning my morning meditation into yet another space in which to berate myself for not being good enough. I want to be a source of compassion, kindness and peace in the world and I can start by offering compassion, kindness and peace to myself.

So it is that, in the midst of my greatest inner turmoil, I begin to make some kind of peace with myself. It is only when I can relax just as I am, without harshness and without deception, that my meditation becomes a transformative process. I decide to meditate every morning, no matter what messy state I wake up in.

Initially I plan to meditate every day for twenty-one days. As the twenty-first day comes and goes, I realize I don't want to stop. Some days these moments on my cushion are calming and restorative. Other days they feel like a battleground. Whichever it is, I find a deep reassurance in the simple mantra I repeat to myself: *just sit*.

My yoga practice is also helping me sleep better and is lifting the dark cloud that hung over me in the weeks and months after Amanullah Khan's murder. Part of what was keeping me awake and causing the depression was the chemicals accumulating in my body from sustained periods of acute stress. As I'm learning from my yoga textbooks, when we are stressed, cortisol and adrenaline are released into the body. If we are exposed to sustained stress, these chemicals can have a depressive effect on our nervous system. This is true especially if they have not been used to either fight or flee the threat that triggered their release in the first place.

In the early days after the Shindand fighting, I sometimes found time to run on the treadmill long enough to feel the worst of the day's tension leave my body. But it was neither regular nor targeted enough to deal with the level of stress I was under. It has only been through a regular yoga practice that I've found a way to use or release those chemicals on a daily basis.

When I get through my yoga practice, I set my alarm for ten minutes and sit on my special orange cushion to practice meditating. I think of it as "practicing," because then I don't worry about whether I am doing it "right." I just do it. I rest my attention on the flow of my breath inward and outward. When my attention wanders off, I gently guide it back to my breath. That's it.

When the alarm goes at the end of ten minutes, I reach for my coffee and my journal and write out the first words and sentences that come to my mind. Some days I write pages of anxious questions about whether Joel can actually love me and whether I'm a fool to keep trying to make this relationship work. Other days I'm full of ideas and plans for the day ahead. Most of the time, though, I'm simply exploring my experience of yoga and meditation, and the effect they seem to have on me. Whatever emerges, I write until I feel like a clean slate, ready to embrace whatever the day holds.

I grow to love my mornings. No matter how early I have to wake up to fit it all in before the start of my working day, I welcome the alarm. Every morning feels like an investment in myself. I am filling my own well, so that I have something to draw on as I go out into the world each day. By the time I go downstairs to meet my boss, I feel nourished, grounded and ready for whatever might be waiting for me in the office.

20
The Christians

*A*s I am sitting on my meditation cushion, undergoing my own spiritual awakening, a different kind of spiritual awakening is taking place elsewhere in Herat.

One morning when I arrive in the office there is an email waiting for me.

> *Dear Mr. Elliott,*
>
> *I need your help. I am a 20 years old man and I live in Herat. Because I love Jesus I have become a Christian and now I must follow Christ.*
>
> *But this is very difficult. I am afraid. My father knows that I have become a Christian and now he will kill me.*
>
> *I know that you are working for the human rights and I need your help to protect my right to freedom of religion. Also I need help to find a church that can help me.*
>
> *Please help me,*
> *M.*

I'm used to being called Mr. Elliott, but the rest of the message stops me in my tracks. Despite having signed international human rights treaties protecting the right to freedom of religion, Afghanistan's constitution forbids conversion from Islam to another religion. The crime—known in English as apostasy—carries the death penalty. Recently an Afghan Christian convert was saved from a death sentence only by being evacuated to Italy. It seems plausible that the shame of having a convert in the family could lead a father to kill his own son. If the email is bona fide then this young man is in serious danger.

My instinct is to believe him, to take the message at face value. But I seek the advice of a colleague at the UN refugee agency. She is Italian and she wastes no time telling me what she thinks of this email.

"Don't believe them, Marianna!" she insists. "Ever since my government made this terrible decision to rescue the Christian from Kabul we get dozens of these messages every week. They all think they can claim to have become a Christian and get a fast trip to Italy. Ha! I don't think they realize what a shithole Italy is these days!"

The Italian government's rescue of the convert from Kabul has apparently inspired other young Afghans who want to get out of the country. According to my friend, UNHCR is being flooded with claims of conversion, many of which they suspect to be false.

"If they knew that they will most likely end up stuck in Pakistan," she continues, "I don't think they would be so keen to become Christians all of a sudden. Tell him the truth, that it is very hard to be a refugee in Pakistan and that he is not going to get a one-way ticket to the United States. If he's faking, he might change his mind. If he's telling the truth then you are just preparing him for reality."

Although her cynical tone is jarring, I can see she is right. There is a chance that this young man is only claiming to have become a Christian in the hope of getting to Italy or the United States. If he is faking, I need to make it clear what will really happen if he decides to pursue refugee status. It is not an easy option. This young man has access to a computer and can write in English, so it is fair to assume that he comes from a relatively wealthy home here in Herat. Life in Peshawar is likely to be a shock. After a reality check about a long, lonely life as an Afghan refugee in Pakistan, I hope he might reconsider his plan. Even if this is a genuine conversion, I can't see any easy way ahead if he insists on his new faith. His best chance might be to fake a renunciation of Christianity and go along to the mosque every week with his father.

I word my response carefully and run it past my boss before I send it.

Dear M,

I am very sorry to read your message and to learn of your very difficult situation.

Of course you are entitled to the freedom to choose and practice your own religion. The importance of this freedom is recognized in international law. Because Afghanistan has signed and ratified those laws the Government has an obligation to protect your right and to ensure that you are able to practice it freely.

However, in Afghanistan the reality falls far short of this ideal. If your father decides to harm you because of your choice to become Christian, there may be very little that the Government can do to protect you. And because the real threat to you right now comes from within your home rather than from the State, there is also very little that I can do to protect you.

All I can do is advise you of some options that may protect you. You have several choices. One is to publicly renounce Christianity and return to the Islamic faith. This may or may not be a true reflection of what you believe in your heart but it may protect you from grave danger and prevent your father from committing a terrible crime.

I can imagine that this option may initially seem impossible to you. I urge you to give it serious consideration. You would not be prevented from continuing to hold your own private beliefs, nor from practicing your beliefs in your own private ways but you would publicly and visibly appear to be practicing as a Muslim.

If you do not think you can do this, then you may choose to leave your home and travel to someplace where your family cannot find you. This could be another city in Afghanistan, or it could be one of the neighboring countries.

If you were to arrive in another country, having fled your home country because of fear of religious persecution, then you could apply to the local office of UNHCR (the United Nations High Commission for Refugees). If they are convinced by your story then you may be granted refugee status. There are no guarantees in this process, however, and it is a difficult and lonely path to travel.

Many people think that getting refugee status will lead to resettlement in Europe or America. This is usually not the case. Please don't embark on this journey with false expectations. If you make it to Pakistan, for example, where it is possible to live safely as a Christian in some areas, then you would probably be expected to live there as a refugee without any resettlement at all.

If you decide that you would like to try to leave the country and need more information about where to go to find the local UNHCR offices in countries neighboring Afghanistan then please let me know. I will do everything I can to help you.

Yours sincerely,
Marianne Elliott
Human Rights Officer
United Nations Assistance Mission in Afghanistan

I feel uncomfortable advising this young man to fake a renunciation of his Christianity. But I want him to stay alive. I hope I've struck the right balance in my response.

In any case, I don't hear back from him. I report the exchange to my boss and record it in the confidential case files that we keep for conversions. These files are only accessible to international human rights officers, not to our Afghan colleagues or even to our international political colleagues. They are probably the most sensitive and inflammatory of all the cases we handle.

As the days go by with no response, I don't know whether to worry about the young man or assume that he was, after all, hoping for an easy trip to Italy. Even if he is in real danger, I have no idea how to find him and I can hardly start asking around town for anyone who recently became a Christian. A few days after my first message, I send another email to his address, asking whether he has any more questions or whether there is anything more I can do to help him. Still I hear nothing.

A week after his email, I see a note in the daily security report that a twenty-year-old man in Herat was killed by his father for converting to Christianity. I feel nauseous. I am convinced this is the young man who emailed me. This explains why I haven't heard back from him.

All day I think about him. I wonder what he thought and felt when he got my email. I wonder whether he tried to renounce his faith. It seems unlikely. Perhaps he began to make plans to escape. Perhaps he was paralyzed by despair after reading my grim email and did nothing while his father plotted his murder. Perhaps he never even read my response.

I can't concentrate on any of my other work. I call the person who wrote the security report and ask him about it. He says the reported murder is unconfirmed at this stage but that he heard it from several different sources so he feels confident it is true. I ask him to follow up with the police to see if they have launched an investigation into the murder. I want the police to know that the UN will be following this case. If I failed my young correspondent in life then at least I can try to press for some justice for him in death.

That night I tell Joel about the case. We drink whiskey and he tries to make me feel better about my failure to help this young man. He blames the missionaries who come to Afghanistan and encourage these young Afghans to convert to Christianity, despite knowing the grave risk it poses to them. I know it isn't my fault this young man is dead, but he reached out to me in his hour of need and I somehow failed him. I feel desperately sad for him. I'm having trouble getting the image out of my mind of him reading my email and becoming filled with despair.

What I am not feeling, though, is the dreadful crisis of confidence that had almost drowned me after Amanullah Khan's murder. I am beginning to accept that all I can do is make the very best job I can of each situation that presents itself to me. Part of doing my very best, I am learning, is taking the time to pay careful attention to the needs of the person who shows up in front of me. Had I paid careful enough attention to his email? On reflection, I feel I did the best I could with very little information.

The next day I get a call from my boss. He has someone in his office who needs to see me. He asks me to come alone, without either my Afghan human rights assistant or a language assistant. This is unusual and I immediately suspect that the visit has something to do with the murder. I put down the phone and walk quickly along the corridor to my boss's office. The door is closed so I knock and announce myself. He tells me to come in and to close the door behind me.

Sitting at the round table with my boss is a blond, fair-skinned man in his early forties. He is dressed "American-style" in cargo pants and a button-down shirt and he smiles warmly at me as I sit down at the table with him. He introduces himself as Jim and explains that he is an American who has been living in Herat with his family for several years. He runs a private business in the city and is also involved in a charitable organization that provides tertiary education opportunities to young Afghans. He begins to tell me about the charity and some of the young people they have helped in Herat.

Because of the secretiveness surrounding our meeting I suspect Jim knows something about the young man who emailed me or about the murder, and I am desperately curious to find out what. But Afghanistan is teaching me the value of listening. So, instead of interrupting Jim to ask him to get to the point, I let him continue at his own pace.

If people are nervous about what they need to tell you, then the first moments of a meeting are an opportunity for them to decide whether they can trust you. If you don't have the patience to listen while they tell you the history of their family, then why would they trust you to hear about whatever they have really come to talk about?

Eventually Jim stops talking. He looks at me, takes a deep breath, and then starts again.

"Through my work I came to know two young men. They were close friends and were studying together at the university. They were in their midtwenties and were already married and each had a child. They told me that they had become Christians and asked me for my help and support." He hesitates, looking at me to gauge my reaction.

"Yes," I say, nodding, "I understand."

"I wanted to help them but I was aware how dangerous the situation was, not only for them but also for my own family. I told them that they had to be very, very careful not to give any signs to their families of the change in their faith, but I agreed that they could come and meet in my home since there was nowhere else safe for them to meet.

"I knew that they were interested in getting out of the country," Jim carries on, "because they asked for my advice and assistance to do so. I spoke to the U.S. embassy in Kabul and was told that there was nothing that could be done while they were in Afghanistan. They would have to leave Afghanistan and then seek asylum once they were in another country." He looks at me, as though to confirm this advice.

"That's right," I agree. "That's how it works."

"Right, so I explained that to them. We talked about what this meant for their wives and young children. They told me about another friend of theirs who had also become a Christian. He was younger than them, about twenty years old, and he had become afraid that his father had discovered his conversion and was going to kill him. I gave them some money for him and told them that they should encourage him to leave Herat as soon as possible. Before he could leave Herat his father killed him."

"Oh," I can't help but exclaim, "yes, I think I know this case. It's terrible."

"Absolutely," Jim agrees. "And now the other two men are terrified. A lot of people know they were friends with the young man who was killed. They are afraid that their families will guess that they too have converted to Christianity. I need your help to get the other two young men, together with their wives and children, out of Herat and out of Afghanistan."

This time I am not going to be skeptical or wary in my advice. I tell Jim what he already knows, that the process of leaving Afghanistan and seeking asylum as refugees in a neighboring country will be difficult and fraught with problems for these young families. But I also tell him that I will do all I can to help them. I will help him find accommodation for the families in a safe and friendly hotel in Kabul. I will give them the directions to the UNHCR office in Pakistan and alert the officer there that they are coming. I promise to document the case of the young man who was killed. When they get to the UNHCR offices in Pakistan or Iran they can refer the investigating officers to me and I will give them all the evidence I have showing these young Christians were in very real danger.

Jim and I discuss all these steps and agree he will take my advice to the young men and get back in touch with me by email. It is best if we are not seen together any more than is absolutely necessary.

As he leaves I wonder why I am not angry with Jim as I am with the other anonymous Christians in Herat who are helping these young people convert to a faith that puts their lives and the lives of their families at risk. For one thing, I reason, if Jim's story is true then these young men approached him after they had already converted. But even if he did play a role in their decision to become Christians, at least he is now doing all that he can to help them. Although my boss and I are both making a contribution, Jim is paying most of the costs of their escape to Pakistan. This is more than can be said for the "friends" of another young man, Mirwais, who turns up in my office later in the month.

When Mirwais arrives at the UNAMA compound, he asks to see me—the human rights officer—alone. He doesn't want any Afghans present, not even an interpreter, as he speaks English. I agree to meet him and arrange to use a private office for the interview. As soon as he starts to speak my heart sinks. Mirwais claims to have converted to Christianity. His father has apparently begun to suspect something is wrong and now Mirwais wants my help to escape Afghanistan before his father kills him.

Given the recent history I have with these cases I want to know who the hell is converting all these young Afghans. I ask Mirwais. He tells me he became a Christian after watching a TV show about Jesus. I don't believe him for a minute and say so. I know there are people in Herat who are encouraging young Afghans to become Christians. I ask Mirwais why he hasn't gone to the people who converted him to ask them for help. I immediately regret my abrupt manner when I see Mirwais begin to sweat under my questioning.

Despite his discomfort, he tells me he approached some people he knows in Herat who have a church and they told him they couldn't help him. I am furious with them. Poor Mirwais bears the brunt of that fury. I tell him, in no uncertain terms, how difficult it is to apply for asylum as a refugee.

Mirwais obviously comes from a relatively wealthy family. He is dressed in expensive clothing, speaks fluent English and is enrolled in Herat University. He is accustomed to a life of relative privilege and he believes I can help him get asylum in the United States. I give him the worst-case scenario.

"The only way you can apply for refugee status is to first get yourself to Iran, Turkmenistan or Pakistan," I say.

"But I don't have my passport with me and I'm too afraid to go home to get it," he responds.

"Well, then you only have one option. You can try to get into Pakistan without a passport."

The western borders of Afghanistan, with Iran and Turkmenistan, were heavily mined during the years of wars in Afghanistan, making it extremely dangerous to try to travel across those areas. Mirwais, if he insists on leaving Afghanistan, will have to travel east with the hundreds of other Afghans who make their way illegally across the border to Pakistan in taxis, private cars and on foot.

I begin to describe what his life is likely to be like in Pakistan.

"Once you get to Pakistan, you'll have to find work. It won't be easy. The Pakistanis won't want to give good jobs to an illegal Afghan immigrant. You might be lucky to find work as a cleaner or a taxi driver."

"I can work," he says, defying my efforts to dissuade him.

"Once you get to Pakistan, that's where you'll have to stay," I continue my depressing litany. "Even if you do manage to get refugee status, which is not guaranteed, they won't be handing you a ticket to America."

"I just have to get away from here," he says. "I have to get away before my father kills me."

His words remind me of the email from the young man who was murdered. No matter how remote Mirwais's chances are of making a good life outside Afghanistan, I can't argue against it any longer. I tell him that he needs money.

"You'll need enough for your fare to Pakistan, maybe some food along the way. You'll probably need to stop in Kabul and then get another bus to the border. It will be good to have a little bit of money to live on once you get to Pakistan; it could take a while to find work."

"I don't have any money on me," he says. "All my money is at home and I can't go back there."

By now he is sweating profusely and I can see his hands shaking. I try my "fake a renunciation" approach with him. I suggest he could start going to the mosque with his father. I even go so far as to say that Jesus will understand why he needs to do that. I know I am speaking well beyond my authority on this point, but the boy is shaking in terror. I really don't think he is ready for life on the streets of Islamabad.

Mirwais is not convinced.

"How do you know what Jesus would think?" he challenges me.

I laugh, which breaks the tension in the room a little.

"You are probably wise to doubt me on that count," I tell Mirwais, smiling and feeling my own body and heart soften. "But I really am just trying to help."

"I believe you," he says, "but I don't think I have any option. I must leave Herat immediately. I cannot go home, not even to get my passport or money."

"Well, in that case you need to get to Pakistan. You can cross the border there without a passport."

"Can you help me get on a UN flight to Kabul?" he asks. "Or Pakistan?" I'm irritated by Mirwais's assumption of privilege. While other Afghans take the bus from Herat to Kabul and then make their way painstakingly by taxi to the border, Mirwais wants me to book him on a UN flight to Islamabad. I know it is unfair, but nonetheless I am frustrated.

"Listen, Mirwais, you'll just have to take the bus like everyone else." In the end the best thing I can do for Mirwais is to give him two hundred dollars, the name of a bus driver who will take him to Kabul, a hotel in Kabul where he can stay without fear of being found by his father, and the address of the UNHCR office in Islamabad. Peshawar is closer but I'm worried that he might be recognized by one of the many Afghans who live in Peshawar.

I go into my office to grab my wallet. Carolina is there. Her three-month posting to New York has become permanent and she is back in Herat for a week to pack up her room and clear out her desk. She asks me how the interview is going. I give her a very brief summary and admit what I am doing with my wallet. She does not approve. For one thing two hundred dollars is a lot of money. It's a lot of money to me, but even more to Mirwais. She's worried about the precedent I might be setting.

"Ah, Marianna," she sighs, "I love you but damn it, you are soft-hearted and naïve. This guy is probably scamming you. How do you know that any of his story is true? You can't start giving money to everyone who shows up here with a sob story."

"I know, I know," I reply. "There may be no conversion, no murderous father. Mirwais may be about to walk away with two hundred dollars of my money, laughing all the way to the bank. But one kid is already dead. I'd rather be taken for a fool than risk making the same mistake twice."

Carolina shrugs theatrically, but smiles at me. I suspect, despite her bravado, she may not have been able to refuse Mirwais either.

I give Mirwais the money and he leaves with directions to the nearest bus station. It is nearly the end of my working day and I am exhausted. I type up case notes from the interview and email a colleague in Kabul who will help Mirwais if he has any problems with his accommodation. Then I email the UNHCR officer in Islamabad to warn him there is another convert on his way. In the end I never hear anything more of Mirwais, either from my colleague in Kabul or from Islamabad. For all I know it was a scam after all. Or his father found him.

After four cases of Christian converts in less than a month I am ready to go on a hunt in Herat to find these missionaries and tell them what comes of their conversions. They must be out there somewhere, yet they are nowhere to be seen when these desperate young people end up in my office.

Ironically, although it is considered a crime for a Muslim to convert to any other religion, I find Afghans are extremely respectful of Christians from other, non-Muslim countries. Their problem is with people who abandon Islam; most Afghans don't seem to have any particular agenda against Christianity. In fact, many people I talk to seem to think Christianity is an excellent religion—for other people.

Most Afghans assume I am Christian. My parents are Christians and I have great respect for their faith and the way they embody it in their lives. I myself cannot believe that Christ is the only path to God, which is a central doctrine of Christianity, so I cannot be a Christian. Still, the fact that I come from a Western country and celebrate Christmas is enough to convince most of my colleagues that I am. Some of them make a point of letting me know that they approve of my religion.

"Christianity is a very good religion, Miss Marianne," says one of the drivers one day as he takes me home. I'm sitting in the backseat, but I catch his eye in the mirror and he is smiling warmly at me.

"Well, yes it is, mostly," I agree.

"Christianity, Judaism and Islam," he continues, "these three are the best religions."

I feel like I'm having a conversation about football teams rather than world religions. He's letting me know that, despite his undying allegiance to his own team, he's willing to acknowledge the quality of my team. I feel it would be churlish to point out that I'm not actually a loyal fan of the side he's complimenting, so I simply agree.

"Yes," I say, "they are certainly tough to beat."

He smiles at me, satisfied, while I wonder whether I'll ever have a better answer to the question I'm asked so often in Afghanistan: What is your religion?

21
Occasional Recuperation Break

March–May 2007: Herat, Afghanistan

*T*hings with Joel have reached a strange kind of stasis. I'm feeling much more stable, which means I don't seek his constant reassurance like I did before. Not surprisingly, as I ask less of him, he feels less driven to withdraw from me. It is becoming easier just to be together. But I can't help but wonder, will I ever be able to trust him to be there for me when I really need him?

A distance has opened up between us. When I think back to our early days in Kabul, and the easy intimacy that grew so naturally between us, I barely recognize the people we are now. We keep each other company, and we still make each other laugh. Yet I feel I have to keep my deepest fears and most profound discoveries to myself. For example, I don't talk to Joel about the difference that my morning meditation and yoga practices are having on my life.

Maybe most disconcertingly, physical affection has almost disappeared from our relationship. During my darkest days there were times when I came right out and asked Joel to hold me, to give me some physical reassurance that I wasn't falling apart. He was reluctant but I was persistent, convinced that my very sanity depended on it. Now he avoids initiating any kind of contact. When I stay at his house for the night, I lie awake, painfully aware of the space between us.

In some ways, though, Joel and I still make a great team. At our best, we work well together on child protection projects and find new ways to get the UN agencies cooperating with the NGOs. At our worst, we indulge in a good long bitch session at the end of an insane day at the office. Between the bitching and the *Buffy* we help keep each other sane even as we are driving each other crazy.

At the beginning of April, Joel tells me he doesn't feel any real connection with me anymore. Apparently he hasn't for months. This certainly explains the growing sense of distance between us, but it doesn't lessen the pain when I hear it. I am not yet willing to let this relationship go, so I suggest that he take some time to think it over. With great effort I stay away from him for a week, making no contact at all. Fortunately for both of us, I am just about to go to London for a week's leave. Every eight weeks we are supposed to leave Afghanistan for an "occasional recuperation break." For once UN bureaucracy-speak is spot on.

I head to London for private meditation lessons at the Shambhala Meditation Center. I found the center via Pema Chödrön's website and emailed them to ask about getting some instruction. In my email I explained that I was doing human rights work in Afghanistan and trying to develop my own meditation practice. My email was passed on to the president of the international Shambhala Buddhist network, Richard Reoch.

It turns out, serendipitously, that Richard is not only an internationally respected meditation teacher but also a human rights advocate with extensive experience living and working in war zones. It just so happens that he will be in London when I visit and he wants to meet me and teach me himself. I couldn't have asked for a more perfect meditation teacher.

Being in London is so much easier than being home in New Zealand was in November. Perhaps it is me who has changed. I feel lighter, and everything about London in spring delights me. I stay with my aunt, who has done development work all over the world, been through a difficult divorce and survived breast cancer. We have long talks over breakfast and I remember that I have the love and support of my family, however alone I may feel in Herat. She lives near Regent's Park, and when she leaves for work I spend hours wandering through the park, enjoying the freedom and ease of movement.

Imogen is also now living in London. We have a picnic in the park, and talk about the psychological and physical toll humanitarian work has taken on us both. The next day we go to a yoga class, marveling at the difference yoga is making to our well-being and resilience.

I also visit my friend Susannah on the south coast of England. Susannah's boyfriend died only eighteen months ago, so she is familiar with the kinds of dark places I've been inhabiting, and she encourages me to go and talk to her therapist, Jill. When I finish telling Jill what I've been through in the past six months, she says I might be experiencing some kind of ongoing posttraumatic stress reaction. Importantly, she says she would be surprised if I wasn't struggling, given what I've been through. Knowing this won't fix everything, but it does help me feel less crazy and less like I'm making a fuss over nothing. It's a relief to have someone say something other than "Toughen up" or "Look on the bright side."

After a week I return to Herat refreshed, rested and with my new meditation techniques in hand, to Joel's announcement he doesn't want to break up. Having expected him to announce that we were done, I accept this reprieve gratefully and we carry on, hoping it will get better. But as the weeks pass, our different approaches to healing our relationship become increasingly obvious. I want to talk about what went wrong and how we can fix it. Joel wants to leave things be and see if the "spark" comes back of its own accord.

On top of that, we finally talk about what our future might look like if we stay together. I am about to turn thirty-five and I'm starting to think about having a family. Joel, however, has decided he won't have any children; there are already too many children in the world, he says. He might be open to the idea of adoption, but refuses to consider having children of his own. This isn't a position he would try to force on anyone else, but for him the decision has been made.

What bothers me about this is that Joel made his decision without me. He has taken a position on the matter and isn't about to reconsider it for me. My reaction probably just makes him even more determined. As usual, I cry.

"You don't seem to even care how I feel about this," I say through my tears.

"Well, that's because how you feel is irrelevant. Choosing to have a child is too important a decision to make based on feelings. It has to be made based on ethics. I don't believe it is ethical for me to have a child when there are already children alive who need parents."

The thing is, I have some sympathy for Joel's ethical position, at least for those of us in the privileged position of being able to control our sexual encounters and having easy access to contraceptives. I am quite open to the possibility of adopting. But I want to know that Joel cares how I feel. Surely, I reason, if he really loves me, my feelings would be at least relevant to his decision. This whole issue about having children seems like an opportunity to assess whether he loves me or not.

Unfortunately, the evidence is all lining up on the wrong side of the table.

I am aware that staying with a man who has openly admitted that he doesn't think he loves me anymore is unwise. But Joel is my best friend, and has been since my earliest days in Afghanistan. Amid all the chaos and newness of my life, Joel is the only constant. Our connection was formed quickly, but that is not unusual in this setting, with the combination of dislocation from all other friends and family and the intense emotional pressure of this kind of work. Given everything else that is unstable in my life right now, I will stay in this relationship at almost any cost.

On the morning of my thirty-fifth birthday, however, I wake up alone in my bed. The night before, Joel helped organize my birthday party. At the party he had quite a lot to drink and before the last guest left, he wandered off and fell asleep on a cushion dragged out onto the roof outside my room. I went to bed alone, berating myself for hanging on so tightly to our broken affair.

In the morning I take time to drink my coffee, do my yoga and meditation and dress in my favorite orange tunic before I wake up Joel. He isn't a morning person at the best of times. Today he seems to have forgotten that it is my birthday. He slept in his clothes, and without even talking to me he straightens his shirt and pulls on his boots before heading downstairs to ask my boss if he can be dropped back at his own compound on our way to the office. I feel a momentary wave of self-pity at this lonely beginning to my birthday. But I don't dwell on it for long. I put on some beautiful Afghan jewelry given to me by a friend in Kabul, remind myself of the many people who do love and support me, and then make my way down to join them.

We drop Joel at his compound and drive out of town toward our office. I'm relieved to get there and busy myself making the final arrangements for our upcoming trip to Ghor province.

22
Flying to Ghor

May 2007: Herat and Ghor, Afghanistan

*I*n the weeks leading up to my birthday, Kate and I have been final-
izing the materials for the Ghor workshop. It was well received in
Badghis, so there are no major changes, but we agree that we should
make the material a little simpler. We also decide to change some of the
case studies to reflect the types of cases I see most often in Ghor province.

Meanwhile I have been working with Asiyah on the logistics of
the workshop in Ghor. Asiyah is going to take over the translation
duties for this workshop and she is also doing a great job of making the preliminary arrangements. She and I have already flown up to
Chaghcharan, the provincial center, to meet with the relevant officials
and to find a venue.

We've had a very good response from the police in Ghor. I've worked
with the provincial head of the Criminal Investigation Department
before and he is quick to get on board with the workshop. He sets
about arranging for the local police chiefs from each district to travel to
the provincial center for the workshop. He also tells us that ten officers
from his own department in the provincial center will attend.

I am impressed. These men have a lot of control over the day-to-day
experience of human rights of people in their districts. In some remote

districts, the police are the only government presence. They are, to the community, the face of the new "democratic" model of government and the new constitution. I am going to have them all together, for almost a week, just to talk about gender and criminal justice. I can hardly believe it, and I'm determined to make the most of this rare opportunity.

Along with the police, the chief prosecutor summons the senior prosecutor from each district and commits to sending a significant number of staff from his own office along to the training too. I realize that our workshop will likely delay criminal investigations and prosecutions in the province by a solid week. This makes it even more important to ensure the event is worthwhile.

Kate's boss again agrees to provide her time to the project free of charge. In order to get Kate to Ghor, I fill out numerous forms explaining why her presence is essential to the workshop and, in turn, why the workshop is essential to fulfilling the UN human rights mandate in Ghor. Eventually we receive word that Kate's passage on a UNAMA flight to meet me in Herat is approved. From here we will fly together to Ghor.

A local legal aid organization that I helped to get funding from the Icelandic government offers us their rooms to host the workshop. The Icelandic development adviser, Heida—who is based on the ISAF military base in Ghor—offers to provide a hot midday meal every day for all the participants. She will also print out copies of the materials and the completion certificates. Little by little I am able to pull in favors to make up for our lack of budget.

But I still need money to transport each district prosecutor and police officer from their district into the provincial capital and then to house and feed them for the six nights of the workshop. I decide that the easiest plan will be to calculate how much this is likely to cost them and then give each person a cash payment on the basis of receipts provided.

I send one of my drivers into the center of Chaghcharan to get estimates of costs for rooms, meals and transport to and from each of the district centers. Based on these estimates I need eight hundred dollars. Given that this will house, feed and transport almost forty men for a week, it is a tiny amount. But I still have to find it.

In a country where literally millions of dollars in foreign money is spent every day on military presence and activity it seems ludicrous that I have to ask my friends and family in New Zealand to donate the money. But that's what I do. I send out an email telling them about the workshop in Badghis and explaining why we want to do another in Ghor. By the end of the following day I have seven responses from people confirming that they want to make a contribution. By the end of the week I have raised more than I need. I am buoyed by my friends' and family's support for the work we are doing. I am particularly touched by a donation from Kate, who is already doing so much to make the workshop happen.

Today, in the typical way of UN missions, all my arrangements have to be remade, as our flights change twice within five hours. Each time they change I have to go through the entire process of getting security clearance and approval for each of the non-UN participants, including Kate, to travel with us.

In the midst of the administrative hell that is rescheduling a UN flight, I am receiving lovely birthday phone calls from New Zealand. When the mail arrives I am thrilled to discover that a parcel sent from Vietnam has miraculously arrived on the very day of my birthday. It is a tea mug with a built-in strainer. I love it. I make myself a cup of ginger tea and sit at my desk while rearranging all the flight clearances for the second time that day.

My new colleague, an English human rights lawyer who replaced Carolina when she was transferred to New York, has been watching me deal with these last-minute changes to my carefully laid plans all day. She tells me she's impressed by my ability to remain calm. I wonder whether I might finally be learning how to cope with the vagaries of planning in Afghanistan and in the UN.

The day passes quickly and by the close of business the entire trip is brought forward by a day. We will now be leaving tomorrow morning; however Kate can't be brought to Herat in time to join us. Instead she will travel the following day, as originally planned, flying directly from Kabul to Ghor.

Toward the end of the day I get a call from Joel inviting me over for a birthday dinner. Whatever the flaws in our relationship, he is a great cook. I'm elated!

For my birthday Joel goes to considerable effort to cook a delicious meal. He finds some frozen fish at the Italian military base and cooks it with fresh herbs and lemon. After dinner we watch *Three Kings*, a movie about the Gulf War. It is hardly light entertainment, and far from romantic, but at least it makes a decent effort to show something of the true chaos and sadness of war. Once the movie finishes, I head back to my place to pack. I make it home in time, for once, to make my radio check before curfew.

In the morning our flight leaves for Ghor. As our little eight-seater Beechcraft plane takes off, I feel my spirits lift immediately. The endless security restrictions of life in Herat mean that I spend most of my days inside one compound or another. Being cooped up is not helping my mood or my efforts to remain sane.

As the plane pulls up and away from Herat, I suddenly have a view that extends as far south as Farah province. I feel an unfamiliar sensation in my chest. It's as though my ribs are being gently pried open. I am inhaling more deeply than I have in days, perhaps weeks. As my diaphragm adjusts to the unfamiliar sensation of a deep breath, my cheeks contort in an equally unfamiliar sensation. I am smiling! Spontaneously, for no reason other than that I'm not locked up in a compound or driving in an armored vehicle, I am smiling from ear to ear.

I breathe in the sense of space as we sweep up and over the foothills of the Hindu Kush. It is early May and the snow is beginning to melt on the mountains, filling the rivers that now rush down through the valleys, bringing new life to each village that they pass. Flying over Ghor province gives the impression that it is entirely uninhabited. Most people in the province live in very small hamlets and villages that are almost impossible to see from the air. The buildings blend effortlessly into their surroundings.

The higher we climb into the mountains of the Hindu Kush the happier I become. I always prefer to live on the top of hills and love nothing better than hiking to the highest point on the horizon. Living in a valley, or in a house surrounded by tall buildings, makes me feel trapped, and life in the enclosed compounds of Kabul and Herat has tested my resilience to the limit. The sight of the mountains of Ghor is like a long drink of water for my parched soul.

We approach Chaghcharan following the path of the Hari Rud River. The pilot flies low over the runway once to check it is clear of wandering animals and then circles back around to make the final approach for landing. I love Chaghcharan and am excited about the workshop. I have moved heaven and earth to get everyone here, and I am sure it will be worth it.

I have arranged for the women in our party to stay in a house owned by Catholic Relief Services. There are five of us. For the workshop itself there will be Kate, my assistant Asiyah, and Faezeh, the head of the Women's Rights Unit at the Afghan Independent Human Rights Commission in Herat, who is also guest-teaching at the workshop. The fifth woman is Suraya Pakzad. I managed to get her on the UN flight so that she can look into setting up a branch of Voice of Women in Ghor. The province is in desperate need of a shelter for women, and I'm keen to do whatever I can to help make that happen.

The men are staying at another guesthouse belonging to World

Vision. We stop in the town center, which is no more than a couple of dusty shacks selling vegetables and tinned goods, and buy some supplies for dinner and breakfast, and then drop our gear off at the house.

I have several errands to run in order to finalize all the arrangements for the workshop, so I leave Faezeh and Suraya to make the usual visits to the governor and other local officials. I go to the ISAF military base just out of town where Heida is waiting to discuss final arrangements for the food. Heida and I get along very well indeed, and working with her is a pleasure. The last time I saw her was when Asiyah and I came up to make arrangements for this workshop, and I have been looking forward to seeing her again.

My driver drops me off at the external gate to the base. I've been to the base several times by now so I know the routine. I have to walk through the first gate, where an Afghan security guard and one Lithuanian soldier check my ID. From there I walk a few hundred meters along a metal road with a deep moat to my left and a high wall, marking the outer perimeter of the base, to my right. It is still daytime so I have no problem avoiding the large concrete bollards that are placed at random intervals along the path. When I visit after dark I carry a torch because the base is completely pitch black. They leave the lights off to make it more difficult for anyone who wants to target the base with a rocket-propelled grenade, or worse.

At the interior gate I shout up to the soldier in the tower above me, telling him that I am from the UN and I have a meeting with Heida. Unfortunately he doesn't speak English and has no idea what I am trying to say. I try speaking to him in Dari, but to no avail. It is disconcerting to be in the middle of Afghanistan and meet someone who speaks only Lithuanian. Actually, he probably speaks a little Russian, which is a language familiar to many Afghans, but I am at a loss with that too.

Fortunately I called Heida before I left to let her know that I was coming, and I can hear her voice on the other side of the gate. She is also trying to speak to the soldier in English. She manages to communicate, perhaps through gestures, that she wants the gate to be opened. I hear the lock on the small door in the base of the gate being slid back. The door swings open and a female soldier gestures to me to enter. She speaks to me, presumably in Lithuanian, but when she sees that I don't understand, she mimes that she needs to see inside my bag.

As she searches my daypack I watch a line of Afghan day laborers being searched as they leave the base. They are carrying bags of wood offcuts. One even has a wheelbarrow filled with remnants from whatever building project they are working on. This is obviously all legitimate because the soldiers searching them pay no attention to the wood. I know how hard it is to find affordable fuel in Ghor, and presume that these men are taking the offcuts home to use in their stoves. This will be saving their wives and daughters many hours of work each day that would otherwise be spent gathering firewood. No wonder the jobs on the military base are coveted, despite the security risks that come with being associated with the foreign military.

It is distressing to think that in some provinces the Taliban make an example of Afghans who work with the foreign military forces, even in strictly civilian roles. In the southeast recently, two men were killed just because they delivered fuel to American army bases. Here in Ghor, where antigovernment forces are still thin on the ground, it seems unlikely that these laborers are in any immediate danger. But in the long run it is a risky job choice and, it seems to me, the willingness of so many men to work here is a sign of the lack of options available to them.

Security checks over, Heida walks me over to the tent where she shares an office with the political adviser to the Lithuanian commander of the base. We double-check the numbers of participants who will need feeding and the time we will be serving lunch each day. Heida lets me check my email on her computer. When I open my email, I find a message that sends my blood pressure through the roof. Apparently someone in Kabul noticed the plane booked to fly to Ghor tomorrow with only one passenger, and that the passenger is not a UN staff member. So Kate's flight has been canceled.

It is too late to try to resolve this by email. I tell Heida I have to go, and rush back to the guesthouse where I have a satellite phone. I call my direct manager in Herat. He is very sympathetic to my plight but explains it isn't his decision to make. He suggests that I call flight operations.

I call the manager at UNAMA flight operations. I have dealt with him many times before and he is an extraordinarily helpful man. He would like to help me, he assures me, but it is a UNAMA rule that there can be no flight without at least one UNAMA staff member. I begin to protest, pointing out this wasn't made clear when all our flights were rearranged yesterday, but quickly realize I don't have time for recriminations. I need solutions.

Flight operations say they can't send a plane unless there is a UNAMA staff member who needs to get from Kabul to Ghor tomorrow. In a flash of inspiration, I decide to create one. I call the Human Rights Unit in Kabul and talk to one of my colleagues. I explain my problem to her and ask whether she has a junior staff member whom she can spare for a week. I promise that if she sends me her human rights assistant I will give him some excellent training in running workshops and in gender justice. To my enormous relief she agrees.

Within fifteen minutes she fills out the official form asking for her assistant to be approved to fly to Ghor tomorrow in order to help with our workshop. She emails it to flight operations. I call my boss in Herat and explain we now have a UNAMA staff member for the flight. I call the flight operations manager and tell him that a form is on its way to him requesting a seat on the flight for a UNAMA staff member. He seems happy that he will be able to help me without breaking any mission rules.

Kate's flight is on again. I've been on the phone for two hours and I feel as though I've run a marathon. It has taken a year, but I am finally learning how to work in the UN system. There are rules that cannot be broken, but there are also ways to work around these rules. I've learned that the people who run operations like the UNAMA flights can be invaluable allies. If I remain courteous, even when my plans seem to be falling apart, it is amazing how far the support staff will go to try and help me. This is a big moment for me, a moment of finally feeling that I fit into the UN system and, more importantly, of finally feeling effective at my job.

I had stashed a little bottle of gin and some cans of tonic in my suitcase to share with Kate. I decide I deserve a drink to celebrate my successful negotiations. So, incongruous as it seems, I pour myself a gin and tonic and sit out in the back garden. It is early evening and I would love to go for a walk in the hills out behind the house, but to do that I would have to take one of the guards. What I need most of all, right now, is solitude.

As I sit watching the sun set over the hills behind Chaghcharan, there is a familiar tussle in my mind between relishing my successful afternoon and wondering why I haven't yet heard from Joel. I shake off all thoughts of our relationship for the moment and savor the victory of my afternoon and the anticipation of the day to come.

23
Workshop in Ghor

May 2007: Ghor, Afghanistan

*T*he Ghor workshop is even more successful, and more chaotic, than the workshop in Badghis. We have a bigger turnout of policemen and prosecutors, more than forty participants in total. We even have one imam, an Islamic religious teacher. He sits in the front row all week and listens thoughtfully to Kate's expositions on what sharia law has to say on subjects like rape within marriage.

Kate's courage in presenting to such an audience deepens my admiration for her. She knows her stuff, on both secular Afghan law and sharia law, and she speaks with the assurance of someone who has read over her material until she knows it inside and out. She is always respectful, welcoming critical feedback. In fact—as she admits to me in the evenings while we walk over the hills behind our guesthouse with the security guard walking in silence alongside us—she often feels intimidated, although she never shows it.

While Kate's teaching is a hit, the food supplied by the military base is not. For our workshop in Badghis, the Spanish development officers paid Afghan cooks to prepare traditional Afghan food. In Ghor, Heida has asked the chefs at the Lithuanian army base to prepare the food. Our participants are perplexed by the crumbed chicken cutlets and mashed potatoes. They don't understand why each person's meal has been separated out into individual serving containers. Eating together, out of one large bowl of rice and meat, is part of the group bonding process. I am going to have to order Afghan-style food from the restaurant in the town center or risk having this strange foreign food detract from the workshop.

Fortunately for me, a little bit of money goes a long way in rural Afghanistan. I'm able to buy a hot cooked lunch for the forty participants for a little over fifty dollars. I can almost cover the cost of the lunches from the extra money I raised for the workshop, and Kate and I agree that we will make up the difference between us. The next day the restaurant delivers large dishes of steaming hot rice scattered with chunks of meat. Everyone is happy.

There are five women on the course from the local Department of Women's Affairs, as well as two female provincial councilors. Together they act as lay advocates for most women who come into contact with the criminal justice system in Ghor. Their participation is essential if our workshop is to have a positive impact for women in Ghor.

And they participate actively. Occasionally one of the women is the first to respond to the questions Kate poses to the group. Much of the workshop is spent in small groups. This gives the women an opportunity to work together, away from the pressure of a male audience. They engage enthusiastically in the role play and case studies, and even allow me to photograph them as they work.

My camera, as it turns out, is a star attraction of the workshop. I am trying to take candid photos of people talking, listening and debating, but many of the participants have never been photographed before, so it becomes distracting. I decide the best solution will be to take photographs of everyone during the lunch break one day. I promise to make prints of the photos the next time I go to Kabul so they can each have a copy. At lunchtime the men all line up for their turn; the women watch from the shady balcony. I take portrait photos of all forty men. Once everyone has been photographed alone, they start requesting photographs together.

"Take a photo of me with my brother, please, Miss Marianne."

"Another, please, of me with my friend here from Dowlatyar!"

"One more please, of all the prosecutors from Chaghcharan."

I snap away for the entire hour. I could keep going all day. I want to see whether I can get the men to smile. It is conventional for Afghan men to adopt a very serious expression for a photo. This is all very well for the images they want to mount on their own office walls, but for my own record, I want to remember them as I have seen them all day— animated with laughter. So I tease them. I call out from behind my camera, telling them their friend looks more handsome because he is smiling. I ask why they are so sad. Some are very good at holding their stoic expressions until I put the camera down, at which point they burst into laughter. Others I can cajole into a smile while I'm still snapping.

These photos capture for me the essence of what makes these two workshops so wonderful. I continue to hear many complaints about the Afghan National Police, and I'm hardly an apologist for their short-comings—it is part of my job to investigate and document allegations of police corruption and misuse of power, and I find plenty of evidence of both. But I also meet dozens of police officers who understand that their role, in theory at least, offers them the opportunity to play a part in rebuilding their war-torn nation. They care about making a differ-ence and they want to do the best job they can, given the constraints on them.

The men and women who attend our workshops are keen to learn. In five days I don't see anyone napping, which is better than I can say for any training I've ever attended in New Zealand. They undertake every small-group exercise wholeheartedly. There are spirited debates, led by the imam, about whether or not we should even be talking about duress, or rape, as a defense to the crime of adultery. The imam is concerned that by discussing these ideas we might be giving women an excuse to run off and have sex with men, knowing that if they get caught they can claim they were raped.

I am struck by how similar this reasoning is to what we used to hear from judges in New Zealand not so long ago. As recently as the 1970s, it was not uncommon for defense lawyers and judges in New Zealand to assert that young women willingly had sex and then later, feeling remorse or regret for their actions, claimed to have been raped. I take comfort in the idea that by opening up the discussion here in Ghor we might be opening the door to the same changes we've seen in New Zealand, where those arguments, though by no means extinct, are increasingly recognized as ludicrous.

There are several participants ready to disagree with the imam. One is Jawid, the head of the Criminal Investigation Department in Dowlatyar district. He argues forcefully that since we all know that rape happens, policemen and prosecutors have a duty to face that ugly truth and learn how to better respond.

Outside the workshop, I am again finding Kate's company restorative. We practice yoga together in the mornings and go for long walks in the evenings, talking over the events of the day and strategizing for the next. We eat our meals with Asiyah, Faezeh, Suraya and the local female staff of the NGO where we are staying. They spread a plastic-coated cloth out over the floor of one of the bedrooms and we share naan, rice and yogurt.

As much as I am enjoying the chaos and energy of the workshop, mornings are my favorite time of the day. I wake early, before Kate or the others stir, and sit out on the back steps of the house to meditate. Every morning I sit for fifteen or twenty minutes. I practice a very simple form of meditation, with my eyes open. I simply allow my awareness to settle on my breath. Inevitably, my attention wanders off to follow my thoughts down winding paths but I gently guide it back to the breath and begin again. It has been several months since I started this practice and I'm beginning to notice its effects in my day-to-day life. Most of all, I'm becoming more willing, and more able, to sit still with the kind of uncomfortable and unpleasant emotions that often arise in my daily life.

When I finish my meditation, I sit on the steps for a little longer to enjoy the view. The house is surrounded, as are all houses in the dusty street, by a mud-brick wall. The backyard contains the beginnings of a small raised garden. It will take dedication to grow vegetables or flowers in this dry mountain climate. Having seen the state of the food market in the town center, though, I can understand why you would try. There are no more than a handful of stalls selling dusty and tired-looking onions, potatoes and, in season, tomatoes. If you want fresh greens of any kind, you have to grow them yourself.

At the end of the yard is the outhouse, a small room built on a raised platform. What the toilet lacks in luxury, it makes up for in location and view. A small window high in the back wall looks out over the hills to the east of Chaghcharan. The hills become flooded with pink light each evening as the sun sets.

This mix of simplicity and beauty is matched in the equally rustic but somehow still luxurious washroom. As in most Afghan homes, the house doesn't have any running water or electricity. Instead there is a diesel stove in the washroom. The stove heats a tank of water, and as the water heats, the small room becomes filled with hot steam. Taking a wash in this room is like bathing in a sauna. It is delicious. It is also quite different from what I have in Herat, where my landlord has installed a Western-style shower with limited success. The water is only hot when the power is on, which is not often. Much of the time I resort to washing in a bucket.

In Ghor, there is a limited amount of hot water to serve the eight women staying in the house, so we are each allocated one bucket of hot water with which to wash ourselves. Last year I spent a bitterly cold winter in Kabul bathing each morning with a single bucket of hot water, which I got by placing a metal bucket of snow on top of my *bukhari*, or stove, each evening. I got used to it, but I was always cold. Here, as I wash with the water in the bucket, the rest of my body is warm from the steam.

On our third day, things are running smoothly at the workshop so I leave Kate to it for a few hours while I sit through a long meeting with the chief judge. He refused to attend the workshop, believing it to be beneath him to take part alongside police officers. He spends most of our meeting complaining about the lack of qualifications and skills among local defense lawyers. He doesn't mention or acknowledge the new legal aid office that has just opened in Ghor, partly as a result of my efforts. I know that, for the first time in many years, he now has qualified defense lawyers appearing before him. Rather than asking him to acknowledge this progress I simply hear him out. I'm frustrated by his negative attitude, but I bite my tongue and let him talk.

I also bit my tongue in the workshop when the imam argued against discussing the law relating to rape; and I bit my tongue when the workshop participants complained about the food. Some things are better left unsaid, but I wonder just how many things I can leave unsaid before it all comes pouring out.

Later that night, Kate and I go to eat at the military base with Heida. There is a television in the dining hall and I see footage on the news of a French aid worker who has just been released by his Taliban captors. He was kidnapped in Farah, where I recently traveled. Now he is frail, with an IV drip in his arm for dehydration and a silver emergency blanket wrapped around him to prevent shock. Despite his frailty, he insists on speaking to the cameras. He says he is relieved to be released but he is very worried about his Afghan colleagues who are still being held hostage.

The thought of them, and of him having to live with the knowledge that he is free while they are not, fills me with sadness. But I am sitting at a dining table with Lithuanian soldiers so I swallow back the sadness and blink back the tears. My unshed tears join all the words I haven't spoken over the past three days, coiling into a tight ball in the middle of my chest.

If I were in Herat I would have headed over to the UNHCR basement to run on the treadmill until I felt my body release. Instead I sit with the tightness as I meditate the next morning, unable to breathe it away, and Kate and I manage to fit in only a few minutes of yoga before we clear up our room to share breakfast with the other women. It's barely enough to work the kinks out of my lower back, and doesn't even come close to loosening the deeper layer of tension that is tightening its grip on me once again.

24

Anger and the Art of Listening

May 2007: Ghor, Afghanistan

On the last day of the workshop, Asiyah pulls me aside and says there is a man to see me. He claims we have met before and he wants to follow up with me about his case. I arrange to meet him in one of the lawyers' offices immediately and ask the young human rights assistant from Kabul to come with me to help translate, since Asiyah needs to get back to supporting Kate.

Waiting for me is a small man sporting a jet-black beard with traces of gray regrowth. It fascinates me how common it is for Afghan men to dye their hair and beards either black, or red with henna. His features seem a little too large for his head. This gives him an elfin appearance and makes him look younger than the gray regrowth would suggest.

He is dressed in a black shalwar kameez covered by a dark green polyester cardigan and a woolen vest. His turban is white and gray with a thick black stripe running through it. He has removed his shoes, as is customary, and is sitting cross-legged on the red carpet. As I enter he stands up to greet me, reaching out an arm to shake my hand. As he does, he looks me straight in the eye with a heart-stopping combination of sadness and desperate hope.

In that moment I recognize him. We met on my very first visit to

Ghor, which happened two days after I interviewed the mothers in Shindand back in November. When we first met, he told me his story. Five years ago he owed some money to the local warlord. When he was unable to pay his debt the warlord sent some men to kidnap his eldest daughter. She was only eight years old. Despite his efforts to get the police to intervene, nobody had been able or willing to challenge the powerful warlord.

This man's wife decided to take matters into her own hands. She traveled, alone, to the home of the warlord and demanded to see her daughter. I don't understand exactly why or how, but she was allowed to meet with her daughter and somehow they managed to escape together. They returned to the family home.

After a few days, however, the warlord's armed men came to the family and took the daughter back again. This time they also took her younger sister. There was nothing the man or his relatives could do to stop them.

The father had told me this story with tears in his eyes. He repeatedly complained, with understandable frustration and anger, that nobody would do anything to help him. Tears were streaming down his face. I was gripped, almost frozen, by the terrible grief and pain I was feeling from and for him, and for his daughters and wife. He had ripped off his turban and thrown it to the ground at my feet. As he threw his turban, it broke the spell of my sadness. I had never seen anyone do that before. His head was shaved beneath the turban. It seemed to me to be a profound gesture of grief and despair.

I had told him that I would document his case and I would need to talk to other witnesses about the case. And I would take the matter up with the local police. He brushed this suggestion away with a hopeless swipe of his hand.

"The police will never do anything," he told me. "They are also afraid of the warlord."

He was probably right but I didn't have anything better to offer him. I would talk to my colleagues and contact him via the prosecutor if I could think of anything more that could be done. I didn't hold out very much hope. Sadly all I could promise him was a well-documented case, which would become an official record in the UN human rights database. If the day ever came when justice actually prevailed in this province and this warlord was finally brought to trial, there would be a well-prepared legal account of this crime.

It wasn't much to offer a man whose need was so great and so pressing. So I was surprised by his genuine gratitude. Since our first meeting I have learned, slowly, that people in Afghanistan don't actually expect me to be able to solve their problems. They have lived with so much injustice for so long that my willingness simply to hear them out is often more than anyone has offered them before.

Realizing this, I also realize something about my interviews with the mothers in Shindand all those months ago. At the time my own depressed state had allowed me only to see what I had not been able to do for them. Now I can see that by giving them the chance to tell their story, and by listening attentively and with compassion for their suffering, I had, after all, offered a service to the women that day, even if my report seemed to have little impact. It is a liberating realization, freeing me, finally, from the residual guilt that has clung to me all these months.

Today the father greets me with warmth and kindness, despite the fact that I have made no progress on liberating his daughters. Until much larger changes take place in Ghor, it is unlikely that he will see his daughters again. I suspect he might be able to negotiate some sort of payment for their return if he had the resources. But I doubt very much that they will ever be extracted from the warlord by force or law. I don't say as much, as I'm sure he knows this better than I do.

I listen as he updates me on his case. His wife was able to visit his daughters again, this time without trying to get them away. The fact that she can visit her daughters gives me a little bit of insight into the dynamics of this case. If she can visit the warlord's compound, alone, then she might be related to him. These girls were taken from their parents, but it occurs to me that they might be living with extended family. I don't want to diminish the terrible suffering of this man and his wife, but I do hope their daughters are being cared for by distant aunts or cousins.

Maybe I am trying to make myself feel better because I cannot do anything to help this man, but I am coming to understand that in Ghor, nothing is impersonal. There are no nameless, faceless bad guys. The men who are called commanders or warlords are all somebody's uncle, somebody's father, somebody's son.

We talk for about an hour. He does most of the talking. When I find myself becoming uncomfortable with the intensity of his pain, I apply what I am learning in my morning meditations. I simply sit with my emotions. As he tells me how sad his wife is and how fearful they are about their daughters, I begin to feel guilty for not being able to do more. I practice just allowing myself to feel that guilt without needing to act on it. Eventually, as I remain focused on the man in front of me, my own guilt passes again. Ironically, my efforts to repress my own feelings have actually been keeping me from moving beyond them. It is by giving myself permission to feel sad, guilty or angry in response to his story that I'm able to be more fully available for him.

As he tells me about the failure of the police to respond to any of his pleas for help, I start to get angry. I sit with that anger, allowing it to be what it is, bringing my attention back to the man who is talking to me. It is a kind of yoga, this approach. It is transforming my ability to be in the presence of profound suffering without closing my heart or leaping too quickly into action.

As I learn to sit with other people's pain, I also learn to sit with my own. I haven't heard from Joel all week, despite sending him several texts. There is a terrible ache in my chest, because my heart recognizes this for what it is—abandonment. My mind, however, leaps quickly into action to explain it away. He is busy, I think, or perhaps he is having trouble getting through to my phone. They are pathetic excuses, especially given that nobody else has any problem getting through to me. Even my boss in Herat understands how important this workshop is to me and calls me every few days to check how it is all going.

My happiness at the success of the workshop is compromised by this creeping awareness that Joel is withdrawing himself from our relationship again. I spend an hour sitting in the back of the workshop while Kate talks, filling page after page of my journal with my fears and frustrations.

As I write, the provincial chief judge suddenly arrives at the workshop. Without asking or waiting for an invitation, he walks straight to the front of the room and begins to speak. He speaks in a soft voice, but it grates on me like fingernails scratched on a blackboard. He doesn't acknowledge Kate, nor does he pause to allow Asiyah to translate what he is saying. I interpret this as his way of signaling he has no time for the foreigners in the room. I can understand very little of what he is saying, although I recognize the words "rights of women," "foreigners," and "Islamic law," each of which he repeats several times. I know enough of his views to suspect that he is subtly undermining Kate and the entire premise of the workshop. And I am angry.

My feelings of respect and warmth toward the men in the room are washed away in a wave of such intense anger that I feel I must scream or weep. I'm shocked by my own anger. In order to not make a scene, I write in my journal, digging my pen deep into the pages— "It's all a waste of time! No matter how hard we all work here, it is all bullshit. These misogynist bastards will continue oppressing, abusing and misusing women." Even as I write, I know I don't believe this; at least I don't *only* believe this. But the small injustices of the week have accumulated, like drips of petrol into a puddle on the floor of my belly. The judge's dismissive words were the spark that turned my puddle into a towering flame. Allowing myself to be angry, even only on the pages of my journal, helps the anger to pass again and I'm able to get through the rest of the day, though I remain unsettled.

The next morning when I sit down to meditate, the waves of anger and sadness move through me again. In the stillness of the morning, I start to piece it all together—I am angry, *really* angry, with Joel. I feel like he's making all the calls in this relationship and I resent the power I've allowed him to have over me. More than that, I'm angry at the power that men have over women wherever I look.

This connection, between my personal struggles as a woman in my relationship with Joel and the general struggles of women in Afghanistan, hasn't occurred to me before now. It's obvious really. I've started to see myself as powerless, when really I have all sorts of choices. I've somehow absorbed the message that I need Joel to protect me, when the truth is I've been quite capable of taking care of myself for many years. On top of that, I have been building up frustration and anger at my lack of power, without being aware of it. Thankfully my anger boiled over in a situation where I was able to contain its impact, though my journal is filled with murderous thoughts toward the chief judge.

I'm still sitting on the back porch in my meditation spot; everyone else is asleep. I allow a small smile to escape: what a potent lesson.

I have to be aware of the impact my own emotional "stuff" can have on my ability to do my job well. Words unsaid, tears unshed, anger and frustrations unacknowledged, they all hang around in my body waiting for an outlet. And they'll show up when I'm tired, when I'm overwhelmed by emotion, when I'm under extreme pressure. When—in other words—I most need to be able to act with clarity. If I want to be able to show up with an "unbiased mind and heart" in my work, then I need to deal with my own shit.

Now I can see how my yoga and meditation practice is helping me in my work, by making me aware of my own motivations. It's the awareness that really matters. I don't have to "fix" myself or change my nature. Just by sitting still, or holding a yoga pose, I can recognize what is going on within me. It's that simple! And once I recognize what is there, whether it is anger, sadness, fear or joy, I can let it be.

This realization has a steadying effect on me, but I'm still feeling fragile. I probably could do with a little bit more time alone in the guesthouse or walking over the hills. Instead I have to head in to the last day of the workshop.

One of my jobs today is to distribute the money to reimburse the participants for their transport and accommodation costs. At the beginning of the workshop I told them what the upper limit for their claims was and asked them to bring me receipts on the last day, which they do. Several of them bring receipts for much higher amounts than what I have allocated. I tell them I don't have enough money to reimburse them the full amount. They start to argue with me. I burst into tears. My counterpart from the Afghan Independent Human Rights Commission sees me, and laughs. I feel foolish.

"Why are you crying, Miss Marianne?" he asks. "You are a strong woman. You must be if you came to Ghor to work. Surely you are not crying about this money. Ignore them, they are teasing you."

I realize he is right. The men are, if not teasing exactly, at least trying to negotiate. I am expected to respond either by insisting that there is no room to negotiate, or by making a counteroffer. I wipe the tears away and smile at them.

"Sorry for the tears," I apologize. "I'm very tired and sometimes I forget that things are done differently here."

They smile, apparently relieved I am not permanently upset with them. For my part, I'm relieved I'm in Afghanistan rather than New Zealand, where stoicism is the national sport, and where any sign of tears can paralyze otherwise perfectly competent adults. The Afghan policemen were concerned, but didn't seem at all embarrassed by my emotion. They happily accept the smaller amount of money.

Kate leaves a day before me, flying directly back to Kabul. I stay around to finish up the payments and to attend human rights training for prison staff organized by the Afghan Independent Human Rights Commission. As passionate as I am about the rights of prisoners, I'm in no state to really take anything in.

By the time I get back to Herat the following day, my entire body is aching with fatigue. I'm ready for some creature comforts, like joining Joel for *Buffy* and some of his good home cooking. I may finally have recognized just how angry I am with Joel, but I'm not very good at staying angry. My analytical mind may be saying one thing, but my lonely heart and exhausted body are saying another. I still want to make this relationship work and I've already convinced myself that all that needs to change is my attitude.

If I feel powerless in this relationship it's only because I've willingly given Joel the "power" to make me happy or unhappy. It's time to take that power, and responsibility, back for myself. In any case, I'm not ready to give up the company of the closest friend I have in Herat. I am looking forward to being back in the same city as Joel again.

25
Crying

May 2007: Herat, Afghanistan

When I finally see Joel, after another long and dusty day of travel and work, he says all the things I don't want to hear.

"I just don't see it getting any better," he says. "I don't make you happy." He pauses. I say nothing. I'm trying not to cry.

"You deserve better," he says. "I'm not even that nice to you. I don't like who I am when I'm with you. I'm tired of this."

"So, does that mean it's over?" I ask. He says yes.

He doesn't say, "You are not good enough to make it worth me trying harder," but that's what I tell myself that night as I lie awake. If only I were a different kind of woman, then Joel would be willing to try harder to make this work.

I torture myself with these thoughts, and as I spiral deeper I wonder, am I good enough to be loved? Truly, deeply loved? All night I wrestle with this fear. A part of me, a little core of wisdom, sees I am creating this suffering with my own thoughts. But they have their roots deep in my being and it isn't easy to slide out from under their weight.

I teeter between wise and wounded. I understand the relationship is really over. It is time for the letting go to begin. But where to start? I can't sleep anyway, so I practice the meditation I've been learning all year.

As the gray morning light makes its way up over the hills, I roll out my yoga mat and start to move, and breathe, through the familiar poses. As my body starts to relax and my mind begins to settle, I reassure myself. I feel as though the bottom has fallen out of my world, yet I know I will eventually be okay. The sun will keep rising every morning, the pigeons on the roof outside my window will keep gurgling their morning greetings. Every morning I will get up and make my way out into the day. It will be okay.

I feel almost lighthearted, as though I have relieved myself of a burden overnight. I'm surprised. The worst has come to pass and yet I feel lighter, freer and more open than I have in months. I ponder this in the sunlight, drinking my morning coffee—Parwaiz's daily gesture of love and kindness. Reaching for my book of Jalaluddin Rumi poems, I flick directly to my favorite poem, "The Guest House."

Rumi reminds me that being a human is like being a guesthouse, and we never know what kind of guests will arrive. Some days it is a joy, some days a sorrow. "Welcome and entertain them all," says Rumi, and "be grateful for whoever comes." Closing the book, I decide to welcome this house guest, this sorrow, with a smile. I know it will pass, eventually.

Welcoming the sorrow means I have to let myself be sad. When the tears come I need to cry them. I have a theory: if I let the sadness come, in all its fullness, then it will pass faster. After Amanullah Khan's killing, I tried to escape my own sadness. I kept telling myself that I had no right to feel sad. The longer I resisted and tried to avoid my feelings, the longer they hung around.

I read a quote from Pema's book, which I wrote down some weeks ago and stuck on the back of my door. "If it is painful, you can learn to hold your seat and move closer to that pain. Reverse the usual pattern, which is to split, to escape. Go against the grain and hold your seat… You become willing not only to endure it but also to let it awaken your heart and soften you. You learn to embrace it."

When I think about moving closer to my pain, I am reminded of a story from *Women Who Run With the Wolves* by Clarissa Pinkola Estés. A man is pursued by a frightful Skeleton Woman. The faster he runs to get away from her, the faster she pursues him. The truth is that the skeleton is attached to him, caught in his fishing net. I remember this story as I think back on the months I spent trying to run away from my own sadness. Like Skeleton Woman, the sadness followed me, entangled with my own bones. Now, though, I am ready to stop running.

Having chosen to allow myself to cry whenever I need to, I proceed to cry nonstop for five days. For the first time in my life, I don't care whether or not people think I am "holding it together" or being a drama queen. As I cry, I see how many unshed tears I have been carrying for years. So often in my life I have felt tears coming and swallowed them back, convinced that it wasn't the right time or place. I feel as though I have been carrying a big heavy sack and I'm finally ready to lay it all down.

I cry in the morning in the shower. I cry in the car on the way to work. I cry at my desk as I write reports and even as I talk on the phone, tears silently running down my face. I cry as I run on the treadmill in the bunker after work and I cry as I sit on my meditation cushion. I cry in our guesthouse kitchen, as I reheat the lentil soup Parwaiz makes for me. I let my tears drip into the soup as I eat it, alone, in my bedroom.

My workmates are watching me with a mix of concern and discomfort, but for once I don't care. For five days I cry. On the sixth day, I wake up feeling lighter. Joel is right. What we once shared, the playful friendship that evolved into a love affair, has changed again. We have been stuck in a painful cycle of expectations and guilt and blame. Yes, it is time to get unstuck. I am more than ready to let go of that cycle.

I'm even grateful to Joel for waiting until he could see I was finding my way back onto my feet before he finally ended things. The past six months have been hard for him, and I suspect he stuck around this long largely to make sure I was going to make it out the other side.

This doesn't mean I have stopped hurting. When Joel emails me to say he has gathered up all my things from around his house and will leave them out for me to collect the next morning, it stings like salt rubbed into a wound. My heart is still broken, still raw and tender, but I am no longer clinging to what has passed. I'm ready to take a break from being my own worst enemy. I'm ready to let it all be.

Part of letting it be, I realize, means embracing the rawness and tenderness of my broken heart. Pema is teaching me that the tenderness of genuine sadness can be a way for me to lower the barriers I've built around my heart, a way to connect more directly with everyone who has ever loved, lost or suffered. A tender, broken heart can humble us when we are arrogant and can soften us when we are unkind. The ache of the heart, she says, is a blessing. I feel that blessing.

26
Tim

May–June 2007: Herat and Kabul, Afghanistan

Mercifully, I am due to go on "recuperation" leave again in June, which is just two weeks away. Perhaps there is some benevolent force watching over my life after all, because I am booked into a yoga retreat in Thailand with two of my closest friends from New Zealand. I couldn't have planned a better way to recover from getting my heart broken in Afghanistan.

Herat suddenly feels very small. Joel and I have all the same friends and our work overlaps enough that we find ourselves in the same meetings. I really want to get away from Joel, but in Herat that's pretty much impossible. This seals my decision to volunteer to head up the new UNAMA office in Ghor province when it opens, which could be as soon as the end of June. I was quietly attracted to the idea even while I was still clinging to the hope of things working out with Joel, but now I am free to pursue this opportunity to move to Chaghcharan, to the mountains.

In the short term, though, I need a good reason to get out of Herat for the next two weeks. I call the director of the UNAMA Human Rights Unit in Kabul. I tell him what has happened, even though it means crying into the phone. I ask if he can help me get out of Herat until I go on leave. He understands. He writes to the head of my office in Herat explaining that he needs me in Kabul as soon as possible. Five days later I am on a plane to Kabul.

In Kabul, Kate is ready to welcome me and invites me to stay with her and her boyfriend, a warm and generous Englishman named Billy. They live in one of the older neighborhoods in Kabul. As I know from reading *The Kite Runner*, this neighborhood was once home to the city's intellectuals and elite. Behind these reinforced security walls lie some beautiful traditional Afghan homes, and Billy's house is one of them. It has a large garden and a beautiful lounge surrounded on three sides by windows that open out onto the yard. I love this room. Around the base of the large windows are traditional Afghan floor cushions where I like to lie with a book in the sun.

I sleep in a detached room out the back of the house. Billy apologizes about the simple nature of the room, but I love it. It has a wooden floor and a lovely box window recessed deeply into the thick wall. There is even room to roll out my yoga mat in the sun that streams through the window in the morning. I am pleased my room is separate from the main house, as I can come and go without disturbing Billy and Kate.

When my director said that he needed me in Kabul for the week he hadn't been lying. There is more work than the head office team can possibly get through on their own. The only reason he hadn't asked for my help earlier is because he knows that our regional office is just as overloaded. I spend the week working like a woman possessed. This suits me just fine, because I'd rather not have any time to think about Joel or about life without him.

I get in to work early, before seven most mornings. The advantage of traveling early in Kabul is that traffic hasn't yet reached peak capacity. I have never experienced traffic like Kabul's before. I admire the persistence and dogged optimism of Kabul drivers. There might be traffic backed up as far as the eye can see but that won't prevent an enterprising driver from squeezing his car up onto the curb to slide along between the traffic and the walls of buildings, or from exploring a side street. Our UN drivers are as adventurous as anyone else on the road and I discover all sorts of previously unknown corners of Kabul as we hunt for the elusive way around the traffic jam. It makes for an educational, and sometimes exhilarating, trip to work.

Of course, traffic jams in Kabul have the added tension that comes from the constant threat of violent death. Some parts of the city are at a higher risk for roadside bombs than others. Certain types of vehicles are also more likely to be targeted. The worst place to be stuck in a Kabul traffic jam is right behind a U.S. military vehicle. Equally suspect are the huge armored SUVs with tinted windows that belong either to an Afghan drug lord or to an American CIA agent trying to pass himself off as an Afghan drug lord.

I generally do a good job of distracting myself from the possibility of imminent death by making small talk with the drivers about their mothers' health or their daughters' education. Sometimes, though, my fears get the better of me and I spend the drive clenching and unclench-ing my fists and breathing as deeply as I can while trying not to hyper-ventilate. I always carry my iPod and sometimes resort to Pema's calm voice. As she talks about sitting still with our fears, I think to myself that these traffic jams are my personal meditation boot camp.

In the early morning the roads are clearer which means I spend less time on them, and that is always a good thing. My office is also empty, which means I can make personal phone calls. This week I talk to my sisters and friends every morning. They all assure me that I am beautiful and smart and good, too good for Joel anyway. One day I'll meet someone who is smart enough to see how lucky he is to get me. It is exactly what I need to hear. It fortifies me for a day of document-ing civilian deaths in a war that seems to be creeping farther across Afghanistan by the hour.

Outside work, Kate has planned a week of social engagements for me. She is also very firmly in the "you were too good for Joel anyway" camp and is determined to get me out and about in the social scene of Kabul. Her plan is for me to meet lovely new men and be reminded that there are, indeed, plenty more fish in the sea. She even has one particular fish in mind for me.

An Australian journalist moved into Kate's old guesthouse a few months earlier and Kate thinks he is perfect for me. I'm not at all interested in meeting other men and feel certain I never will be, but Kate's description of Tim intrigues me. She describes someone with a gentle spirit and a strong intellectual curiosity, qualities I find deeply attractive.

"He's also tall, dark and handsome," she tells me, "and he's going to be cooking at a party at my old house tonight. Everyone there wants to see you again. I think we should go."

Tall, dark and handsome is good, but a man who cooks is irresistible. Despite my loyalty to my heartbreak, I experience a flutter of excitement about meeting Tim. I'm also keen to see Kate's old housemates, whom I've stayed with during trips to Kabul over the past year, on visits to the head office or on my way out on leave. I agree to go along to the party after work.

By the time I get to the party, I've had a long and relentless day of counting the dead and I have lost my appetite for small talk with strangers. But I notice Tim right away and we are introduced by one of the housemates. Kate was right about him being handsome. When he smiles at me his brown eyes crinkle with kindness, almost melting my bad mood. I even like his beard. Before I moved to Afghanistan, I was never keen on beards, but that has changed in this country where even weak-chinned mummy's boys from the suburbs of the West can be transformed, by a desert tan and a Taliban-friendly beard, into ruggedly handsome sand warriors.

As attractive as Tim is, all I want to do is curl up on the couch by the outdoor fireplace and talk to the handful of people at the party who know me well enough already to understand my melancholy mood. Despite myself, I'm drawn into conversation with a Kiwi security contractor who seems determined to make me laugh. He is having some success with a story about his hapless attempts to do something brave and useful, when Tim comes over to join us. We chat for a while but my bad mood still hasn't evaporated completely. When Tim makes a throwaway comment about the arrogance of people who come to Afghanistan to preach "Western values," which I interpret as "human rights" whether he intends it or not, I take offense and go and find Kate.

An hour or so later, I've had a few restorative glasses of wine and an easy chat on the sofa with my friend Jan, who is also an Australian journalist. I feel bad about cutting short my conversation with Tim. I take my glass of wine and wander over to the bar where he is now sitting. We start our conversation over again and this time things flow easily, probably because he lets me do most of the talking. I have plenty to say about the international community's failures in Afghanistan, and it is nice to have an attentive audience. I decide I might like this Australian after all.

A few days later, two days before I am due to leave for Thailand, Kate and Billy decide to host a dinner. Kate makes a point of telling me that Tim is invited. I'm not ready to embark on any kind of new romance, but I can't deny I am looking forward to seeing Tim again.

The day of the party I have a disagreement with one of my colleagues from the Political Affairs unit. He complains that all our talk about human rights only causes political problems.

"Our job," he tells me, "is to promote stability and security in Afghanistan. Human rights officers, like you, who insist on investigating reports of human rights violations by prominent members of

President Karzai's cabinet are just stirring up trouble. Afghanistan isn't stable enough for that kind of investigation."

"But these men are responsible for countless murders, rapes and kidnappings!" I argue. "Allowing them to continue to hold positions of official power in the government actually undermines security for ordinary Afghans. What kind of stability are we promoting if people can't feel safe?"

When I first arrived in Afghanistan I had worked for the Human Rights Research and Advocacy Consortium in Kabul. In 2006 we published the results of a national survey of Afghan citizens about security. I am glad I can refer to those results now, to reinforce my argument.

"The number one reason people gave us for feeling unsafe was the presence of armed warlords and 'commanders' in their province or in positions of power," I tell him. "I am not sure whose version of security you think you are creating by protecting these men from prosecution but I am sure it isn't that of the average Afghan."

He laughs at me. "You human rights people are so naïve! Do you think that generations of the rule of the gun in this country are going to end because you run around in Ghor writing reports about warlords kidnapping ten-year-olds?"

"No," I say, furious, "I don't think that I'm going to change entrenched patterns of abuse of power and violence with my reports. But I do think it is our responsibility to listen to those people in this country who have the least power. That's the only way I've ever seen anything change anywhere, when new voices begin to be heard and new forms of power begin to emerge."

"Those are lovely ideas, Marianne"—he smiles at me condescendingly—"but I've been working in Afghanistan for more than fifteen years and I know that this will never change. We can only try to create enough stability for the government to function. We can't hope to see real transformation. You and the other human rights officers don't seem to understand this and as a result, you just create more problems for the rest of us."

I realize that I'm not going to change his mind, so I drop the argument, but it leaves me seething with anger. By the time I get home to Billy's place I am ready to let off some steam, so I sneak out to my room for a quick yoga practice before I help Kate get ready for dinner. A dozen sun salutes later I feel altogether calmer, although doubts linger about staying with a UN mission that nurtures, and apparently promotes, that kind of attitude.

If the only thing we really care about is a government stable enough to hold off the Taliban, no matter whether it meets the needs of its citizens, then whose interests are we really here for? Perhaps he is right. Am I naïve to even think that we are here to protect and promote the interests of ordinary Afghans?

I enjoy helping Kate set up the table outside. She has kerosene lanterns to place around the edge of the patio and candles for the table. It looks magical. Billy is a diplomat, so he has access to fresh foods and wines that are generally impossible to find in Afghanistan. The evening is shaping up to be a real treat.

Despite Kate's not-so-subtle matchmaking efforts, I don't end up sitting next to Tim. It's not until dinner is over, as the evening cools and we retreat inside, that we finally find our way next to each other. We recline on the floor cushions in Billy's beautiful lounge, turning toward each other so that we can talk over the music. There is no room for anyone else to join our conversation, and there's every excuse to lean in closer to hear each other.

We talk about Afghanistan, mostly. Tim is here researching a book about opium. He has just returned from Jalalabad in the east where he went to see the poppy harvest. There, he talked to local farmers who grow opium poppies to supplement their income and to feed their families.

"The U.S. is spending big money on projects to 'eradicate' poppy crops," he says, "and these poor farmers are the people hurt most when the crops are destroyed. It seems like the perfect way to drive them all to support the Taliban, really."

The farmers, I know, live from harvest to harvest and have no savings to protect them from the impact of losing their only cash crop. The Taliban offers a salary to anyone who joins as a foot soldier. I agree with Tim: these eradication efforts seem likely to drive people into the Taliban's open arms.

"I've seen the same in Farah and Ghor," I tell him, "families who plant a small cash crop of opium as insurance in case the food crops fail. If they lose that, they lose everything and they really have no choice but to take any paying job they can find—which may very well be as a Taliban soldier."

We talk about the argument I had earlier in the day, whether Afghanistan is yet stable or secure enough to address past human rights abuses.

"The Afghan people I meet and work with each day tell me they will never feel safe as long as the men who murdered their families are not punished," I tell him.

"I can understand that," Tim says, "but haven't the trials so far been disappointing? From what I've heard people don't feel that justice has been done."

"It might not be time yet to have human rights trials," I concede. "The court system may not yet be robust enough to give everyone confidence in its decisions. But there are other ways to address past human rights violations, and people in this country have spoken, they've told us that this is what they want to see in order to feel safer. I'm tired of hearing Western 'experts,' especially the ones in my own organization, say that they know better than ordinary Afghans about this. I'm tired of being told that I'm naïve for thinking that we should at least be trying to support some kind of justice."

Tim is very sympathetic to my arguments. "I've barely been here four months," he says, "but I'm already sick to death of all the people I meet who claim to have all the answers for this country. It seems pretty obvious that they don't have all the answers and that things are not going according to the plan that the international community laid out for this place. Maybe it's time to admit that we don't know half as much as we'd like to think we do."

"Well," I say, "I'll drink to that."

We've been talking for a long time. The other guests are beginning to leave. Kate comes over to ask if Tim wants to leave with the others from his house. There is an awkward moment as we say good-bye. Had we been alone, we might have kissed. I think about creating the opportunity, but my heart is still so turbulent. I have enjoyed our conversation, and the closeness of our bodies as we talked, and for now I want to leave it at that. Perhaps I need more time to let go of Joel. In any case I hope this won't be my last chance to kiss Tim.

27
Improvised Explosive Device

June 2007: Kabul, Afghanistan

*T*he next day is my last in the office before going to Thailand. I go in very early to make a start on the long list of things I have left to do before I can escape with a clear conscience. By midafternoon I am making good progress. I get an email from Tim inviting me to join him for drinks that night. I have plans for a farewell dinner with Kate, who will leave Afghanistan for good while I'm in Thailand, so I ask for a raincheck and promise to get in touch on my way back through Kabul from Thailand.

As I finish typing the email, a UNAMA security guard comes into our office and tells us all to leave, immediately. There is no time to gather up our bags or belongings. This is not a drill. We are led through the compound to the back wall where a small door connects our compound to the UNIFEM (the United Nations agency for women, now called UN Women) compound behind us. As we are hurried away from our offices he tells us there is a fuel tanker parked outside the front gate of our compound. An IED (improvised explosive device) is attached to the fuel tank. If the bomb goes off, the blast will flatten our entire compound.

I am accustomed to the constant threat of danger in Afghanistan, but even for Kabul this is high drama. I wonder whether the wall between the UNAMA and UNIFEM compounds is solid enough to keep us safe if the fuel tanker blows. Dwelling on my fears makes no difference to my own safety or the safety of anyone else, so once we are safely inside the UNIFEM compound, I decide to get on with my work.

I have wanted to catch up with some UNIFEM colleagues about a joint project on violence against women that I am managing for UNAMA. I take this opportunity to talk with them. I guess we are all pretty accustomed to working with a threat of danger, because nobody seems to think it odd that I request a meeting while we are all waiting to see whether the fuel tanker bomb can be defused.

I tell them the report is coming along well. I have collected information about more than two hundred cases of violence against women documented by UNAMA human rights officers. More than half of the officers have not yet responded so I expect to double that number by the time I'm done. My job will be to read all the cases and write a report describing the trends and key issues that emerge. UNIFEM, in the meantime, will enter the cases into its national database, combine them with cases documented by NGOs and by the Ministry of Women's Affairs and do some statistical analysis of the cases. Together we will produce a national report on violence against women in Afghanistan.

Given the spread of the fighting across the country, donor countries increasingly want to spend their money on projects directly related to "security." Unfortunately, most of them don't include preventing violence against women in their definition of security. I'm worried that funding for projects focused on women's rights will dry up, and people like Suraya at the women's shelter may struggle to find the money they need to keep their projects going. I want this report to give donors a reason to continue to fund those projects.

Along with the workshops Kate and I ran in Badghis and Ghor, I'm proud of my contribution to this report. I've worked hard to establish the relationship with UNIFEM and to convince the other human rights officers to help by sending me their cases. UNIFEM doesn't have any staff in the regions, so human rights officers like me act as de facto women's rights officers. We are their eyes and ears on the ground, and our contributions will help the report tell a much more accurate story about violence against women. In this project I've found a way to bridge the gap between my past experience in research and national-level policy and my current work with individual human rights cases.

By late afternoon I've done all the work I can at UNIFEM. We are still not allowed to return to our offices. As I stroll around the compound looking for a coffee, I see a man wearing an ISAF army uniform with the New Zealand flag on his arm. I walk over and introduce myself. He is the commander of the New Zealand PRT in Bamiyan. I sit down next to him and we talk for an hour or so about how we could improve collaboration between UN civilian staff and the ISAF military forces.

"The most important thing," he says, "is that we actually respect each other's role."

"Yeah," I agree, "it seems so obvious but in reality it takes a lot of effort to avoid falling into stereotypes. It does for me, at least."

"What we really need from you guys," he says, "is advice on how to spend the discretionary funds I hold as commander for small-scale development projects in the province."

"I'll tell you what you could do with your discretionary funds," I tell him enthusiastically, reflecting that these are my own tax dollars I'm talking about. "There is a great project in Bamiyan I've heard about from some of my colleagues. It's human rights training for women who provide lay representation for women in the court systems. I've done something similar in Ghor and it was a big success. It should only cost a couple of thousand dollars. We did it in Ghor for under one grand."

"Sounds good," he says. "Tell your colleagues to get in touch with me. I have a few thousand dollars sitting around looking for a good home."

Despite my concerns about the increasingly blurred lines in Afghanistan between military operations and humanitarian and development work, I would have happily taken his money for Ghor. But I know he has to spend it in Bamiyan, where the New Zealand government has focused all its efforts, and I'm happy to point him in the direction of a good project. As we talk I'm aware how much my confidence in dealing with the military has increased over the time I've been in Herat.

Evening falls and we are still not allowed back into the offices. Most people have already given up and hitched a ride in a UNIFEM vehicle back to their guesthouses. I am holding out, hoping we will eventually be given the all clear. My handbag is in the office, with my passport and wallet, and I am due at the airport at seven the following morning.

The compound security manager eventually tells me I might as well go home. She won't be letting anyone back into the office tonight. I feel fatalistic about the whole situation; there is nothing at all I can do about it. I might as well go out for dinner instead. This is one of Afghanistan's lessons for me, I think—finally recognizing when I am not in control, and learning to let things be.

After a farewell dinner with Kate, whom I'm going to miss terribly, I go home early. I have ordered a car for 5:30 a.m. in the hope I will be able to get back into my office. I need to finish one final report that I promised to my boss, collect my passport and get to the airport by seven. I have no idea whether any of this will be possible. Only a year earlier, this situation might have thrown me into a craze of anxiety. Now it seems quite normal.

At five thirty the next morning I am standing at the gate of Billy's house. I know that if the car turns up, there is a good chance the office compound is open, because most of the cars were locked up inside the compound the day before. When the driver pulls up alongside me, I give him an especially enthusiastic greeting. He confirms that the bomb was finally rendered harmless in the early hours of the morning and the compound is open. We speed away to the office and I begin to think maybe the travel gods are on my side after all. By six thirty I have my passport and am on my way to the airport. At the airport, I finally let myself relax. I'm off to Thailand where a week of yoga awaits.

28
New Beginnings

June–July 2007: Kabul, Herat, and Ghor, Afghanistan

By the time I get back to Afghanistan after a week of yoga, detoxification and deep, blissful sleep in Thailand, I am a new woman. My appreciation for yoga has deepened, my body has been released and I'm once again equipped with new practices to help me stay well here in Afghanistan.

In Kabul, on my way back to Herat, I bump into Joel. He is heading out on a holiday himself. We agree to go out for dinner, to make peace over Lebanese food. I'm pleased, and a little surprised, to discover this does not make my heart ache. Partly this is because my future just opened up again and anything is now possible. Partly it's because I'm feeling uncharacteristically light about everything. I credit the yoga for that.

I also manage to catch up with Tim, who takes me out to dinner and somehow gets me talking about my desire to have children.

"I always thought that I wanted to have children, to have babies of my own," I say, "but now I wonder whether it's the ethical thing to do. There are so many children already in the world who need parents." Even as I say it, I'm aware of the extent to which Joel's reasoning is leading me to doubt my own desire to be a mother.

"Wanting to have a child is a perfectly natural desire," Tim says, "and it's neither ethical nor unethical in itself. If you want to have a child, if that would make you happy, then you should feel free to do it. And then you do your best to raise your child in an ethical way."

It's such a compassionate response, and such a stark contrast to the conversations I've had with Joel on the topic. I leave Kabul for Herat even more confident that it is time to let Joel go, and even more grateful to Kate for introducing me to Tim. As I fly into the now familiar airport in Herat, I feel ready to move on to the next chapter of my life.

Before leaving for Thailand I volunteered to be the sole international staff member at a new UNAMA provincial office to be opened in Ghor province. When I land in Herat, my boss asks if I can be ready to move up there by July 10, which is in only two weeks. I'm happy to get out of Herat; as much as I'll miss my friends and colleagues, I won't miss being just two hundred meters down the road from Joel's place. The timing of this move couldn't have been better.

I have also grown to love Ghor. I'm a sucker for the underdog and for the great outdoors, so Ghor suits me perfectly. While this may be one of the poorest and worst-served provinces in an already poor and poorly served country, it is also home to some of the most spectacular scenery I have seen in my life. It's just what my body and spirit need right now.

Opening the new office is effectively a promotion. As well as my human rights work, I'll be overseeing all the work of our mission in Ghor and helping the other UN agencies to do their work in the province too. As far as my career goes, it is a great opportunity. It's also timely: it will be a great way to get some distance from Joel. I can't help smiling at the realization that I chose career over relationship when I moved to Herat, and I am now moving on from the failure of that same relationship by making yet another "great career move."

When the day comes to make my move up to Ghor there is a limit on my luggage, so to make room for my beloved books of Persian poetry and my yoga mat, which I can no longer live without, I leave behind a trunk of winter blankets and clothing. I also manage to find room for two dozen cartons of soy milk and six months' worth of Italian coffee from the military base. My priorities are clear.

High in the mountains of the Hindu Kush, our helicopter comes in to land over Chaghcharan, the provincial capital and my new home. Perched on the banks of the Hari Rud River, Chaghcharan is a small town, home to no more than ten thousand people. I find the town beautiful. The river is clean and clear with a bed of smooth gray pebbles. The town is surrounded by rolling hills that give me a sense of great spaciousness, a feeling that has been conspicuously absent in my life lately.

For all its beauty, Chaghcharan is desperately poor. It has one of the saddest little markets I have ever seen. The market holds only a handful of stalls, perhaps five or six on each side of a narrow, dusty street. Whenever I visit, ever hopeful of finding something appetizing for my dinner, I find pitiful little piles of tired, dusty onions and tomatoes. Sometimes there are a few bruised eggplants or some green potatoes. Very occasionally I find a wrinkled apple.

The vegetables and fruit are imported from Iran or Pakistan, because the prices are slightly lower than for those grown in the fertile plains of Afghanistan. They then travel by truck from Herat or Kabul, a journey that takes at least two days in each direction, if the conditions are perfect. More often, conditions are not perfect and the trucks are stuck for days waiting for an opportunity to pass through the most treacherous sections of the road. By the time they reach Chaghcharan, the vegetables may have been traveling for a week or more. They look roadweary and I wonder whether they have retained any of their nutritional value. Of course, most people in Ghor can't afford to buy any fruit or vegetables from the market anyway. They survive on what they grow themselves, and in many cases that is only wheat.

A UN World Food Program (WFP) consultant comes to stay with us in Ghor while he makes an assessment of the food shortage in the province. He informs me that more than 80 percent of people in Ghor eat only bread for more than eight months of the year. I can't quite believe it's possible to survive on such a limited diet, but he insists it is true. Even children, he says, often have only bread to eat through the harshest months of winter.

It is no wonder the children—and the adults for that matter—all seem so small for their age. Many of them are severely malnourished. This is also the reason, he explains to me, for the fair reddish hair of many children in Ghor. I assumed it was a genetic tendency of the Aimaq tribe that makes up the majority of the population.

Ghor has been hit hard by the many years of erratic rain in Afghanistan. There has been rain, so it isn't technically a drought, although many call it one. But the rains come later than usual and all at once, in massive downpours that wash away the fertile topsoil and destroy rather than nurture the crops. It is exactly what climate scientists predicted would be the effect of global warming.

In Ghor I begin, for the first time in my life, to really understand the connection between the environment and basic human rights. I have always admired and respected environmental activists but saw them as being interested in and committed to a different cause from mine. I care most about the suffering of other humans, while they care most about the planet. It seems absurd, now that I think about it, that I ever imagined there was a distinction between the two.

In Ghor I finally understand that if we don't protect and preserve the environment then there will be nowhere left for people to live. I also realize that as we degrade the planet, the first people to feel the effects of that degradation are also the ones least equipped to adapt to the changes. While in the West we go merrily along consuming more than our fair share of the earth's resources and polluting what remains of its beauty, the poorest people on the planet, who rely most directly on the environment for their survival and who are most exposed to the effects of extreme weather, are already suffering the impacts of our excesses. I came to Afghanistan a human rights activist, and Ghor is turning me into an environmentalist.

When I arrive in Ghor we have only two weeks before we are due to open our new office and compound. The head of our mission, Tom Koenigs, is flying up from Kabul for the big event, as is Sima Samar, the fearless leader of the Afghan Independent Human Rights Commission, who will open a new office for the AIHRC at the same time. This joint opening is a big deal because it signals a shift in our mission's emphasis toward supporting local institutions. I am honored to be a part of it but wonder how on earth we are going to be ready on time.

One week from the opening, the main office building structure is complete but it still needs to be painted and furnished. Our accommodation units are still being built. The entire compound is strewn with construction materials and there is a huge hole in the outer security wall that will have to be repaired before we can open.

The Ghor office is one of twelve new provincial offices that UNAMA plans to open this year. Each will have one international staff member—either a political, human rights or development officer. The conditions at these provincial offices are considered to be harsh. The staff member posted there, in this case me, will be isolated from other international staff and will live in very basic conditions.

There isn't much for me to do on the building site. It is messy, noisy and chaotic, and just being in the space makes me anxious to impose some kind of order. I've always liked to keep my spaces tidy, and mess triggers the part of me that needs to feel I have things under control. I throw myself into a round of meetings with our new staff.

The most senior staff member is Haji S., the national head of office. He will work alongside me to establish the new office. The plan is for him to eventually take over. This transition period, during which I am to support and advise him, is considered necessary because of the subtleties of our office's political role. My role is to model the UN's political "impartiality," a concept that is met with a degree of skepticism by many Afghans. Afghans understand only too well that human behavior is driven and guided by allegiances and in times of conflict those allegiances only become more important. The idea that the UN has no allegiance to any particular tribe or political group seems improbable to most people. Perhaps they are right.

The second most senior staff member is our political affairs officer, Fahim. From my very first meeting with Fahim, I am impressed. He has perhaps the kindest eyes and warmest smile of anyone I have ever met. Like many Afghan men, he dyes his hair and beard. With his jet-black hair and sparkling eyes, it is hard to believe he is really in his late fifties, as his CV claims. But he was the governor of Shahrak district, in the west of Ghor province, during the Soviet government in the 1980s, so he couldn't be much younger.

He wears a perfectly white shalwar kameez, which I imagine his wife must spend a lot of time cleaning, given the dusty, dirty landscape in which we work. In fact, as he eventually admits to me, he has two wives. He seems reluctant to tell me this, perhaps assuming I will be shocked. Actually I am not surprised at all. Fahim is a well-respected elder in the community and he has a well-paid job; it might be more surprising if he had only one wife. Given the gentle, kind spirit he brings to our work together, it seems quite likely his wives are both happy with their match.

In the short time we spend together before the office is officially opened I begin to rely on Fahim's advice. He seems to know everyone in the province and, most importantly, surprises me with the tolerance and goodwill with which he talks about everyone but the cruelest warlords. He himself is Aimaq, a Tajik tribe, but he is quick to tell me that families who inhabit a Pashtun settlement on the outskirts of Chaghcharan are very fine people.

This small Pashtun community, a minority in this predominantly Aimaq area, immigrated to Ghor many years ago and, according to Fahim, have been upstanding members of the community ever since. They are intelligent and hardworking, he tells me, pointing out the large swathes of irrigated wheat fields and beautiful rows of cypress trees that ripple out beyond their settlement.

He is just as careful to point out the strengths of the Hazara minority in the province. They are very committed to educating their daughters, he explains admiringly, and held their ground against the cruelty of the Taliban. I have been in Afghanistan for a year and a half now; I know how difficult it can be for people to look beyond the pain of many years of ethnic and tribal conflict and see the best in the "other side." Fahim is a man of unusual compassion.

I am disconcerted, therefore, when he doesn't show up to work on the day of our office opening. We all agreed to meet at the office early in the morning to make any final arrangements before the VIPs arrive. I ask Haji S. where Fahim is. He claims not to know. I don't have time to worry—there are last-minute arrangements demanding my attention, including the seating arrangement in the cars carrying our distinguished guests from the airstrip to our office, a distance of perhaps five hundred meters.

It seems ludicrous to send a convoy of six big white 4x4s to carry them such a short distance, but we can't ask the chief human rights commissioner of the Afghanistan Independent Human Rights Commission and the special representative of the secretary general of the United Nations to walk. I'm sure neither of them would object personally, but our security team would never allow it. They must travel by convoy.

The head of the new provincial office of the AIHRC, Mr. Ansari

Baluch, is going to join us in the official welcoming party. I have met him many times in the weeks leading up to the opening. I see the joint opening of our offices not only as a signal of our organizations' commitment to work more closely with each other, but also as an opportunity for me to start things off on the right foot with Mr. Baluch. It's a chance for me to practice what I preach: that Afghan organizations should lead this work with support, when invited, from international organizations like ours.

The opening ceremony, which we hold in the town hall because there isn't room for everyone at either of our offices, goes beautifully. Tom Koenigs and Sima Samar both speak glowingly of the work we have done to set up our new offices in record time, and all the local officials welcome us very warmly.

As we drive back to our compound, a group of protestors blocks the passage of our convoy, demanding to speak to Mr. Koenigs. I know he can't get out of the car for security reasons, so I jump out instead. The protestors are from a camp of displaced people not far from our office. I have already been over to meet them so I know something of their plight. They are Hazara, the ethnic group that suffered some of the Taliban's harshest treatment.

Almost eight years ago, a tribe supported by the Taliban, who governed Afghanistan at the time, threw these families off their land. For the past eight years they have been traveling, homeless and landless, in a country that is becoming more dangerous and less hospitable by the month. They have taken their case through the courts and, a few months ago, they returned to Ghor with a Supreme Court decision confirming that the land in dispute is legally theirs and ordering that it be returned to them immediately.

Unfortunately, the tribe living on their land refuses to acknowledge the decision. They argue that the decision isn't valid because not all the Supreme Court judges took part in it. Or perhaps it's because not all the Supreme Court judges agreed on the decision. I haven't been able to get this clear from the translation of their complaints. In any case, they refuse to move.

So now the displaced families are petitioning the local governor to help them return to this land. The governor, knowing that the tribe currently on the land is ready and willing to fight local police, is reluctant to force the issue. In my first days here, these families asked me to help them in their fight for justice. I haven't yet made the progress they were expecting, so I'm guessing they hope they will have more success by getting my boss's attention.

Women and children gather around me shouting and waving improvised placards. My colleague Abdul-Karim helps me explain that Mr. Koenigs cannot get out of the vehicle for security reasons. Some of the elders implore him to help them. I understand enough of the conversation to know Abdul-Karim is vouching for my honesty.

"Miss Marianne is committed to helping you. That's why she has come to live in Ghor," he tells them. "If she says that she is doing all she can to help you, then it is true. You don't need to embarrass her in front of her boss."

The elders accept his argument and agree to come see me at the compound the next morning.

I climb back into my vehicle, relieved, and the convoy continues. As soon as we are safely back at our compound, Tom Koenigs's personal adviser, Ramon, approaches me.

"Mr. Koenigs wants a written report about the situation, as soon as possible," he says, "and an explanation of what we are doing to progress the case."

By "we" he means me.

"I'll do it as soon as I can," I assure him.

Thanks to the protest, Mr. Koenigs has taken a personal interest in the case. This means he is going to be more aware of, and interested in, the details of my work than he would otherwise have been. Even though I feel the added pressure of this, it also strikes me that I now have access to the advice and support of the most powerful man in the UN mission in Afghanistan. The protestors knew what they were doing!

29

The Past Catches Up

July 2007: Ghor, Afghanistan

A s Ramon walks away I wonder how on earth I'm going to actually help the displaced families. I'm about to follow him to join the afternoon tea with Tom Koenigs when one of my Afghan colleagues from the Herat office, who made the two-day drive to help us with the big day, pulls me aside.

"There is a very good reason Fahim didn't show up for the opening today," he tells me, whispering.

"Yes," I say, a little impatient with the subterfuge. "What is it then?"

"He is hiding in the hills outside Chaghcharan because he has been accused of murder."

I am stunned. Surely I can't be so wrong in my character judgment.

"But Fahim seems so gentle and peaceful! I can't imagine him killing anyone."

"Oh, no, Miss Marianne. He is not accused of having killed anyone himself. The allegations date back to the time when he was district governor of Shahrak."

"Oh," I say, a little relieved, "so this isn't something recent?"

"No, it's about a local man who was arrested and shipped off to Kabul on the orders of the Soviet leadership. He was never seen again.

Fahim just carried out the order from the provincial governor to have the man arrested and sent to Chaghcharan."

I'm simultaneously relieved and exasperated. I'm very relieved that Fahim hasn't killed anyone, but it seems ludicrous to me that he could be held responsible, thirty years later, for following the orders of his superiors. Even as I think this, however, I realize I effectively argue for the same thing when I argue that victims of human rights abuses during Afghanistan's many years of civil war have a right to see their oppressors held accountable for their crimes. I am caught in the net of my own human rights convictions. If there is a case to be answered then I can't justifiably argue that Fahim should be spared the investigation just because I think he is a lovely man.

"I want to talk to him as soon as possible," I say. "I need him to contact me and tell me himself why he didn't show up for work so that I can make a case to the UN administration for his job to be held open for him while the situation is, hopefully, resolved."

My informant promises to find a way to pass the message to Fahim. In the meantime I have to keep up the façade that nothing is amiss while I meet with Tom Koenigs and all our other staff.

"You've all done a wonderful job so far," he says, smiling, "but the real work is only beginning. You now have the responsibility to represent the United Nations well to this province."

I hardly need reminding of this responsibility and it only reinforces my concern about the possibility of a senior staff member being accused of murder in the first days of our operation.

Fahim phones me early that evening, after our VIPs have flown back to Kabul. He repeats what I have already heard. Although his English is a little halting, I know enough of the story already to understand him.

"Please, Fahim," I ask him, "will you come to the office and meet me so that we can solve this problem?"

"I'm so sorry, Miss Marianne, but I can't do that. I trust you, I do, but if I come to town, they will arrest me and I am afraid they will lock me up. I was in prison before," he explains, "during the Taliban time."

We both fall silent for a moment. The news of his past imprisonment isn't really surprising given his history as a government official during the communist regime. When he speaks again, his voice is shaky.

"I was treated very badly last time I was in prison," he says. "I can't do it again."

His explanation helps me understand why he appears to be over-reacting to the allegations. I can't argue with him. I want to tell him he can't be arrested without evidence, that there is no way he can be held without proper charges, and that he would be in no danger in prison. But I can't, because I know that none of those things can be guaranteed.

"I'll be here," I promise him, "watching the investigation and trial like a hawk. I will make sure that all the officials involved know that I am watching them."

"I know you will do everything you can, Miss Marianne," he says. "I believe you and I trust you. If you are with me they will be more careful about what they do. But it won't be enough to keep me safe. For now, the only way for me to stay safe is to stay hidden."

He is probably right. We agree to talk again the next day. In the meantime, members of his extended family are going to approach elders from the family of the man who was killed. He suspects they really want money, which would explain why the complaint is only now being made after all these years, just after Fahim got a new and well-paid job. Fahim is hopeful they can reach a settlement of some sort.

It seems a bit dodgy to me, negotiating away a murder charge, but it might work. As for me, I want to talk to the chief of police about these allegations. First, I need to get some legal advice myself, so I go back to my as yet unfinished room and make a few calls to locate the UNAMA lawyer.

Whereas my job is to monitor the extent to which the people of Afghanistan are given the protection of their own laws and international human rights law, this guy's job is to make sure that UNAMA staff don't break the law. If someone does, in the course of doing their job, it is also his job to establish their immunity from prosecution or to defend them.

Given that the alleged crime took place long before Fahim joined the UN, there is no possibility of immunity. My question is how far I can go to support Fahim without placing the impartiality of our office in jeopardy. I have come up with what I think is a legally sound reason for me to closely monitor Fahim's case. Since the alleged crime dates back to the communist era, the investigation comes under the Action Plan for Peace, Reconciliation and Justice in Afghanistan. Part of my job is to monitor progress in implementing this plan. I wouldn't be monitoring the case as Fahim's employer. I would be monitoring it as a human rights officer.

Luckily for me—and for Fahim—the lawyer in Kabul agrees. As Fahim's employer we have no role to play in this trial, but as a human rights officer, well, that's a different matter.

"If you have an interest in the trial as a human rights officer then there is nothing to stop you monitoring it, as long as you make the distinction clear to all the relevant officials."

I thank him for his advice and hang up, quickly dialing another number. This time I'm calling the personnel department. I want to let them know that Fahim missed work, but that he has a very good reason. I am hoping they will hold the post open for him until we get things sorted out. By now it is late in the evening and there is no answer. I leave a message asking them to call me back first thing the next day. I then sit down to write a report to my boss and all the relevant managers in Kabul explaining Fahim's circumstances and what I have done about it.

There is one detail that I have not included in my report. I need more time to think about it before I can decide what to say about it, if anything. Before lunch someone approached me whispering that he had something to tell me about Fahim. I have very little time for intrigue and my first instinct was that this person meant to stir up trouble. But I didn't know him or anyone in the office well enough yet to be sure of my judgment, so I asked him to tell me what he had to say.

"Haji S., the head of our office, is the one behind these allegations against Fahim," he whispered. "He is connected to the man who made the allegations against Fahim and it is really Haji who wants to make trouble for Fahim."

I groaned and told him that I really couldn't be drawn into rumors. But as he walked away I knew that there might be more to this than just a vicious rumor. I stopped to consider the possible origins of his claim.

Piecing together what I already know about Haji and Fahim's history, it makes sense that Haji could be connected in some way. The man who disappeared all those years ago, presumably killed by the communists in Pul-e-Charkhi prison near Kabul, was a religious leader. His son is the one who has suddenly returned to Ghor, after growing up in Kabul with his mother, to now make the allegations against Fahim.

Haji, the head of our office, is a mujahedeen, one of the commanders who supported the Islamic clerics against the Soviets and eventually overthrew the communist regime. It is highly likely that he would have known the man who was killed because he is from the same district. It also makes sense that the son, when he came back to Ghor, would have sought out Haji in order to find out what happened to his father. Given all this, it is possible it was Haji who told the son that Fahim was the district governor at the time and that Fahim had his father arrested. He need not have had any malicious intent at all; he may just have been answering a simple factual question.

It all makes sense, which only makes it more worrying. What a mess. I wonder what my illustrious superiors were thinking when they hired a mujahedeen as our head of office and an ex-communist district governor from the same bloody district as our political officer. The combination was always going to be explosive. I wonder why they didn't even bother to warn me! It is too late for recriminations now, though. And I suspect it is impossible, in a province with a population as small as Ghor's, to hire two competent, qualified, senior political staff without them being either too closely aligned, or having some kind of complex or deep-rooted conflict.

There is nothing more I can do, so I head to the military base. I am staying there with Heida until my room is finished. Like most people on the base, Heida sleeps in a large tent divided into small individual sleeping spaces by hanging canvas sheets. Because there are so few women on the base, there are spare beds in Heida's tent so I'm sleeping right across the "hall" from her. It's summer now so the tent is hot and stuffy. In the winter these tents are actually quite warm, heated by giant air heaters at the entrance. I've stayed here in the past and am always struck by the lack of privacy and personal space. It's one thing for the soldiers who come only for six months, but Heida is here for two years. I admire her commitment.

As badly as I need to talk about it, I can't tell Heida what is going on with Fahim. Instead we talk about the opening ceremony, which she also attended. I go to bed with my worries still keeping me company. As I lie in my bed, mulling through the day, I realize this is the story of Afghanistan. The challenge facing these two men, and our small office, is the challenge facing the entire country. Will it be possible to find a way past the betrayals and pain of the past? Is it possible to forgive someone who was responsible for the suffering of your people, your tribe? Is there any shared vision for the future that is compelling enough to motivate people to work together despite that suffering? Is it even possible to trust each other enough to work together?

I don't know what the answer will be between Haji and Fahim any more than I know what the answer will be for Afghanistan. But I know that here in the UNAMA office in Ghor, unlike on the national scale, I have the opportunity to play a supportive role. Maybe this is the opportunity for which I stayed in Afghanistan. Maybe this is my chance to understand what our role, as supposedly impartial outsiders, can usefully be here. If during my time in Ghor I can help Fahim and Haji find a way to work together to make this new office a success, then I'll be satisfied. If I can also do something to help the displaced families living in tents across the field from our new compound I'll be even happier.

30
Slowing Down, Letting Go

July 2007: Ghor, Afghanistan

The Hari Rud River winds through Chaghcharan, which is surrounded by miles of rolling brown hills that will explode into green as soon as the rains come. Still a farm girl at heart, I feel at home here.

Our compound is about a kilometer from the center of town, on the eastern side of the river. The river functions as both laundry and washroom to the population. While women and girls squat along the banks of the river scrubbing clothing, men bathe and swim. Some of the younger boys strip off their tunics and swim just in their loose cotton trousers, but most men in Ghor are as modest as the women and bathe fully clothed.

In one section the riverbank gives way to a small pebble beach. Locals drive their dusty jeeps right into the river to wash them. Once a week the drivers from our office take our big white 4x4s down for a clean. The water comes up just past the top of the tires and the men use a bucket to throw water all over the vehicle while they rub it down with a wet rag. The road from the river to our compound is unsealed, so the cars are dusty again by the time they make it back. This persistent cleaning in the face of relentless dust seems to epitomize the kind of perseverance needed to survive in Ghor.

To my huge relief, I am allowed to go out for walks along the river, as long as I take one of our security guards with me. As soon as I am done with my work for the day, I pull on my walking shoes and the biggest scarf I own and head out the front gate. These walks convince me that moving to Ghor was a good idea. I love the independence I have in the small provincial office. I enjoy the intimacy of a small town, allowing me to develop deeper relationships with a small number of local officials and activists. But it is the walking that restores me to full mental health.

We have eight security guards who work shifts in groups of three. One of the guards is older than the others, perhaps in his late forties. His name is Rahim. He is tall and broad, reassuringly solid, with a beard and thick black hair, and eyes that are at once sad and kind. I trust him instinctively and think of him as an uncle.

When Tom Koenigs came to Ghor for our office opening, he met all the security guards and asked them what they thought about the safety of our office. Rahim was the only one confident enough to respond.

"The office is in a good location, Mr. Koenigs," he answered, "but we are vulnerable to rocket attacks from the west. It would be good to ask the police to set up an additional checkpoint along the ridge of those hills."

His quiet, almost reluctant, confidence gave me the impression of someone who knew what he was talking about.

Rahim takes a special interest in my safety. Whenever he is on duty he insists on being my companion as I stroll along the river. Missing my treadmill, I am desperate to get some real exercise from these walks, but with this gentle giant beside me I can't bring myself to force the pace. So we stroll, mostly in silence, and I watch the people of Ghor as they wash their clothes and their cars and themselves, sluicing away the dust and fatigue of life in these mountains.

Sometimes we chat a little, within the limits of my poor Dari. I am able to understand that Rahim worked as a policeman for many years until the Taliban came into power. Losing his job under the Taliban, he found work as a security officer for a French NGO. He tells me that during those times there were other foreign women living in this town. He speaks about the French women with a warm smile and although I don't have the language to ask, I have the impression they were kind to him. I hope he will remember me with the same warmth.

As we walk farther away from the town there are fewer and fewer people. I enjoy the quiet, hearing the gentle sounds of the river and the birds, but I sometimes get nervous about our safety. One day, far from the town, I see a group of four men walking toward us. My body stiffens in fear. I look up at Rahim and ask whether we should turn around. He smiles at me.

"Miss Marianne, you never have to worry when you are with me. You are like my sister. I will take care of you. If there is any danger I will tell you. You can relax."

As he speaks I feel tears coming to my eyes, but I don't want to embarrass him so I blink them away. I don't have brothers of my own, but I miss my father, cousins and brothers-in-law. I am never really relaxed outside my room; without even noticing it, I am always scanning my environment for anyone or anything that looks out of place. In truth, I have little chance of noticing anything unusual or suspicious, since I hardly know what is "normal." It makes much more sense to relax and let Rahim take responsibility for our safety.

I enjoy our walks even more as I learn to relax into his care and let my mind take a break. These walks become my refuge; I watch the river flow past, noticing the brown, pink and gray rocks that line the riverbed. I watch dragonflies swoop down over the surface of the water. I notice the changes in the landscape we walk through. As we get farther away from the village we begin to pass fields planted in wheat. Every day I see subtle changes in the plants as they grow and ripen.

Just past the wheat field there is a kind of vehicle graveyard. Rusted skeletons of old Russian tanks and military jeeps are slowly disintegrating into the grass. It is a stark reminder that even in this bucolic river scene, we are never far from the chaos and bloodshed of war. There is a strange, eerie beauty in the rusty shapes. Rahim waits with a bemused smile as I pull out my camera and photograph our shadows on the side of an old tank; mine looks especially slight alongside his substance.

It surprises my friends back in New Zealand when I tell them I am learning how to slow down in Afghanistan. "There must be so much to do," they protest. "Surely you are working around the clock." Of course there is always more to be done. At the end of a long working day there will always be a child still locked up in an adult prison, families sleeping in tents because they can't return to their homes, and women in the hospital who need more doctors, more medicine or simply more food. There will always be more to do. Somehow, this becomes liberating. If it is impossible to ever do "enough," then what I can do will have to be enough for me.

Under "normal" circumstances I may never have loosened my stranglehold on my own life, demanding the very best of myself at all times. But here in Afghanistan, I couldn't pick out one day when I measure up to the standards I once thought were inviolable. I now miss deadlines and hand over reports that I once would not have allowed to see the light of day, I drop balls and I fail over and over again and—lo and behold—despite it all I am still making a positive difference. I am still doing a good job.

I haven't been for a run in three months. The careful control I maintained over my exercise and eating in New Zealand has long been abandoned and I see little, if any, physical evidence that my body is about to fall apart as a result, despite my secret fears to that effect.

I still think that striving for excellence is great, that taking care of my body and meeting my commitments to others are important. But in learning to survive here I've learned to release my grasp on those unrelenting standards and expectations for myself and others.

Instead I work as hard and as well as I can, starting at 8:00 a.m. and finishing at 6:00 p.m., then I shut my office and head out for my walk. I learn to take time to cook myself a proper dinner, or the closest I can get to a proper dinner when the only things in the market are tired potatoes and wrinkly tomatoes. I learn to take time every morning for my yoga and meditation and to savor a cup of well-made coffee while I read my personal emails before logging in to the madness of my work email for the day.

I even learn to take a weekend, despite often not being allowed out of my compound for the entire two days. I spend my days off writing, reading, befriending the stray cat in our compound, and slowly coaxing her kittens to let me pet them. I learn to sit still and do nothing even when there is so much to do. I learn that the most important part of my job is listening, and that I listen better when I am rested and nourished. Listening may become an even bigger part of my job in the weeks to come, as I try to make sense of radically different accounts about how the displaced families came to be forced from their land.

31
Making Peace

August 2007: Ghor, Afghanistan

*F*ahim has reluctantly returned to work after I got an assurance from the chief of police that he would not be arrested, though he remains worried about the investigation into the allegations against him. We have several long conversations about his history, his experiences under the Taliban and his fears about what might happen if he is arrested again. We discuss the rumors flying around town that Haji is somehow behind the allegations. I feel it necessary to play peacekeeper, telling Fahim there are good reasons why Haji might have been talking to the young man who brought the complaint against him.

"None of this means he was acting maliciously," I insist.

One day Haji comes to my office to discuss Fahim's situation. Haji is about the same age as Fahim, with graying hair and a short, neatly clipped beard. He wears a pakol, the traditional woolen hat worn by the mujahedeen who fought against the communist regime in Afghanistan, and made famous by Ahmad Shah Massoud, renowned mujahedeen leader of the Northern Alliance. Haji's manner with me seems to flip from a slightly pompous formality to an almost ingratiating humility, leaving me unsure which is contrived. Perhaps neither.

It's harder for me to relate to Haji, with his military bearing and stern concern for authority and hierarchy, than to Fahim, who is more poet than soldier and who was drawn to support the Soviet regime because of its emphasis on education, especially for women. But I'm mindful of the risk of allowing my affection for Fahim to cloud my judgment or undermine my ability to play a useful mediation role between these two men, so I work hard to see things from Haji's point of view.

Haji is concerned about the impact of Fahim's situation on our office's reputation, and keen to make sure I know that he had nothing to do with the allegations. His concerns about the office seem legitimate to me, although I can't help wondering whether he is exaggerating them a little to justify his suggestion that Fahim be placed on suspension until the allegations are investigated. Again, I try to set aside my own tendency to trust Fahim, and I listen with an open mind to Haji's concerns.

The next day Fahim spends hours unburdening himself to me about his concern that Haji has it in for him. I have sympathy for both of them. But their distrust of each other runs deep. Can they take the risk of trusting each other enough to have one honest conversation? Had I been in their shoes, I'm not sure that I could. I want badly for them to find a way to work it out.

To their credit, and despite the distrust, they are able to work together. I know that I am very fortunate to have two men of such experience and wisdom on my team. Ironically, the same political differences that lie behind their distrust of each other are a real asset in our work. They bring radically different perspectives to our political work; between the two of them, I can access an incredible range of knowledge and advice about the cases that come to our office.

One case that is taking up much of my time for the moment is the land dispute that displaced the Hazara families who protested in front of Tom Koenigs's car. Local police have been out to try to enforce the

Supreme Court decision in favor of the Hazara families, but the people on the land repelled them with resolute defiance and homemade weapons. The police retreated and are now reluctant to return.

The provincial governor has asked my office to make a peace-building trip to the district. I am already making regular visits to the camp of displaced Hazara families, helping them secure access to the local school for their children. They too have asked me to help them find a peaceful resolution to the conflict over the land.

In preparation for my visit to the district I've been learning as much as I can about the conflict. I've interviewed local officials, the Hazara elders and some distant relatives of the people who are currently on the land. I'm beginning to realize that this conflict is part of a much bigger land conflict and that I'm going to have to get my head around the whole thing before I can be of any help.

The roots of the conflict lie in Dowlatyar district, about three hours' drive from Chaghcharan. Thirty years ago, the now protesting Hazara bought land in Dowlatyar from the Sardarha tribe, who claimed to own the land. The Baiboqa tribe, who later forced the Hazara families off the land, claimed that they were the rightful owners and that the Sardarha had stolen it from them.

The conflict between the Sardarha and Baiboqa dates back to the days of King Amanullah Khan (1919–29). The dates of specific incidents are difficult for me to pin down since they vary from one account to another. From what I have pieced together from various accounts of the conflict, the Baiboqa were the original inhabitants of the area. When people speak about them, they use a Dari word that translates into English as either "peasant" or "indigenous people." The Sardarha, on the other hand, were feudal lords during the reign of King Amanullah. The king granted them control over much of the land in the district. Herein lies the root of the current conflict.

Although the conflict is almost ninety years old, it has taken on a new urgency in recent decades as changing climatic conditions drastically reduce the arable areas in the district. At the same time, population growth means both tribes need more and more land to support their people. The indigenous Baiboqa and feudal Sardarha tribes have been fighting over a reducing parcel of fertile land. Unfortunately for the Hazara families, they walked into the middle of this conflict when they bought their parcel of land from the Sardarha thirty years ago.

Many people before me have tried to broker a peaceful resolution without any lasting success. So I have modest expectations for my own peace-building mission. Fahim, however, insists we should make the trip. He seems to believe we can do some good. He also insists that I must come.

"A foreigner," he says, "will be seen as neutral."

I agree and we plan our trip.

32
Conflict Stories

August 2007: Ghor, Afghanistan

*B*ased on what I know of Afghan custom and the advice of people, like Talatbek, who have lots of experience in this kind of thing, I've pieced together a picture of the "right" way to approach solving age-old tribal conflicts in Afghanistan.

Step one is to meet with elders from each of the different tribes involved in the conflict and any neutral tribes in the area. During this stage the would-be peacemaker listens to all sides of the story, asking the elders what they have experienced, what the conflict has cost them and what they want to see happen. The goal, at this stage, is to gather lots of information, to identify any areas of common ground for future peace and, most importantly, to build trust. This is the goal of my mission to Dowlatyar. Fahim is coming with me, together with one of the human rights officers from Mr. Baluch's office.

The first day of our mission goes well. The district governor lends us the local jail to use as a meeting room. It is a small room adjacent to the district governor's office, surprisingly comfortable for an Afghan jail, with warm carpets on the floor and windows that fill the room with natural light. There are no prisoners in the district at the time, so we have the room to ourselves.

We have arranged for the different tribal groups to meet us at different times throughout the day. The governor chose the times depending on how far the elders had to travel. The first group is from a village near the district center. There are six men in the delegation, three elderly men with white beards and delicate silhouettes and three younger men, still thick with the solidity of youth. All of them are dressed in cotton shalwar kameez suits, woolen waistcoats and turbans. They remove their shoes at the door and take a seat in the chairs the governor has set out for us.

We begin by greeting each other, one at a time around the room. I place my right hand over my heart as I nod toward each of our hosts, greeting them with *"Asalaam u aleikum. Chetor asten? Jona jorast? Familetan khubas? Shuma khub estan? Zenda geetan khubas? Familetan khubas?"*

It's not uncommon in a formal meeting like this for these questions, which translate roughly to "How are you? How is your health? How is your family? Are you well? Is life well? Is your family well?" to be repeated twice or even three times for each person. It amazes me how quickly my Afghan colleagues can reel them off, sometimes so quickly that I wonder if I can really be expected to respond. Fahim, however, insists that I should so I learn to answer rapid-fire: *"Tashakur, khub astum. Familema khubestan. Nam-e-khuda. Besyar khub. Tashakur."* "Thank you, I am well. My family is well. God is good. Very well, thank you."

Our discussions start well. We drink green tea made by one of the governor's nephews. Fahim explains that we want to hear about the longstanding conflict between the Baiboqa and Sardarha tribes. The elders talk and I listen. I take lots of notes.

We follow this process twice in the morning. The first group of elders is loosely aligned to the indigenous Baiboqa tribe; the second group of elders is from the Baiboqa tribe itself. Although it is clear that each tribe's version of local history reflects its own allegiances and

interests, there are enough repeated threads for me to begin to piece
together a common picture.

I notice how particularly graphic stories of injustice have been carefully preserved and handed down through the generations. One such
story is about the feudal Sardarha forcing men from the indigenous
Baiboqa tribe to work their grindstones in the place of oxen, whip-
ping them beyond the point of exhaustion until they collapsed and
died beneath the massive stones. This happened during the reign of
the king, when the Sardarha held the upper hand in the district. The
victimized tribe tells us this story, but so does the other group of elders,
using almost identical language and phrases.

Another story emerges about members of the feudal Sardarha tribe
using the Baiboqa as targets for shooting practice. This gruesome tale
is repeated to me not only by the Baiboqa elders but also by a variety of
government officials in Dowlatyar. These shared trauma stories play an
important role in maintaining the momentum and heat of this conflict.

After the first two meetings I am beginning to get sleepy, so after
lunch I ask Fahim to come with me on a quick walk to refresh myself.
We wander over to a tent school near the governor's office. The local
children share the tents; boys taking classes in the morning, and girls in
the afternoon. Under the hot August sun, there are hundreds of young
girls being taught Dari, Arabic, English, math, and history.

The tents are worn thin and ripped in places. It seems unlikely these
tents will survive the coming winter. The teachers show me the rips and
beg me to help them get new tents for their school. I am probably one
of few foreigners to visit this district in recent years and it doesn't surprise me that they ask for my help. With Fahim's help I try, as always,
to lower their expectations. There may be little I can do. I do know
Heida is in the process of getting new school tents for Ghor, so there is
a chance that I will be able to do something in this case.

After lunch we talk to two more groups of elders. One is a subtribe of the Baiboqa and the fourth group has peaceful but frosty relations with the Baiboqa and more sympathy for the feudal Sardarha. I learn nothing new, but it is helpful to keep hearing the same accounts over and over again. I'm beginning to get a sense of the history of this conflict. More importantly, I'm getting an idea of how the conflict continues to play out today. What happened in the past is less important than what is remembered of that past. If the decreasing parcel of arable land is the igniting spark of the current conflict, these stories of grievance and trauma that I've been hearing all day are its primary fuel.

In the evening we are invited into the village to eat with the relatives of one of my colleagues. As the only woman in the group, I am separated from my colleagues and find myself spending the evening in the company of our host's mother and several of her grandchildren. She is full of questions.

"How often do you pray?" she asks me.

"Most days," I reply.

"How do you pray?"

"Sometimes sitting, sometimes moving." I'm thinking of my meditation and yoga practices.

"Do you fast?"

"Sometimes." I have been known to do cleansing fasts.

"How often do you fast? For how long?"

"It varies."

"But what is the correct way, in your religion, to fast?" She is obviously perplexed by my vagueness.

"It varies," I repeat, wishing my Dari were more sophisticated.

"Hmmm," she seems unconvinced. "Do you eat pork?"

"No. I don't eat meat."

"Ah, so you are Hindu!" she declares, pleased to have finally made sense of me.

I am unsure how to explain in my kindergarten Dari that no, in fact

I am a budding Buddhist (thanks to Pema Chödrön's teachings) who practices yoga.

"Something like Hindu, I guess," I say.

"So you are from India?"

I am resigned by now to my lack of linguistic ability. Close enough, I think.

"Yes," I say. "I'm from India."

"Ah," she says, satisfied. "I like the Indian soap operas."

Having invented a new religion and nationality for myself, I then settle the matter by doing a few sun salutes alongside her evening prayers. This isn't the first time I've been mistaken for an Indian or a Hindu. In theory it would be better to be taken for a Christian, which is a religion honored by the Prophet Mohammed and respected, as a rule, by Muslims. As it is, it's not surprising that Afghans have trouble pinning down my religion. I am muddled myself.

I find extraordinary power in Pema Chödrön's simple yet profound Buddhist practices and teachings and I've begun to read other Buddhist writing as well. Perhaps Afghanistan is the right setting to be introduced to the Buddha's teachings on the four noble truths. There is certainly no avoiding the first of them; that life is suffering. But I had been struggling to accept the second noble truth; that suffering is caused by attachment, or craving, and aversion. I have no problem seeing how my suffering is caused by these two tendencies. But I struggle to see how the suffering of a mother who can't feed her child might be caused by her own attachments.

I'm still confused by some of these teachings, but perhaps it is not my job to understand why other people suffer. My job is only to do what I can to ease their unnecessary suffering, just as I learn to ease mine. And amid it all, I find clarity in my own practice. Every time I sit in meditation or get on my mat to practice yoga, I see my own attachments and aversions more clearly. I am also coming to see that I am not just my own preferences, my ideas or even my feelings—although they are so strong sometimes that it is easy to identify with them. My sense of identity itself is beginning to lose its solidity. Surprisingly, for someone who was raised in a culture obsessed with the identity of the individual, this is a great relief.

The family invites me to stay overnight at their home, but when I radio my security officer back in the compound in Ghor, he is not happy. I know it's not a battle I can win, so we say good night and my group heads back up to the police station.

The normal arrangement on trips like this is for us all to sleep in the main hall of the station on the floor cushions that line every meeting room in Afghanistan. It doesn't make for a peaceful night of sleep, mostly because of the snoring, but there is safety in numbers and my colleagues prefer to have me nearby.

When we arrive at the station, however, I find a familiar face. Jawid, the head of the Criminal Investigation Department, was a participant in the workshop on gender and criminal justice that Kate and I ran in Chaghcharan three months ago. He was the man who argued with the imam, insisting that since we all know that rape happens, it is the responsibility of justice officials to learn how to investigate and prosecute it. I recognize him immediately and am thrilled to see him. He's also happy to see me and proceeds to tell everyone in the station about the wonderful training he did with "Miss Marianna" and "Professor Katerina." I make a mental note to tell Kate her legacy has spread to Dowlatyar.

He insists that I sleep in his office, where he keeps a small cot for emergencies. I am grateful. I will have privacy and a locked door. Our driver comes with me to make sure that the room is indeed empty, that the door is properly locked and that there are no other possible entry points. If I'm not going to be sleeping in the common room with the rest of them, then, in his self-appointed role as my chaperone, he wants to be very sure that nobody can get into my room.

He also accompanies me to the outhouse toilet. There is no door in the mud structure that houses the drop toilet. As I squat over the filthy hole in the ground, he stands at the door, with his back to me, to shield my modesty from prying eyes. Outside, I rinse off my hands and brush my teeth with a little of my precious supply of bottled water. I go to bed fully clothed in case I need to get up and move quickly in the night. You don't want to be caught out in a flimsy nightdress in an Afghan police station if there are incoming rockets.

The next morning we start early again, to get on the road before word can spread about our movements. We have two stops to make on our way back to Chaghcharan. In each place we will meet another group of elders to hear their accounts of the conflict.

The first group is from an unaligned tribe, supported by neither the Sardarha nor the Baiboqa. They arrived in Dowlatyar more recently than the other groups and have no strong allies in the district. They are, however, aligned with powerful tribes in adjoining districts and have therefore managed to secure the support of a local NGO to build a new school for their village. We meet them in an empty room of the newly constructed school.

One of the eldest men in the group sits quietly, sucking on his gums and occasionally nodding in agreement with the reports given by his companions. I wonder whether this fragile-looking old man might have been alive at the time of the alleged atrocities we heard about the previous day. I don't want to direct my question at him too obviously, so I ask generally whether anyone from their tribe had witnessed the alleged mistreatment of the Baiboqa peasants by their Sardarha masters. All faces in the room turn to the old man and in a raspy, breathless voice he starts to talk.

He shares the same stories I heard from the Baiboqa elders, about people being shot at for target practice and hunted like animals. He repeats the story of people harnessed into grinding machines in the place of oxen and worked until they themselves were ground to death on the massive stones. His face and voice give little away about what he might feel about these terrible stories. Still, even listening to them now, many years after they took place, I feel my heart rate accelerate with emotion.

Perhaps because he is not aligned with either tribe, he is also willing to tell me more recent stories in which the tables of power have turned. The Soviet regime, predictably, preferred the peasant workers over the feudal lords. So after the Soviet invasion, the Baiboqa tribe gained considerable power, and land, at the expense of the Sardarha. He tells me that at the height of their power, during the Soviet regime, the Baiboqa attended a purported peace meeting with the Sardarha only to turn on their hosts, killing up to thirty people.

Despite the horror of these tales, my visit with this tribe is a relaxed affair. They have remained relatively neutral throughout the generations of this fighting and therefore have managed to escape the endless cycle of violence and revenge in the district.

The second group we go to meet are the elders of the Sardarha tribe, once feudal lords of all the land in the district. They were unwilling to meet us in the district center for fear, they claim, that their Baiboqa enemies would ambush them. By the time we pull in to the dirt road leading from the main road up to their fortified village, I have heard tales of this tribe's alleged cruelty for two long days. I'm aware of the impact this must be having on my ability to approach them with an open mind and heart, and I try to clear my head of everything that has gone before.

We are running late and need to keep the visit to a strict time limit if we are going to get back to our compound before sunset. UN security rules forbid us from traveling on the road after dark. I enter this meeting with two challenges: keeping an open mind despite all that I've heard, and remaining patient and attentive in the face of a sinking-sun deadline.

As we pull up outside the walled village, a delegation of elders comes out through the gates to welcome us. Our drivers and security guards (we travel with two vehicles of armed police officers in convoy at all times) are taken away to wash, rest and drink tea in a special room dug into the thick exterior wall for exactly that purpose.

Meanwhile, Fahim and I are led in through the massive gate and up a set of stairs molded into the interior side of the wall that surrounds the entire village. At the top of the stairs is a room recessed into the wall; it sits directly above the entrance gate. This is the space set aside for receiving delegations of men from other tribes. If the story about the Baiboqa attacking the reconciliation meeting and killing Sardarha men is true, then I guess it took place in this room.

The mud floors of the room are covered in carpets, and foam mattresses covered in red fabric line the floor around the edges of the room, making a comfortable square around which we all sit, cross-legged on the mattresses. I pull out my notebook. We begin the meeting, as always, with a round of greetings.

I sit quietly while our host welcomes us and gives a relatively short speech, filled with rhetorical flourishes about the troubles his tribe has faced in recent years. There is no denying that their fortunes have fallen considerably from the heights of their reign as the royally designated feudal lords of all the lands in the district. Despite my natural tendency to sympathize with the peasant rather than the master, it isn't hard to feel genuine compassion for the hardships that these dramatic changes in fortune have brought to them.

Fahim and I have conducted five of these meetings in two days and my Dari is improving, so I am familiar enough with the specific vocabulary of this district and its conflicts to follow the discussion without simultaneous translation. Fahim still stops the speaker every few minutes to make sure I understand the key points and to translate anything that I haven't understood.

When my time comes to speak I start in Dari, thanking them again for meeting with us, and then ask permission to speak in English. Everyone nods in agreement and, with Fahim now translating, I start by explaining what my role is and what I am trying to do with these visits.

"I am not a judge or a jury," I emphasize. "I will not be making any decisions about who is right or wrong in these matters. Our office is neutral. We have no allegiance to, or preference for, any side in this conflict. Our job is simply to try to understand what has happened and what the situation is now."

Although it is unlikely that they will have guessed at my own socialist leanings, the Sardarha elders almost certainly know that Fahim was a district governor under the communist regime. They have every reason to suspect he will be more sympathetic to the Baiboqa and I want to do my best to reassure them.

Fahim and I take turns leading the questioning. I like to listen to his approach to interviews. Sometimes it seems that he is wandering off the topic, straying into a discussion about unrelated or irrelevant issues. But I learn to wait and see where the line of discussion leads us. It usually becomes apparent that he knew all along where he was going, but understood that a direct approach would never get us there.

I am learning, but I am far from being fully adept at this slow and indirect approach. I still lose patience with people who seem to be purposefully obstructing the course of a discussion with delays and distractions. Sitting in the Sardarha meeting room, I notice my impatience rising—not only impatience with the time it is taking to listen again to stories that I have already heard three or four times in the past forty-eight hours, but also at having to listen to tales of woe from these men, whose own tribe is widely reported to have been bitterly cruel to those less powerful than them when they themselves were in power.

As I sit and listen to them talk, I notice my skeptical reaction to their stories and feel myself shift from the openness of listening toward the rigidity of judging. At one point in the interview, the elders of this tribe tell me they have killed only one person over the decades of the conflict. I've heard from many different sources that the number of fatalities at their hands is closer to three hundred in the past thirty years. I roll my eyes in frustration and disgust at their dishonesty.

The "right" approach to building peace does not involve me rolling my eyes, even at stories that I find deeply improbable. Nor am I supposed to shift about uncomfortably in a way that suggests I want to get out of the room, fast. I've given up on any opportunity to generate trust in this room. Now I'm just watching the clock.

Fahim has worked with me long enough by now to notice I am out of sorts. With concerned glances in my direction he lets me know that my fidgeting and skeptical body language are not helping. I understand his unspoken message. We need to stay with this process. We need to let these men talk for as long as they want. But I am uncomfortable and I am in charge so I make the call to leave. To his credit, Fahim does his best to extract us from the situation with the least possible insult to our hosts.

As we arrive back at the gate on our way out, Fahim tells me that the women of the tribe want to meet with me as well. In a move that goes against everything I claim to believe about the essential role of women in peace-building, I tell him we don't have time to meet the women.

It is strictly true. We are now running late and it would be irresponsible of me to allow the safety of all eighteen people in our convoy to be put at risk. But would it really be so bad to stop for even ten minutes to meet these women? What could I learn about the conflict if I make the time? As we drive away, I wonder what they make of my refusal to meet them. Maybe they assume I think they are not as important as their men, with whom I spent over an hour.

I am furious with myself. I know I behaved badly by losing patience in the meeting and refusing to speak with the women, and I have plenty of time to berate myself on the drive home. I choose to ride in a different car from Fahim, as I am not ready to face his questions about my poor behavior. He asks anyway, using the two-way radio built into the vehicles.

"What is wrong, Miss Marianne?"

I don't answer, cutting off the conversation, claiming we need to keep the radio channel free for communication with our base.

When we get back to our office in Chaghcharan a few hours later, I send the police escort and my colleagues home to their families and head to my room. In the weeks since I moved into this little unit I have set myself up with some essential home comforts. I make myself a cup of herbal tea and reflect on my behavior. As disappointed as I am, I try to keep some perspective.

I have only ever been one small player in this story. It helps to remember that. I might have blown my chance to build real compassion and trust with the Sardarha tribe, but I haven't blown the tribe's chances at peace. It would be ludicrous and arrogant to imagine that I have that much influence. At the same time, I do believe that in each small moment, there is the possibility of creating more peace and ease, rather than adding to suffering and confusion. This is all I really want to do in Afghanistan and I failed to do it in that meeting in Dowlatyar.

What I had felt was anger. I'm not very comfortable with being angry. I tell myself that I should always remain calm, hold my tongue and maintain equanimity. But I get angry with people who don't want to be honest about the past, who won't see that the world has changed and that they need to change with it. I get angry with men who deny ever having killed anyone despite being in the midst of a bloody conflict almost a century old. I get angry that people continue to choose war over reconciliation.

All my legal training hasn't prepared me to deal with anger. It hasn't prepared me to sit in a room with men who are accused of terrible crimes, while remaining open and compassionate toward them and all they have to say. I have been taught how to evaluate whether or not they are telling the truth, but not how to sit still and remain open-minded even if they are not.

But the fact that I am so disappointed with myself shows that I know there is a different way. I have been developing the skills I need to sit in the presence of suffering and remain open. I have been practicing it by sitting with my own discomfort and pain in the weeks since Joel broke up with me. I practice it each morning as I sit on my meditation cushion and hold my seat even when I am assailed by doubts and the thought that I will never be any good at meditation. Today I've been reminded that I'm only human, I'm not always going to be able to listen with an open mind. But I'm doing my best and I head to bed with a sense of peace.

33
Four Men and a Gift from the NATO Gods

August–September 2007: Ghor, Afghanistan

Life in Ghor settles into a reassuring rhythm. I wake early every day and practice some yoga and meditation. Before I sit down to meditate, I put the coffee pot on and put a small pot of my precious soy milk on the stove to heat so that there is a soy latte ready for me as I finish my practice. I drink my coffee at my wee kitchen table while I write in my journal.

Overall, I feel well here. Between my morning routines and my afternoon walks with Rahim, I'm as balanced as I've ever been in my life. It's ironic, really, that the space I needed to take care of myself is finally created here, in the midst of a country at war. I've never found, or made, this space before, not even in New Zealand where I always had "so much to do." Why is it that here, in the mountains of Afghanistan where there is so much work to be done, I am learning to slow down and nurture myself?

Part of what has made this possible is the restriction on my life. There is a simplicity to my outer life here in Ghor, a simplicity that I may never find again, though I hope that I can remember the powerful effect of this simplicity on my inner life.

As I settle into the simple routines of my life in Ghor, I miss Joel.

We've begun to chat over Skype in the evenings. He still makes me laugh when I'm taking my work or myself too seriously. But I don't have to rely solely on Joel for my sanity. Tim is also keeping me company on email, which is both good and, given my ongoing contact with Joel, a little bit confusing. My email exchanges with Tim are the most intimate conversation I'm having with anyone at the moment. I write to my girl-friends back in New Zealand and their responses are a great source of comfort much of the time. But sometimes they struggle to relate to my experiences in Afghanistan and it is only with Tim that I feel I can talk freely of my doubts and fears about my work and life here.

I'm getting to know him better than I knew the people I lived with in Herat. Tim makes me laugh, but his humor comes wrapped in an understanding that we are up to our necks in strong emotions and we both need to share them with someone we can trust.

If I could start afresh, Tim would have my undivided attention. He and I are made of the same stuff; we *get* each other. Joel and I, on the other hand, are different in almost every way. But I'm not starting afresh. Despite all we've been through, Joel can still make me laugh and I still feel safer just knowing that Joel is in Afghanistan with me.

So I continue these two conversations, deeply grateful for Tim's friendship and yet ever hopeful that Joel will change his mind and decide to give us, give me, another chance. If someone asked me why I want to be back with Joel I would have trouble explaining it. The truth is, I don't really know. Maybe it's no more than the appeal of the familiar, but I can't deny I'm holding out hope for a reunion. This hope makes no sense, and yet it persists. What has changed is that I realize that I'll be fine whatever happens. And the part of me that is getting stronger, calmer and saner by the day recognizes the folly of my hopes.

Fahim and I are almost inseparable, working closely on human rights and political cases throughout the province. After Fahim, my closest col-laborator in Ghor is Ansari Baluch, the director of the Afghan Independent

Human Rights Commission office in Ghor. The first time we met, Fahim introduced him as Mr. Baluch, using the English "mister," so that's what I always call him, on the assumption that it is his preference.

A couple of times a week I head over to Mr. Baluch's office to discuss any new human rights cases that have come to either of us. AIHRC's offices are closer to the center of town and its compound is much smaller and more modest than ours, with a mud wall in place of our high fence, barbed wire and security lights. I yearn to blend in as they do, but accept that the security fence comes with the UN gig. Like the big white 4x4s, the wire and lights are part of the UN "minimum operating security standards," or MOSS. These four letters rule my life.

When I visit, Mr. Baluch welcomes me at the door and, although he is from Kandahar in the conservative south of the country, he always insists on shaking my hand.

Mr. Baluch is a tall, thin man. Always impeccably dressed in either traditional Afghan clothing or a Western-style suit, he carries himself with dignity and has elegant manners. I wonder if he is from a wealthy family, although it certainly isn't unusual in Afghanistan to meet men who dress carefully and are well mannered, no matter what their socio-economic background. Good manners and grooming are the norm rather than the exception.

Like every office I've seen in Afghanistan apart from our own at the UN, the AIHRC office is furnished with a comfortable lounge suite. I often wonder what visitors make of our uncomfortable Western-style office chairs. As I settle back into the cushions, Mr. Baluch asks one of his assistants to bring us tea. We take a few moments to chat, asking after each other's health and family. It is customary to precede any actual description of health or family with the phrase *"Alhamdulallah,"* meaning "Thanks be to God." Even in Afghanistan, where Arabic is not generally spoken except by religious scholars, this phrase is always said in Arabic—the language of the Quran. My basic knowledge of

Arabic, dating back to my time in Gaza, gives some people the misleading impression that I am a devout scholar.

"Alhamdulallah," I say. "Thanks be to God, my health is good and my parents are well. And you, how is your health? How is your fine family?"

"Alhamdulallah," he replies. "Thanks be to God, we are all well." Once we settle in, he gives me a rundown of their human rights cases.

It makes for depressing conversation. There is always at least one person who has been in the local prison for months without being brought to trial, at least one underaged girl forced into marriage, at least one illegal seizure of land by a local warlord and several complaints about police corruption or brutality. There are no easy solutions to any of these cases, but I am finding new energy for my work in Mr. Baluch's enthusiasm and his tireless efforts to seek justice for those oppressed around him.

Mr. Baluch always makes it clear that he sees a real advantage in my role. There is no sense of competition between us—the local and the foreign human rights defender. As far as he is concerned, two human rights lawyers are better than one. Sometimes he suggests I should take the lead on a case, especially if it involves complaints about the Lithuanian soldiers or one of the international organizations.

Even where there is no international angle to the case, he still prefers that we work as a team. We talk about the cases at length, agree on the legal status and then plot out our strategy for getting things fixed. If we need to meet with the chief of police or the governor, we agree on who will speak first, what we will say and what our approach will be.

Working with Mr. Baluch is a genuine collaboration and I get the sense this is how this UN mission is supposed to work. People in Kabul talk about "supporting local actors" a lot. Here in Ghor I'm putting those words into action and it feels good.

One day in early September I get a request from the governor to attend an emergency meeting to discuss the fate of the displaced

Hazara families living in the tents near our office. It turns out somebody in Kabul has taken an interest in this case. Somebody powerful.
The governor has received word that he, together with the chief of
police, must implement the court decision and return the Hazara to
the land. It is a seemingly impossible task and the governor is putting
together his own *Mission Impossible* taskforce. I am both nervous and
flattered to be on it.

I arrive to the meeting late; most of the others are already seated
around a long table in the governor's office. I notice the new Lithuanian
PRT commander is here. He arrived to take over command only a few
weeks ago and although I've met him on several occasions, this is my
first chance to see him in action. I'm hoping for an improvement on
his predecessor who, although he may have been an excellent military
commander, was difficult to work with and dismissive of the role of
civilians in Afghanistan.

Heida is sitting next to the commander. This in itself is a good sign.
Heida has been in Ghor for almost a year so she knows more about
the province than the new commander, or any of the military advisers
he brought with him for that matter. The previous commander had
been reluctant to take Heida's advice even on matters that were clearly
humanitarian. Seeing the new commander lean over to talk to Heida
as the other guests settle, I think civilian–military relations may already
have improved under his command.

Apart from the commander, the chief of police and the head of the
National Directorate for Security are also at the table. The local head
of the Red Crescent Society (the Islamic equivalent of the Red Cross)
is there, as are the local directors of World Vision, Catholic Relief
Services, Afghan Aid, and Madera—a French NGO. Together they
make up the entire aid community in Ghor. One advantage of being
poor, remote and ill served as a province is that it is so much easier to
get everyone in the same place, simply because there are so few of us.

The heads of various local government departments are also present, including the head of the Ministry of Works. I have a lot of respect for this man. We have worked together on a plan to keep Ghor's roads open through winter so that food and emergency assistance can get through. From what I've seen, he is genuinely committed to serving the needs of the poorest and most vulnerable people in his province.

As I arrive, the governor is outlining the history of the land dispute that displaced the Hazara families. There is nothing new or surprising in the governor's overview. The Supreme Court found in favor of the Hazara families because they purchased the land in good faith from the Sardarha tribe, who have papers establishing their ownership of the land. The court declared the land should be restored to them as soon as possible. In theory, this is fantastic news for the Hazara families. In practice, things don't look quite so bright.

The chief of police gives us a briefing on the police's previous efforts to dislodge the Baiboqa from the land. The Baiboqa stood their ground against the police—women and children together with their menfolk, some of whom were armed—and threatened to kill anyone who tried to take the land from them. I have no doubt they are capable of carrying out their threat. Although the families on this parcel of land alone are no match for the police, they could call on the support of their tribal brethren. If it came to that, I would estimate the full force of the Baiboqa tribe in Ghor province would easily outgun the police.

The chief of police is suggesting as much himself, without actually conceding any weakness on the part of his force. He insists he is ready and willing to go into the area and will succeed in removing the Baiboqa from the land, as long as he and his men are properly equipped. It doesn't surprise me he is using this opportunity to make a plug for more men, guns and vehicles. It's a fair plea, but the governor isn't impressed.

"We will enforce this court decision," he reiterates forcefully, "and we will do it with the resources we already have."

He seems uncharacteristically agitated and I suspect that some kind of ultimatum was issued from Kabul. The governor's job may even be on the line.

All eyes turn to the new Lithuanian commander.

"Perhaps you could supply a military escort for the police?" the chief of police asks him.

"Or," suggests the governor, "maybe you could send military trucks and an escort to transport the Hazara families back to the land."

I watch nervously for his reaction. This is the first real test I have seen of his judgment. If he agrees to help with this mission, without first taking time to consult with Heida and me about the humanitarian and political implications, then we are no better off than we were with his predecessor. If he asked, I would tell him he could put the lives of all the Hazara families at risk by associating them, in the minds of the population, with the foreign military. The stakes are high for his first public utterance.

"I will certainly give careful thought to your request, Governor," he begins, "and I will be as supportive as possible. But I need to consult with the relevant UN agencies and with my own humanitarian adviser before I can give you a definite response."

My sigh of relief is probably audible to everyone in the room. A military commander who insists on consulting with UN humanitarian agencies before getting involved in a humanitarian mission is a gift from the NATO gods. I had heard that such men existed, but up until now I hadn't met any.

Having reached a dead end in his efforts to enlist military support for the operation, the governor turns to the aid agencies. He has already enlisted one of his staff members to draft up a list of the resources needed to relocate the families. The initial assessment includes food, fuel and tents.

"Can the aid organizations help fill this list?" he asks.

I am confused about the tents. There are houses on the occupied land, the houses the Hazara used to live in, and I assume that the whole point of getting the Hazara back to their home before winter is so that they can get out of the tents and into proper houses. I ask the governor about this.

He explains, "The Baiboqa have threatened to destroy the houses if they are forced to leave the land. Even if we can get the Hazara families back onto the land, they will still be in tents." He shrugs. "But at least we can get them some better-quality tents."

Having drawn attention to myself, I become the first victim of the governor's efforts to enlist a commitment to contribute something on his list. I dodge his request by talking about procedure. The established procedure is for the Provincial Emergency Response Committee to meet and conduct a needs assessment. This would be jointly coordinated by my office, representing the aid community, and the local government officials. I can't go to the UN agencies with a wish list unless it has been approved by the joint committee and based on a proper needs assessment. UN work is full of procedures, most of them there for good reason.

I will also need to get a "protection assessment" from UNHCR, the UN agency responsible for refugees and internally displaced people. They will have to assess whether or not it is safe for the Hazara families to be returned to their original land. If UNHCR decides it isn't safe, then none of the UN agencies will contribute to their repatriation.

I explain all of this with some trepidation. The governor is obviously under pressure and wants to act quickly. My explanation of the various checks and balances built into our emergency response system is going to frustrate him. But they are not optional; this is how it works and there are very good reasons why the system has been designed this way. Many well-intentioned efforts to return displaced people to their place of origin have gone horribly wrong in the past. If we return the

Hazara to their land and they are then attacked by hostile Baiboqa, their blood will be on our hands.

To my relief, several others in the group speak up in support of my position. The head of the Red Crescent insists the Provincial Emergency Response Committee should first meet to conduct a more thorough assessment of the situation. He also agrees that the UN agencies will not be able to support the operation unless UNHCR determines it is safe for the displaced families. And the NGOs tell the governor they are, in principle, ready to contribute to the operation but they too need to see a formal needs assessment from the provincial committee and a protection report from UNHCR before they can go any further.

The governor sees he won't get much further with any of us today. He asks us to start work as soon as we can, and orders the Provincial Emergency Response Committee to meet immediately to conduct the needs assessment. I know I will be called on to take part in that process, but I need to get back to my office as fast as I can so I can get in touch with my UNHCR colleagues in Herat. They need to get up to Ghor as soon as possible and I've organized enough missions to Ghor to know I have no time to lose. The governor appears to be under so much pressure that, if I'm slow to act, he may go ahead and return the displaced families despite my misgivings.

34

Not Without a Fight

September 2007: Ghor, Afghanistan

*I*t takes me a while to get hold of the right person at the UNHCR office in Herat. I have a good friend who works there as the senior protection officer and hope he will understand and support the need to get someone up for an assessment mission as soon as possible. He agrees immediately. We decide on a joint mission, a human rights officer from my office with a protection officer from his office and, ideally, someone from the AIHRC. I leave him to draft up some terms of reference for the mission while I get busy requesting a flight and preparing the paperwork.

I call in all my favors with the air operations team and manage to set up a flight to come to Ghor the next day. Meanwhile my friend over at UNHCR has arranged for one of his Afghan protection officers to undertake the mission. We are in business!

Shortly afterward, I am summoned to the PRT to talk to the Lithuanian commander about the governor's request. When I arrive at his office, a converted shipping container on the military base, I am pleased to see he has again invited Heida to join us. I explain that plans are in progress for an assessment mission by UNHCR, and tell him that until we have the results, none of the UN agencies will act. He is happy to take the same approach and asks me to let him know as soon as the assessment is completed.

Then he surprises me.

"I noticed during your last visit to our dining hall that you liked chocolate." He hands me some chocolate bars.

A military commander who listens to civilian advice *and* who notices that I like chocolate?

"Where should I make my request that you never be rotated out of this place?" I laugh.

The next day the plane arrives carrying one UNHCR protection officer and my newest human rights assistant from the Herat office, whom I recruited just before leaving. We haven't had much chance to work together but I'm confident she'll be great. She is mature, in her forties, and has good judgment and excellent people skills. Mr. Baluch sends over one of his staff as well, and after a briefing from Fahim and me on the background to the land conflict and the current situation in Dowlatyar district, they set off, with Fahim as guide, to visit the disputed land.

They arrive back from their mission late that afternoon. My new assistant from Herat interviewed women all day, and reports that the women told her that if the Hazara families try to take back their land, the Baiboqa will kill them. Fahim reports the same from the older men and, he tells me sadly, even from children. The Baiboqa families will not leave without a fight.

I ask if they really believe these threats; are the Baiboqa really going to kill any Hazara who try to return? Maybe they are bluffing in the hope that they will convince us it is unsafe to enforce the court decision? The UNHCR field officer says he has no doubt that they will do what they say. The Baiboqa currently on the land recounted a story of a young man from their tribe who was tortured and killed by the Hazara before they were run off the land. The Baiboqa are ready to avenge his death and are convinced the Hazara are cruel and ruthless killers.

The story seems far-fetched, given my own experience of the warm, welcoming Hazara families in the tents across the field from our office. Then again, when I met the indigenous Baiboqa tribal leaders in Dowlatyar they were equally warm and welcoming. This is a vicious cycle in which old wounds, fears and hatreds are passed down from one generation to the next, and no one is immune from the violence.

The results of the assessment mission are unanimous. The members all agree it is not safe enough to return the Hazara families to the land. I am not surprised by their conclusions, but I don't look forward to telling the governor, particularly when his job may be on the line. This means the UN agencies will not be able to help him in his efforts to repatriate the families. I had better go to him with a proposal of some other way that we can help.

I wonder if we can ask the UN agencies for support to find housing for the families in Chaghcharan over the winter. The governor could explain it was a short-term solution to keep the Hazara families warm and safe. He could tell the families there would be more work opportunities for their men in town. In the meantime, during the winter months, he could initiate negotiations with Baiboqa leaders in the larger tribe, of which the families living on the land are a relatively small subgroup, about leaving the land.

Fahim agrees this is the best approach, but Mr. Baluch is less enthusiastic. "We should insist on upholding the rule of law by enforcing the court decision," he argues. Fahim reports the findings of their assessment and Mr. Baluch concedes.

Together we go to see the governor in his residential quarters, on the top floor of the municipal building. He has changed out of his formal wear into a white cotton tunic and pants, and from his freshly washed face and hair, I guess we have arrived just as he finished his evening prayers.

As I expected, he is not pleased with our position. As I have also come to expect from this man, he maintains his calm demeanor and impeccable manners.

"I have no choice in the matter," he says. "It is my legal duty to implement the decision of the court, with or without your support."

I try to convince him that the safety of the Hazara families must be paramount, but again I am left with the impression he has been told in no uncertain terms to make this repatriation happen. I realize I'm not going to change his mind tonight. We leave him to get on with his evening. I go home to heat up some tinned soup for dinner and to catch up with Joel on Skype.

Joel and I are now talking most nights, sometimes for hours. It's telling how willingly I embrace this return to our former intimacy; there's a familiar comfort in it. I'm still guarded, though, and I keep any fear or sadness to myself lest he suspect I'm falling back into the darkness. It's not all I hope for in a relationship, but it's what I'm familiar with and, for now, that is what I need.

I'm not even really sure why I still need it. Life in Ghor is good. My work is challenging and fulfilling. I am increasingly confident of my place and my usefulness. My colleagues are teaching me more about Afghanistan each day and I know they trust and respect me. I practice yoga and meditation every morning and write in my journal regularly. I even have a real friend in Heida. Do I really need Joel anymore?

35

Mission Accomplished

September–October 2007. Ghor, Afghanistan

*T*he next day I hear from the governor. He has spoken to his superiors in Kabul and convinced them of the wisdom of our proposal. He is now ready to talk to the Hazara families about delaying their repatriation.

"I expect you to be at the meeting," he says, "since it was your report that convinced us it isn't safe for them to return just yet."

I have already been over to talk to the Hazara families about the UNHCR mission, so this won't come as a complete surprise to them. They are, understandably, frustrated and insist they want to return to their land, threats and all. I'm not sure whether they are crazy and prepared to die, or bluffing. Either way, I am worried.

I walk over to the tents where the Hazara families are living. On the way I pass Heida, who is out checking on progress for a new children's center to be built near our compound. Whenever she leaves the base she has to wear a camouflage-patterned bulletproof vest and helmet. She looks decidedly uncomfortable. We have vests and helmets back at the office too, but they are UN blue and, thankfully, we only have to wear them when we travel into particularly dangerous parts of the province.

Today Fahim is walking with me, which means I don't need a

security guard. As we arrive at the tents, I wonder what kind of welcome I will receive. As far as they are concerned, I have let them down and they have every reason to be angry with me, but they are warm as ever. I follow the elders into one of the tents, sit on the ground and accept a cup of green tea.

One of the elders asks after my family and I inquire after his health. While we wait for the governor to arrive, I ask if he has given any more thought to the dangers of rushing their return to the disputed land. He nods gravely and makes noncommittal noises. He is waiting to see what the governor has to say about the situation.

The governor arrives and is offered the place of honor on the only cushion in the tent. He also accepts tea and asks after the health of everyone in the room. Once everyone has been greeted he sits in silence for a moment before he speaks. I appreciate the gesture; it shows his reluctance to relay the bad news. He explains the situation to the men and women gathered in the tent, emphasizing he has not given up on restoring them to their land.

"I propose," he says, "a postponement rather than a cancellation of your return."

The gathered elders sit in silence.

He makes the same arguments that I made to him yesterday. "It isn't safe to return yet. The Baiboqa have threatened to kill you if you return and, even if we send in the army, they threaten to destroy all the houses. Your families will be left in tents for the winter." He pauses, waiting for a response, but the elders remain silent.

"It would be better to stay in town, in proper houses, for the winter," he continues. "I will use the time to negotiate with senior Baiboqa commanders. With their support we can go ahead with your relocation in spring, without the threat of violence and without the risk of being stuck in tents for the winter." Again he pauses; the elders simply nod. They are not yet convinced.

"Miss Marianne," the governor turns to me, "please tell them what your assessment mission found."

I do so very briefly since I have already discussed it in detail with these men. When I am finished he asks the elders to respond. They remain silent for a moment longer and then Hassan, the most senior representative of the families, speaks quietly.

"We understand the problem," he says, "and we accept the logic of your proposal. But we are worried that if we agree to stay in town for the winter, delaying the implementation of the court decision, this might be interpreted as a relinquishment of our rights. We are willing to endure the cold and even to face the threat of violence in order to be sure that we don't lose our hard-won advantage."

He is right. Their position isn't crazy at all. There is a risk that an agreement to stay in town for the winter will be interpreted by the Baiboqa as a capitulation to their threats. Afghanistan is full of impossible situations and diabolical choices, and Afghans are among the most resilient and strategic survivors I have met anywhere.

Hassan continues in the same quiet, calm voice. "If you had been willing to support us, we would have taken whatever risks we had to in order to return to our land. But without your support that option has been taken from us."

He pauses. I feel uncomfortable under his gentle but constant gaze.

"We would prefer to return to our land, no matter the challenges, but if you are not going to help us do that, then we will be grateful for your help to find better housing for our families."

I leave the tent camp with very mixed feelings. I agree entirely with my UNHCR colleagues: it is dangerous for these families to return to their land as things stand and I'm not convinced they would survive a harsh Afghan winter in tents. I feel much more comfortable about housing the families securely in Chaghcharan for the winter while we negotiate a peaceful return to Dowlatyar. But it is not what they want, and I wonder whether it is fair to overrule the sovereignty of this small but determined community by denying them our support for their return.

On balance, I can live with our decision. We are not preventing the families from returning; we are choosing not to give our assistance and resources to an operation that carries a high risk of loss of human life. At the same time we are doing all we can to offer the families a decent alternative, a safe and habitable place to live for the winter.

Fortunately for my troubled conscience, we don't have to wait long before we can go back to the tent camp with better news. By the end of September, the governor finds seventeen empty houses in Chaghcharan and leases them all for the Hazara families. Some families will be sharing, but the houses are built to house large extended families so they won't be too cramped. I work with UN agencies to get blankets, fuel and stoves for each house and the NGOs provide cooking oil, wheat flour, sugar and tea for each family. I am relieved.

Like a schoolgirl, I mark the day of the move, October 5, with gold stars in my diary. When I wake up that morning I walk expectantly across to the tent camp as they are packing down. One particular mother and child have been on my mind as I lobbied the governor to find houses and I want to know how the mother feels about this outcome. She tells me she is relieved to be able to move her three-month-old baby into a house before the first snow arrives. She says nothing about regretting not returning to their land. It is a deep relief to know that she does not feel betrayed by our compromise. She invites me to come with her to see where she will be living. I get directions and tell her I will meet her there. There is something I want to do first.

I drive to the pharmacy. Over the months I've been visiting these families I have been bothered by the raw, cracked skin on the children's hands and cheeks. It was hardly their top priority, but now they have homes to protect them from the biting cold and dry winds of Ghor, I want to see what I can do about their skin. I buy every tube of cream the pharmacist has, twenty-five in total.

When I meet her at her new home I give my friend the cream and show her how to rub it into her own face and on her baby's hands and cheeks.

"There are twenty-four more tubes for you to share with the other women," I say.

She laughs at me, but there are tears glistening in her eyes. I may be a crazy foreigner, but I'm one who cares about her and her baby, and that is a basis for friendship anywhere in the world.

36
The Ex, Drugs, and CSI: Ghor

October 2007: Ghor, Afghanistan

*F*inally, in early October, I pluck up the courage to talk to Joel about what's happening to our relationship.

"I'm keen to give us another chance," I say, aware that I risk being rejected yet again, but confident of myself no matter what the outcome.

"I'd like to give things another go too," he says, "but I don't know if we can get back to where we were and if it doesn't work out, you'll be heartbroken all over again. I don't think it's fair of me to let that happen."

"Listen," I reply, "there are no guarantees in life and there is no way to avoid pain. All I ask is that you are honest with me, and that you give this a real chance." As I say it, I feel relief from having regained a sense of control in our relationship.

We make plans for a holiday together. We are both due to take leave and I had already planned to take mine in California with friends. Joel was planning to go back to Oregon. So we agree that I'll spend a week with my friends and then fly up to meet him.

Soon after we settle on this plan, though, I notice a drop in the frequency of our evening chats. I suspect Joel is retreating again. My first instinct is to pursue him, but something has shifted in me. I realize that as much as I want to be with Joel, I don't need him. I resist the urge to call and instead occupy myself with the latest local drama.

The police stopped a massive shipment of opium as it passed through Ghor. The seizure is hugely controversial, and the town is afire with rumors of police corruption and allegations about who owned the seized opium. One police officer was killed during the seizure, and some of my informants allege that he was the victim of a breakdown in a clandestine deal between traffickers and police.

Local police, who speak to me only on condition that I meet them in well-hidden locations and don't reveal their identities, tell me that they believe the drug runners made a deal with the chief of police, and that this shipment should have been allowed to pass through the province. The stumbling block in this cunning plan was the deputy chief of police.

The deputy is originally from another province and is widely regarded as the straight man in an otherwise fairly corrupt force. I take pride in the fact that he, the best policeman I've worked with in Afghanistan, was trained by New Zealand police.

He has a small number of his "own" officers, young policemen who traveled with him from his home province. It was one of these young men who was killed during the seizure. I hear from some that his death was a message to the deputy to stop interfering. Deals between drug lords and senior police officers need to be respected!

I speak to the deputy chief by phone.

"My own boss is working with the drug lords!" He is furious. "My soldier died because of this corruption. What am I supposed to tell his family?"

I have no idea what to tell him, so I say nothing, waiting for him to continue.

"And now they are threatening to kill me!"

"Who?" I ask, fearful for him.

"Several people," he says, "people connected to the drug lords. The kind of people who won't hesitate to do what they say."

"Call me," I insist, "anytime, if there is anything more that you think I can do. For now I'll write a report to go to Kabul."

He thanks me and we hang up.

The next day is Friday, which is supposed to be my day off. I generally use the time to clean out my little unit, read, play with the kittens, wash my clothes and write emails to friends and family. But I spend this Friday morning writing my monthly report. It is nice to have some good news, for a change, about finding homes for the Hazara families. Most of the report, however, is taken up with my findings about the opium seizure.

Just before midday I get a call from the deputy chief. He wants to talk to me in person and alone. When I explain that I will need a colleague to translate if we are to be sure we understand each other, he names the only member of our staff he trusts, a young security officer who wouldn't normally accompany me as translator. I agree and call the staff member. He brings a car to collect me from the compound and we drive to the southern end of Chaghcharan where the deputy chief lives. I recognize his compound by the number of armed police officers standing outside the gate.

The heavy police presence at the entrance to his building suggests it will be difficult for his enemies to get close enough to kill him in person, therefore the most likely form of an attack will be a rocket-propelled grenade into his compound. I am walking into the current target of the local drug lords. It doesn't make me feel safe. As we talk, sitting cross-legged on the floor of his front room, I am agitated, aware of the danger. I try not to hurry our conversation too much, but I am not keen on staying here any longer than I have to.

He talks us through the opium seizure with the sort of attention to detail that you would expect from a detective. Our security officer does a great job of translating.

"My officer was killed after the drug traffickers had been arrested," he says. "They should have all been disarmed and handcuffed in the other police vehicle. The shot that killed my officer, however, was fired from the vehicle where the arrested criminals were held."

He shows me the type of weapon carried by police officers in the province. "The bullet that killed my man came from a different kind of gun." He demonstrates the angle at which the gun must have been fired. I feel like I'm in an Afghan version of *CSI*.

"My theory is that one of the drug runners was released from his handcuffs and rearmed so that he could shoot and kill the police officer."

He pauses to gauge my reaction. It is an unsettling scenario, but not beyond the realms of possibility. I nod.

"This means at least one, and probably more, of the other police officers collaborated in the murder."

As he talks I write rapidly in my notebook. When he is finished I tell him, "You need to decide whether you want me to report your suspicions to my superiors in Kabul. It could be dangerous if word gets out that you have made these allegations."

"I want you to tell the international people in Kabul," he insists, "but I don't want you to share this information with your Afghan colleagues here in Ghor." He pauses again and looks at the young man whom he instructed me to bring to the meeting. "Apart from him," he says, "I don't trust them."

This puts me in a very awkward position. This isn't the first time I've had to navigate the murky waters of distrust and suspicion that often prevail in Afghanistan.

"I won't say anything to my local colleagues for the moment," I assure him, "but eventually I will have to tell them something."

As I leave I turn to him. "I'm so sorry about your young officer who died." As I speak I feel a deep sadness for the family of this young man and tears well up in my eyes.

He looks at me quietly for a moment before he responds. "If more Afghans cared as much about the lives of their own people as you do about this man you didn't even know," he says, "then our country would have a chance."

37

A Rude Awakening

October 2007: Ghor, Afghanistan

*B*ack at my compound I write up the report with all the new details from this meeting. By the time I finish it is late afternoon. I'm leaving on a road mission to the remote district of Lal Wa Sarjangal early tomorrow morning, so I go over to eat with Heida in the D-Fac, military shorthand for "dining facility."

The D-Fac is a large tent with a cafeteria where the soldiers line up to be served processed American food. Fortunately for all of us, the food at the D-Fac in Chaghcharan is given a life-saving injection of flavor by the predominantly Mexican chefs. One of them, Miguel, always greets me with a broad smile and, because he thinks I am too thin, encourages me to take extra servings of corn, beans or potatoes.

The D-Fac is also the only place in Ghor where I can get fresh lettuce, apples, cucumber, cracked pepper and yogurt, all of which are flown in to the base fresh every week in military planes. If it were not for this my diet would be limited to what is available in the local market. Before I started coming regularly to the base to eat, I lost several kilos from my already slender frame. I realized that I needed to put aside my concerns about the financial and environmental cost of flying in all this food, and eat one meal per week at the military base.

Miguel encourages me to fill my daypack with tubs of yogurt, fresh fruit and muesli bars from the selection laid out for the soldiers to take out on patrol. The commander keeps up his charming habit of tucking chocolate bars into his pockets to give me when we meet.

Tonight I load my pack with muesli bars and packs of dried fruit and nuts. I'll be traveling for five days to get to Lal and back, and as a vegetarian, I often struggle to find food I can eat on the road. Once I have stocked up and said good-bye to Heida, who will have gone on leave by the time I get back from Lal, I head back to my compound. All is quiet; only the radio operator and the security guards at the front gate are still around and even they seem to be napping. I take out my laptop: before I head offline for a week in Lal I'm keen to check in with Joel. He's online so we chat about our holiday.

We are discussing flights when I hear the first explosion. Actually, I *feel* it as much as hear it. The walls and floor of my room shake with an almighty boom. My brain registers that in the seconds before the explosion, I had heard a high-pitched squealing pass overhead. Hell! A missile has passed directly over me, landing somewhere nearby.

I type Joel a quick note.

"An explosion! Really loud! Really close!"

As I type with one hand, I grab my radio and call the radio control room.

"What was that?" I ask the radio operator, hoping he can tell me it was nothing to worry about.

"I don't know!" He sounds disconcertingly alarmed. "But it was very loud, and very close. I'm trying to find out what it was."

Meanwhile, Joel has written back asking what's going on. Before I can respond to him I hear a high-pitched squeal pass overhead and then a second explosion. This one is just as loud.

I type quickly. "Another explosion! Right over my room!"

Joel is typing. His reply pops up: "Go to the bunker!"

He knows that I have a concrete reinforced bunker for exactly this kind of situation. I wonder why I didn't think of the bunker myself.

"Going now!" I type and shut the laptop.

I am at once terrified and very calm. I must get into the bunker immediately, before the next missile lands right on top of me. And yet strangely, I feel I have all the time in the world, as though everything is happening very slowly. I find my sleeping bag, my phone and my radio and open the door of my room to head out.

As I open the door I see a group of my colleagues, the security guards who are on duty that night, running toward me. Rahim is walking close behind them. I am relieved to see that Rahim is on duty. His quiet, calm manner reassures me.

We all go to the bunker, which is only about twenty meters from my door. It is dark and we have to step carefully to avoid tripping on the loops of barbed wire that are strung across the ground in the compound to protect the expensive satellite equipment. After what is probably no more than thirty seconds of excruciatingly slow progress, we arrive in the bunker.

I get a call on my radio from our local security officer.

"I'm safe at home," he reassures me, "but I heard the explosion and want to make sure you are okay."

"Yes," I assure him, "I'm in the bunker with the guards. Rahim is here."

"I'm going to call the police officers stationed outside our gate and tell them to get into the bunker as well," he says.

"Yes!" I cry. "Tell them to get down here as soon as possible." I hadn't even thought about them in the rush to get into the bunker. As I wait for them to arrive I listen fearfully for the sound of another explosion, praying they get here safely.

They arrive quickly and intact. We close the bunker door. I

double-check that everyone is accounted for and report back to the security officer. "There is nothing more to do but wait," he tells me, so I sit down in a corner, wrapping myself in my sleeping bag.

There is one more explosion, but by now I feel we are relatively safe. We are protected not only by a concrete ceiling but also by several layers of heavy sandbags. I curl up on the ground and go to sleep.

Sometime later, I wake myself up with a loud snorting noise. I realize that I have been snoring and look around to see seven Afghan men staring at me with a mixture of surprise and amusement. I'm not sure what surprises them more—the fact that Miss Marianne snores or that she can sleep in a bunker under incoming fire.

"Have you heard anything new?" I ask.

"Our security officer is talking to the chief of police," Rahim responds.

"There have been no more explosions, but we are to stay in the bunker until he calls us to say otherwise."

I turn on my side in the hope that it will keep me from snoring and go back to sleep.

❖ ❖

In the early hours of the morning my colleagues wake me up to take a radio call from the security officer.

"The chief of police assures me they have identified the spot where the missiles were fired from and they have secured the area." He tells me where it is.

"Huh," I say, "so the missiles were launched from the very spot that Rahim has been concerned about since we moved into the compound. He knows what he is talking about, doesn't he?" I'm digging a little, because I suspect the young security officer, who is Rahim's supervisor, thinks he knows more than the older man.

"The police are confident that there will be no more explosions tonight," he continues, refusing to be drawn. "You have clearance to leave the bunker and return to your rooms."

I know Joel will be terribly worried about me and I should probably call him right away, but it is very early in the morning and he may be asleep. I check my phone, expecting to find a message from him telling me to call as soon as I can to let him know I am okay.

There is no message.

I flick on my computer to see if he sent me an email. Again, there is nothing. I am surprised and disappointed but too tired to think about it now. I go straight to bed and sleep solidly until my phone rings at quarter to nine in the morning.

The call is from the head of the Herat office. Even though I have transferred to Ghor, I still come under his overall regional responsibility. He is calling to see how I am doing. It's nice to know someone cares. While I am talking to my boss, I log on to my laptop to check for a message from Joel. Still nothing. Have I dropped off the radar? Has my life become so consumed by work that my boss is the only person to call me to check I'm alive after a missile attack?

In an effort to reassure myself that I haven't completely disappeared into the UN rabbit hole, I open Facebook and update my status: "Spent the night in the bunker. My Afghan colleagues seemed more scared of my snoring than of the incoming rockets."

I'm being purposefully lighthearted. My sisters read my Facebook updates and I don't want them to know how scared I was. I certainly don't want them to tell my mother that I'm in any real danger. But I do want my friends to know that I've been through a frightening time. I do want some sympathy and some attention. Where is Joel?!

My boss's voice interrupts my thoughts: "You'll have to postpone the trip to Lal until we know whether or not the attack targeted us specifically."

"It seems more likely," I say, "that we were in the wrong place at the wrong time. The NATO army base is about five hundred meters to our west and the Afghan National Directorate for Security compound is no more than two hundred meters to the east. We are probably the victims of the inaccurate guidance systems of homemade missiles."

"Probably," he agrees, "but until I know who fired the missiles and why, I don't like the idea of you being out on the roads of Ghor, an easy target for another attack."

When he puts it that way, I am happy to comply.

38

Maybe He's Just Not That Into You

October 2007: Ghor, Afghanistan

So instead of heading off on a trip to Lal province, I go straight into an emergency security shura with the provincial governor, the chief of police, the head of the National Directorate for Security (NDS) and the commander of the Lithuanian base.

Although the explosives landed closest to our compound, everyone seems to agree that the missile attack was probably targeting either the Lithuanian or the NDS base. So these two men want to know who is attacking them. The most common theory I've heard this morning is that the attack was carried out by the drug lords whose shipment was recently captured. The very same drug lords with whom the chief of police is rumored to be collaborating. The governor, meanwhile, is generally understood to be complicit with the chief of police.

From where I am sitting the governor and the chief of police seem to be on one side of an invisible battle line, while the head of the NDS and the Lithuanian commander are on the other. Everyone is tired. I'm not the only person who spent the night in a bunker. Tensions are high and tempers are frayed.

This is one battle I do not want to be drawn into.

"We all know who was behind these attacks"—the head of the NDS is not so reticent—"and what I want to know is why you"—he stares pointedly at the chief of police—"are doing nothing to stop them."

The chief of police appears unruffled by these accusations. He replies firmly but calmly, "I am doing everything I can to find out who was behind the attacks. If you have evidence you would like to share with my investigation, we would be grateful to receive it."

To my horror, my colleague Haji chimes in with his own allegations:

"We all know who fired those missiles, and we all know why they were fired." He looks at the chief of police. "You certainly know more than you are letting on. Why don't you come clean?"

"If the UN has concerns about my performance," says the chief, "I'd like to know about them."

All eyes turn to me and I find myself furiously backpedaling. I do, of course, have concerns about the police chief's performance, but there is nothing to be gained from revealing that now.

It is an exhausting two-hour-long meeting. When it is finally over I am shunted immediately into another. Between meetings I check the messages on my phone. There is still nothing from Joel, but there is a message from Tim. He saw my Facebook update and texted to see how I am. Exactly the kind of attention I've been craving all morning. I quickly text back, "I'm okay, rattled but unhurt, more worried about how the All Blacks are doing in the Rugby World Cup."

I am underplaying my fears, but I trust Tim will read between the lines. I hope he'll understand that I was scared, but unwilling to be drawn into that fear too deeply.

His reply confirms this: "Hiding in the bunker won't save you from the unavoidable fate of the All Blacks," he writes. "Call me if you want to talk."

"Can't talk now," I reply. "But will call soon to commiserate on the dreadful performance of the Wallabies."

I head into my next meeting buoyed by the sense that I have not been completely forgotten by the world.

This meeting is with the provincial council. The ostensible purpose of the meeting is to consult with the elected representatives of the local people about the attack and to assure them of the UN's continued commitment to being present in Ghor province.

The real purpose, although we can never say so, is to meet with the man who we suspect might be behind the attacks; one of the members of the provincial council is also the most powerful drug lord in Ghor. Some people claim that he is the very man who made the deal with the chief of police to allow the drugs to pass through the province.

It is an unusual meeting. I am sitting across the room from the man who may be responsible for firing a missile at my bedroom. He waxes eloquent about the scourge of drugs in his beloved country. I wonder whether it pricks his conscience to know that his attack put not only my life at risk but also the lives of those Afghan men whose job it is to protect me. I guess not. This man is making himself rich and powerful at the expense of many others. His conscience must have been silenced long ago.

As we leave the council office I get a call from the Lithuanian commander asking me to meet with him. I ask the driver to drop me off at the outside wall of the military base and then send him home to get some rest while I go in to talk to the commander.

When I enter his office I see that he has a large piece of twisted metal sitting on his coffee table. I look at him questioningly. He explains that some of his officers, forensic explosive experts, offered to help the local police in the investigation of the attack. Their offer was accepted in theory, but in practice they were prevented from seeing or doing anything that might actually help to progress the investigation. The Lithuanians did, however, find the casing of at least one of the missiles. The large mass of twisted metal is the remainder of one of the missiles. It is huge, much bigger than any explosive I have seen in Ghor before.

"We've had rocket-propelled grenades fired near the compound before," I say, "but this looks bigger."

"You're right," the commander tells me. "This is not a grenade; this is a much larger kind of missile."

For the first time since the attack, I take a minute to imagine what would have happened if one of the missiles had hit my building. I would have been instantly killed. For a moment, I see the image of my broken body in the rubble of my beloved room. I feel my heart rate spike and a wave of adrenaline rushes through my body. As it passes I feel weak. I am glad I am sitting down.

The commander watches me carefully and offers me a cup of tea. I add sugar to the tea because I am afraid I might be about to faint. I sip my tea slowly. We talk about what was said in the earlier security meeting. I tell him what I know about the drug seizure and he tells me what his intelligence officers have found out.

Ours is a strange collaboration, and one that illustrates the challenges of the parallel but quite separate structures of the civilian (UN) and military (NATO) components of the peacekeeping mission in Afghanistan. Before coming to Ghor I was never really comfortable working closely with the military, mainly because my role requires me to monitor its actions and assess whether or not they are consistent with the international laws of war.

Here in Ghor I have taken on some of the political and coordination functions of the UN mission as well, so I need to work more closely with the military. Based on my experience of previous commanders, however, I continue to be suspicious of the quality of military "intelligence," and I sometimes doubt their understanding of the broader political context in which they are working.

But this commander has already proved to me that he understands, better than many military officers, the humanitarian principles that bind me in my work. He has earned my respect and, more than any other military officer I have worked with, my trust. Sitting in his office I also feel a sense of solidarity in the face of the intrigue and deception that seem to dominate local politics. I feel myself relax a little for the first time today.

By the time I get back to my room it is late in the afternoon. I've been in back-to-back meetings all day long and although I've left messages on Joel's phone, we haven't actually spoken. I am exhausted and tired of having to be brave and strong and in control. I am looking forward to talking to Joel, to allowing myself to just be someone's frightened girlfriend for a while. When I get back to my room and switch on my computer I am happy to see that there is a message from Joel. I open it and my heart sinks.

"So the dude says we need the routing number. Maybe that's what you weirdos call a 'swift' code. Gay name. Anyways, he gives it below. OnPoint Credit Union. Let me know if you need more information."

Less than twenty-four hours after sending me off to the bunker to hide from incoming missiles, my boyfriend's only communication to me is an email about a bank transfer? I can't quite believe it. I am shocked. Angry and hurt, I fire off a response.

"Okay—will do. And no—none of the rockets hit me, thanks for asking."

Despite the snarky tone of my email, I am aching. I am sad and tired. I feel lonely and abandoned, and the one person who was always my best friend in Afghanistan is missing in action. I read back over his email and my response and decide I was too harsh. So, fifteen minutes after the first response, I send another.

"Oops. Sorry, read back and that came out bitchier than intended. I'm a bit rattled and I guess I thought you might be worried…but I didn't mean to be nasty about it."

I call his phone and get his answering machine. I leave a message. I try to distract myself by reading but I can't concentrate. I pull on my running shoes and go for a run. It is a sign of how desperately uncomfortable this waiting is making me because going for a run means making circuits of the compound. I can't even run around the entire compound. That would take me past the room where the security guards sit drinking tea and watching the front gate. Even in my agitated state I have no intention of making a spectacle of myself. I run only in the walled-off section of the compound set aside for my accommodation. Our Afghan staff only come into this area when they need to check the generator or pass a message to me, so I can run around in track pants and a loose T-shirt without offending anyone. One circuit of my compound takes about twenty seconds, so it gets repetitive very quickly. But I plug myself into my iPod, crank up Tina Turner, and persevere for twenty minutes. By the time I do some stretches and shower I've passed an hour.

By now it is 7:00 p.m. and there is still no response from Joel. I give in and curl up on my bed for a good long session of weeping. I am angry with myself for caring so much about hearing from someone who obviously doesn't care about me. The absurdity of the situation leaves me feeling foolish. I try to sleep but I'm too agitated. Joel has an email and a phone message from me, so he must be choosing, perversely, not to call me. Why is he making me suffer? I get up and switch on my computer again.

Joel has emailed me. Finally.

"I saw in the morning that you had updated your Facebook status, so I knew you were all right. I went to a barbecue at the World Vision compound. I didn't check my phone till I got home."

I am stunned. My boyfriend saw that I had updated my status on a social networking site, confirming I was alive, and that was all he needed to know before happily spending the day with friends? He didn't feel any need to call me. He didn't even text.

I write a long email in reply but don't send it. Instead I write another email, an outpouring of all my anger, sadness, loneliness and fear. I send it to two of my closest friends. Then I go back to bed and sleep.

By morning it occurs to me just how strange it is that I am more upset and angry with Joel for not calling than I am with the men who fired the missile over my compound. In the midst of the drama of corrupt police and trigger-happy drug lords, I am caught up in my own personal drama. And I wonder if it was a mistake to get re-entangled with Joel.

The self-pity and soul-searching don't have time to take hold. I have lots of work to get on with trying to unravel the layers of allegation and counterallegation from the local officials so that I can write accurate reports about the whole affair. I also have the go-ahead to reschedule the Lal Sarjangal trip. I am keen to get underway as soon as possible. It seems to me that I will be safer away from the compound; the more likely targets of the attack are still, after all, our uncomfortably close neighbors.

39
Don't Ask About the Poppy

October 2007: Ghor, Afghanistan

I am especially keen to get up to Lal so I can meet the family of
my colleague Abdul-Karim. Abdul-Karim is a bright young Hazara
man who left his wife and three young daughters in his brother's care in
Lal to take up his position with UNAMA. He is only in his midtwenties, an age at which my friends in New Zealand were still spending
most of their time and money on music, partying and travel. Abdul-
Karim has the responsibilities of a man. He'll be coming with me to
Lal, which means he'll get to spend some time with his family and
show me around his hometown.

We set off early in the morning in a couple of old Land Rovers.
Abdul-Karim and I travel in separate vehicles so that if one breaks
down in a spot where it isn't safe to stop and repair it, we can leave it
behind and all get away safely in the second. This is UN policy and for
once, I have no complaints.

As we leave town Ahmad, the driver of my vehicle, looks across and
notices that I am crying beneath my sunglasses.

"Why are you crying, Miss Marianne?" he asks in Dari.

Although the stress of the rocket attack plays some part in my sudden attack of the weepies, I am crying mostly about Joel. I don't know

how to explain this to Ahmad, in Dari or in English. But it turns out he doesn't really want an explanation. He just wants me to stop crying: "It isn't good to see you cry," he says matter-of-factly. "Please stop."

That's as good a reason as any to stop crying. I smile at Ahmad and tell him I'll do my best.

"I'll put on some music to cheer us up," I say.

The drive from Chaghcharan to Lal Sarjangal takes seven hours and runs through some dangerous areas. A few hours into our journey we are about to head into an area that Ahmad warns me is not very safe.

"We shouldn't stop anywhere along this section of the road unless there is an emergency," he says.

I ask to make a toilet stop before we start this section.

There are very few trees in Ghor and in this spot there aren't even any shrubs or rocks to hide behind. Taking a toilet stop here means I have to squat on the side of the road in full view of my colleagues and the entire police escort, which is made up of two police Land Rovers carrying eight armed officers. In midwinter I can sometimes stomp my way into a deep snowdrift to give myself a little privacy. Though it is early winter now, the snows have not yet arrived and I am reduced to using the fabric of my long tunic as a kind of tent within which I can squat and pee.

Done, I jump back in the jeep. The armed policemen who spread out around me to ensure my peeing was not interrupted by the Taliban follow suit. We are well into the "dangerous" section of the road when my satellite phone starts ringing. We use radios in the vehicles for communications within the convoy and with the base. The satellite phones are just there as backup. I have never had a call on my satellite phone during a road mission. Given recent events I wonder if there is some new emergency, a major security incident back in Chaghcharan or on the road ahead of us.

I answer the phone but can't hear what the caller is saying to me.

Ahmad explains that the phone will work better if I get out of the car. He stops the car so that I can climb out. I feel like a sitting duck as I squat alongside the car. I can hear the driver of the other car calling Ahmad over the radio, asking what on earth we are doing stopping in such a dangerous spot.

I try to stop worrying about whether there are Taliban watching us from behind the nearest ridge so that I can concentrate on the call. What if there has been an explosion on the road ahead or, worse, a tip-off about a roadside bomb? I need to hear the message clearly.

Finally I understand who is calling and what he is saying to me. It is our regional security manager calling from Herat. He is calling to remind me to make hourly radio checks with our base in Chaghcharan, and to tell me what the security arrangements are once we arrive in Lal. All of this was discussed and agreed upon before we left our compound. I am furious that I have stopped the convoy in an unsafe place to take a call that turns out to be unnecessary. I end the conversation as quickly as I can and tell Ahmad to get us moving again.

It is a spectacularly scenic drive that takes us through long, deep river valleys where tiny clusters of mud-brick homes mark the points where there is good river access or where traditional irrigation systems have survived. I carefully make note of the state of food crops and livestock in each community. Where it is safe to do so I call the convoy to a halt and Abdul-Karim and I approach some of the local farmers to ask about their crops.

The news from the farmers is mostly grim. The rain came late in the season and even then, it was too short. Many farmers report yields one-third the size of those obtained in an average year. They are worried about food stocks for the winter and want to know whether we can help get them food aid or some kind of short-term credit so they can buy food for their families. As usual, I promise to do my best.

Along one stretch of the river we notice that families have tried to protect themselves against the impact of the unseasonable rains by planting a section of their land in opium poppies. The opium can be sold for cash, which will be used to supplement food for the winter and to buy seed stock for the new season. I wonder whether these local farmers will be hurt by the recent drug seizure in Ghor. I worry that the drug traffickers might pass on the costs of the loss to these small producers, who are the least able to bear it.

This is a particularly Afghan conundrum. I am deeply impressed by the courage of the police commander who ordered the seizure, and, of course, I stand behind his efforts to bring law and order to the province by facing down the drug traffickers. But at the same time I am concerned about the impact of the seizure on the incomes of local subsistence farmers who rely on their small poppy crops to supplement a bad season of food production.

I don't ask the farmers about the poppy crops. We will have to pass back through this valley in a few days and I prefer the word on the street to be that we are investigating food shortages, not opium production. I pretend I haven't seen the poppies and leave the farmers to continue harvesting their wheat crops. They stack the wheat by hand and use oxen and donkeys to thresh it. Apart from the lack of trees and the brown mountains stretching away as far as the eye can see, the scene could be out of one of the pastoral paintings of nineteenth-century England that used to hang in my grandparents' hall.

Eventually we cross the river, stopping briefly midstream to wash off the heavy coat of dust the vehicles have collected along the road. The men wash themselves too, but I stay in the car for the sake of modesty and safety. Then we arrive in the town of Lal Sarjangal. Our first stop is at the police compound where we leave our police escort. They will be provided with a warm meal and a place to sleep for the next few nights. I feel a sense of relief as we continue on escort-free. I'm not a fan of guns, generally. It might seem a difficult position to sustain in

Afghanistan, but many NGOs here have a gun-free policy and rely on their good work and community relations to keep them safe. I accept the security requirements that are placed on us as part of the package of working with the UN, but I am never comfortable with the idea, let alone the experience of being part of an armed convoy.

40
Learning from Lal

October 2007: Ghor, Afghanistan

As we drive through the small town that is the district center of Lal, I notice there are many women in the streets. Lal is home to a predominantly Hazara population and Hazara women generally have more freedom to participate in public life. I watch a group of local women walking along the road in front of us. Ahmad pulls the vehicle up alongside them and winds down the window. He speaks to one of the women in Dari. I understand that he is asking for directions to the home of the foreigners who run the local hospital, where I will be staying. To my surprise the woman replies without hesitation, looking Ahmad right in the eyes.

Wow, I think, these Hazara women really do have much more social freedom than the Aimaq women in Chaghcharan. Then I realize the woman has asked for a ride. She and her companions are climbing into the back of the Land Rover. Now I am really shocked. I've never seen that happen in all my time in Afghanistan. As they climb into the back of our vehicle I turn around to welcome them. Suddenly I see what I had missed before. These women are not Hazara at all.

"You must be Marianne," one of them says to me in English. "Jane told us that you were coming. How was the journey?" Jane is the young New Zealand nurse with whom I have arranged to stay. Suddenly it all makes sense. These women are Jane's colleagues, all foreigners like me. Unlike me, however, they are completely fluent in the local Hazara language, which is close enough to Dari for Ahmad to understand them and vice versa. Their clothes are indistinguishable from those of the other women I have seen in the streets. One of them is visibly pregnant and another is carrying her baby in a cloth sling across her back. It takes me a few seconds to take all this in before I can respond to her question.

I am deeply impressed. Their presence here couldn't be more different from mine in Chaghcharan. Where they blend into their community, I am set apart in almost every way. Of course, I understand that the UN vehicles and security regulations are the trade-off I have to accept in exchange for the access I get into prisons and police cells and for my influence, such as it is, with judges, police commanders and even local warlords. But after the recent rocket attacks, I am feeling tired of it all. I find myself craving this simple, unpretentious community presence.

Before I came, Jane and I talked a little bit about their living situation, so I know that their children attend the local schools. The parents supplement their schooling at home; keeping them up to speed with the subjects and languages they will need to be able to transition, eventually, into the education systems in their countries of origin. And every day the kids go off to join their Afghan friends and playmates to learn the history of Afghanistan and the teachings of the Quran. There is a world of difference between this approach to expat life and the expensive international schools in Kabul.

One of the women explains to me that the team lives in several different compounds. The couples with children have their own homes but I am going to stay with Jane and several other single women. As we pull into the gate I compare their simple mud-brick fence with the razor-wire-topped monstrosity encircling our compound back in Chaghcharan. Apart from the solar panels on the roof, the exterior of their home is indistinguishable from their neighbors'.

On the inside it isn't much different either. The solar panels feed the computers and radio base. They have Wi-Fi service throughout the compound and each room has one low-wattage light bulb that can run for a short period every evening off the solar panels. Aside from that they live as their neighbors do, without electricity or a generator. They use a traditional root cellar to keep their fresh food cool and a bukhari to heat their water. The water comes from a well that their organization built outside the house so that everyone in their neighborhood could share it.

It all makes beautiful sense to me and I feel immediately at ease in the compound. For the first time in almost eighteen months, since I joined the United Nations, I feel free of the nagging unease that comes from being placed in a position of unwarranted privilege in relation to my neighbors and colleagues. I'm grateful too that my Afghan colleagues were invited to stay in one of the family compounds during our time in Lal: Abdul-Karim had also invited our drivers to stay with him at his family compound just across the river.

Jane shows me to my room, which belongs to a young nurse who is on home leave in the United States. The bukhari in my bathroom is lit, in recognition of my long, dusty drive. I am glad to have a hot wash before dinner. Using a small tin cup to scoop up the warm water from a bucket on top of the stove, I wash my hair and body. I happily watch the brown, grimy water drain away at my feet until the water begins to run clear.

I love the bucket approach to bathing. In Chaghcharan my accommodation unit is purpose-built and includes a high-pressure shower that is undeniably luxurious, and is an object of considerable envy among other expats who visit Chaghcharan. The amount of water it uses, however, and the need to have the generator running in order to heat the water, seems an indulgent use of scarce resources.

I dress warmly and head into the kitchen where Jane and her housemate Sophie are preparing dinner. Jane and Sophie both work for a Christian organization that has run health clinics in Afghanistan for more than three decades. They have invited some of their colleagues over for dinner. As we chat in the kitchen some of them grill me about the failings of the UN in Lal district.

"The WFP's 'Food for Work' program has been an abject failure in Lal," one woman tells me. "The food has been left to rot on the side of the road because the WFP staff haven't been up here to supervise the distribution."

"That is frustrating," I acknowledge. "Part of the reason I'm up here is to find out how our new office in Ghor can help ensure that things run more smoothly."

"It's an unforgivable waste," she insists, "and we are tired of UN staff coming in for a day or two to make yet another assessment. Nothing ever seems to change."

I can see why they are frustrated and try to gracefully accept their criticism, which is—understandably—directed at me.

"That's not completely fair," Sophie intervenes. "The new office in Ghor only opened a few months ago. We should give Marianne and her colleagues a chance to get things right."

A part of me wants to drop my professional façade altogether. I want to tell these people that I'm more like them than they realize. I was a missionary kid myself and worked with NGOs until only a little over a year ago. I want to tell them that I am still new to the UN, and I am also frustrated by the inefficiencies of the system. I suddenly want to be on their team, part of this close-knit community. I want to fit in to my community as they do, in a way that I will never fit in as long as I live in our big white-walled compound and drive in our big white 4x4s. Instead I stick to the official script, telling them that we acknowledge the shortcomings of the UN's performance in Ghor to date, and assuring them that the opening of our new office is intended to improve the situation.

Funny how only six months ago I wanted to drag the missionaries of Herat out of their hiding places and unleash upon them the full force of my fury at their ill-considered efforts to convert young Afghans to Christianity. Yet here I am, craving the fellowship these young Christian women obviously share. I realize just how lonely I really am in Chaghcharan, and how isolated from the local community I still feel, despite the massive improvement over life in Herat.

There is also a lot to admire and a lot to learn from this organization's approach to development work, especially because they are very clear that their staff must make no attempt to convert Afghans to Christianity. For one thing, the members of the health team in Lal are all likely to stay in their posts for at least five years. Some of the senior team members have been here for several decades. They are here for the long term. They care about the well-being of the community because it is their community.

I do have some doubts about their approach. I can't help but wonder why, after thirty years, the team hasn't yet handed the hospital over to the care of well-trained locals. Their approach may not be perfect, but whose is, in Afghanistan or anywhere else? In any case, I feel comfortable with them.

After three days it is time for us to head back to Chaghcharan. I've chased local officials for food shortage data. I've delivered copies of the Afghan criminal laws to the local judges, prosecutors and police. Banking on the goodwill I earned for delivering the laws, I've harassed the local police and prosecutors about not doing enough to prosecute men for beating their wives. And I've met Abdul-Karim's family and taken photos of his wife and daughters. As comfortable as I am in Lal, I must go back to Chaghcharan.

As Ahmad and I drive back, I realize that somewhere in the midst of my time in Lal I reached a major decision. It seems paradoxical, given that I am now happier in my job than I have ever been, but I am ready to leave Afghanistan. It snuck up on me, without any anguish or confusion. There are logical reasons for my decision, most importantly the realization that my presence in Afghanistan—unlike that of the nurses in Lal—comes at a cost I'm no longer sure can be justified by the benefits of my work. But, beyond logic and reason, I have a feeling I can't yet put a word to, but it is clear: it is time to leave.

This clarity extends to Joel as well. I know, suddenly and without a doubt, that it is over. It may not have been the kindest or most courageous way to let me know, but by not calling me after the missile attack Joel finally got the message across; he doesn't care about me in the way I care about him. He is looking for a way out of it, whatever it is; and now I realize I don't want it either. Not like this.

41

BBC, a Six-Pack, and My Laptop

October 2007: Ghor, Afghanistan

I arrive back in Chaghcharan on Saturday. Before doing anything else, I call Joel.

"Hi, Joel. It's me."

"Oh, hey. You back from Lal already?"

"Yep, just got back this afternoon. Listen, Joel, I think we need to talk." I have no interest in making small talk. This is going to be hard enough as it is without dragging things out.

"Uh-huh. We probably do. What do you want to talk about?"

"Well, I've been thinking about the fact that you didn't call after the missile attack." I feel my chest constrict a little just mentioning it. "I don't want to go over that again," I insist, wary of getting into a debate about what has now passed. "I'm not trying to make you feel bad about it. But maybe it was a sign." I pause and take a deep breath. "It showed me that you really don't want to be with me." Another breath. "At least not the way I want to be with someone." I stop, proud of myself for saying it out loud.

"Uh-huh. Okay, um, so are you saying…?" I've caught him on the back foot and he apparently doesn't know what to say.

"I'm saying I don't think it's unreasonable for me to want my boyfriend to call me the day after I've been bombed." I stop, but there is no reply. I try again. "I'm saying that instead of trying to convince myself that what I want is unreasonable, it might actually be time to admit that you just aren't interested in meeting my needs." I trail off; my voice is getting higher and I don't want to sound like I'm whining. My throat is contracting with emotion and although I'm trying to remember to breathe, I can't actually smooth out my voice.

Joel's voice, on the other hand, sounds flat and unemotional when he speaks. "Right. That makes sense."

"I don't think you actually love me, Joel," I squeak, terrified of what I am about to ask but no longer willing to go on without knowing. "Do you?"

There is a pause while Joel gathers his thoughts. I bite my lip to keep myself from begging him to answer me quickly, to put me out of my misery.

"Well, no, perhaps not," he finally says. I feel my chest contract and my throat tighten around the pain that this admission generates, despite knowing it was coming.

"I'll be honest with you," he continues in that infuriatingly calm voice. "I knew you wanted me to call you…but"—he stumbles stumbles for an instant, giving me a glimpse of the possibility he may not be feeling as calm as he sounds—"I just didn't want to. I couldn't really understand why I was resisting it, but I was." He pauses and I take a deep breath to keep myself from weeping.

"I was afraid that the feelings would never come back," he continues, "but I hoped like hell that they would. They didn't. I guess that means I don't love you."

I know he is telling the truth, but it still hurts to hear it. I would love to be able to speak clearly now, to give Joel the impression that his words neither surprise nor pain me. But I can't. As I begin to speak again my voice cracks.

"I guess that's all I need to know then," I say, tears rolling down my face. "Let's just end this right now."

"Yes, that seems like the only thing to do," Joel agrees.

He is driving me crazy. How can he sound so calm, so unaffected by this conversation? I have lost all semblance of control over my voice and I'm sobbing.

"I need to go now," I say before hanging up the phone and collapsing onto my bed. The constriction in my throat and chest is so painful; I have to release this tension. I open my mouth wide, throw back my head and howl.

I cry for over thirty minutes. I must be loud because one of the security guards knocks at my door to ask if I am okay. I apologize, deeply embarrassed, and invent the death of a much-loved relative in New Zealand.

It is early afternoon but I head back to bed. I take with me the entire box set of the BBC *Planet Earth* documentary, a six-pack of beer and my laptop. The beer was delivered by a generous Australian ex-soldier. He had driven all the way from Herat with my winter clothes and two trays of beer in the back of his truck. I hadn't had the heart to tell him that I wasn't really drinking much alcohol anymore, having discovered that yoga, meditation and writing were doing a better job of keeping the demons at bay. Today, however, I am grateful for the beer. I intend to throw my good habits out the window for a while.

It's difficult to wallow in self-pity when you are watching a documentary about the beauty and brutality of the natural world. Within five minutes I'm engrossed. For the next four hours I drink my way through three beers while marveling at our planet.

I text Tim for an update on the Rugby World Cup. He keeps me entertained for most of the evening, providing live commentary on the day's games via text message. I also send out a cry for help, via email, to my girlfriends around the world. They may not always have been able to understand the challenges I've faced in my work in Afghanistan, but a breakup is the sort of experience that translates easily into any setting. No one is online tonight, though, and eventually the effect of three beers on an empty stomach, combined with the emotional exhaustion of the past week, sends me into a surprisingly deep sleep.

I wake, Sunday morning, to the realization that I am absolutely and completely beat. Between the missile attack, the trip to Lal and breaking up with Joel I have wrung myself dry. I don't even know if I can get out of bed.

Sunday is a working day. I'm expected in the office. I do something I have never done before, not even in the darkest days after Amanullah Khan's murder. I call in sick and take a "mental health day." I have no intention of getting out of bed for at least one more day. I have an internet connection in my bedroom, so from my bed I make a cursory effort at a weekly report. I send it off to the head office in Kabul with a note explaining I've reached my personal exhaustion point. "I need to stay in bed for at least a day. Maybe longer. I will get back to work saving the world as soon as I can."

I am probably too honest. Most people would claim a stomach bug. But I am too tired to come up with a better excuse than exhaustion. Let them know the truth, for once. They need to know that sometimes it all gets to be a bit much out here. Let them think I'm weak. Right now, I don't care.

Confession out of the way, I open my personal emails to find a series of compassionate, funny, encouraging messages from friends in New Zealand together with a loving but somewhat exasperated note from Kate, who was never keen on the idea of me getting back with Joel in the first place. Buoyed by their support, I switch off the internet and turn on BBC *Planet Earth* again. I spend the next six hours completely absorbed.

By Monday morning I'm ready to get up and back to the office.

There is plenty of work waiting to be done, and I'm due to head off on my holiday to the United States in just over a week. It's time to get back into life.

42
Time to Take Action

October 2007: Ghor and Kabul, Afghanistan

I write up my report on the Lal trip, visit local officials to discuss the food shortage in Lal, and follow up on a couple of serious cases of violence against women that I was working on before the missile attack. Feeling on top of my workload, I request an early flight out of Chaghcharan to Kabul. There is only one UN flight in and out of Ghor on Wednesday each week and even that flight seems to arrive only half the time. If I want to be sure to catch my international flight next Thursday it would be safer for me to get the flight this Wednesday. This will give me an extra week to spend in Kabul, and there is always plenty of work for me to do in the office there.

Kate has left Kabul so I need to find somewhere else to stay. I know where I want to stay: with Tim. I'm just not sure if I have the brass to ask. He has always made it clear that I am welcome to stay in the spare room at his guesthouse. I've stayed there in the past and I am friendly with his housemates, so it's a very tempting option. Since then, though, our flirtation dimmed when I told him that I was unavailable due to my ill-fated efforts at a reunion with Joel. I'm not sure whether the offer still stands.

Tim and I have been playing Scrabble on Facebook for the past few days. At the moment we are in the middle of a game in which he is, typically, well ahead. I send him a message on Facebook: "Other than the All Blacks dipping out of the World Cup, my great regret of the season is passing up the chance to make out with the hottest man in Kabul in order to pursue a doomed reunion. If I come to Kabul will you let me take you out for dinner and see if I can convince you to give me another chance? If not, let me buy you a drink for your birthday at least."

This will be the first he knows that things are finally over between me and Joel. I hope that this will be good news. Fortunately, I don't have to wait long for his response. He says he is "pleasantly surprised" by my email and will gladly take me up on my offer when I come to Kabul. He invites me to stay in the spare room at his guesthouse. It took all the cheek I had to make the offer in the first place; I hope I now have the courage to follow through!

Joel has also talked me into coming to meet him in Portland after all, so that we can break up in person. It could be a form of masochism, but breaking up by phone just seems half-baked. I want to do this thing properly and that means making peace with Joel. I believe his attempt to give things another go with me was well intentioned. I'd like to find a way to let him know that I can see that.

First, though, I'm on my way to Kabul. As our little plane takes off from Chaghcharan I look back over the town. When I think about leaving Afghanistan I feel a sense of relief, like anticipating taking off a heavy backpack after a very long hike. But when I think about leaving Ghor my heart constricts. I will miss this place and these people terribly. It's tempting not to think about it, but what I'm learning is that the beauty of life is in living it, not distracting myself from it. So I sit on the plane with tears rolling down my cheeks and allow myself to feel all the love I have for this place and its people.

By the time I land in Kabul I've shed my tears, and I am ready for a change of pace and scene. After today, there is only one day left before a four-day weekend for Eid. A year has passed since Amanullah Khan's murder. This year I'm looking forward to spending the holiday weekend in the relative luxury of Kabul, such as it is, but first I have one day of work to get through. I want to make some progress on the report on violence against women that I'm still working on with UNIFEM.

I go directly from the airport to the office and spend the rest of the day reading case summaries collected by other human rights officers from all over Afghanistan. There are more than four hundred cases in total, and they all document extreme acts of violence against women. In one case a man threw his wife into a dry well and then threw a grenade in after her. The violence is so visceral that I have trouble reading the case summaries.

I come across a case that I know well. A warlord in Ghor kidnapped and beat a nine-year-old girl. She was made to work as a slave in his home but she was not allowed to sleep with the other women of the house. He forced her to sleep outside with the dogs. This is the kind of case that keeps me awake at night. I go over and over it, wondering what more I could and should be doing. Perhaps I should simply get a car and go out to the warlord's compound, and demand to take the child away with me.

The problem with this plan is that the warlord wouldn't let our car get anywhere near his compound. He's already repelled an approach by the U.S. army. If the U.S. army can't penetrate his defenses then what hope do the Afghan National Police have? What hope do I have? None.

So I do what I can. I write up the report. I try to make it clear that the security challenge in Afghanistan today is not just about the Taliban. For many women, the risk is much closer to home. All afternoon and into the early evening I write, I write because it is the only thing I can do and because it is better than doing nothing.

By the time I'm done for the day I am exhausted. I call Tim and tell him that I am on my way. He's at home after a long day of research for his book. He spent his day with opium addicts who live in the bombed-out shells of buildings in old Kabul and he sounds as weary as I feel.

When the driver drops me off outside the guesthouse, Tim meets me at the gate. He is as lovely, as reassuringly solid and warm as I remembered, and for a moment I almost collapse in to him. Then I remember where I am and who might be watching. I smile at him, hoping that he knows how grateful I am to see him right now, yet suddenly too shy to say as much. He takes my bag and walks me into the house. He has set me up in the spare bedroom. As tempted as I am to throw myself into his embrace, I am grateful for his considerateness. He knows I've been through a lot recently. I may have told him of my plan to seduce him, but he is leaving me the space to do so in my own time. I just hope that I get up the courage to make my move before our small window of opportunity passes.

On Thursday, after another full day of writing about violence against women, I arrive back at Tim's house in time for drinks. Tim shares a house with another Australian journalist, Sophie. Sophie is a funny, smart and big-hearted woman who has been in Afghanistan for many years. Every Thursday night, to mark the beginning of our weekend, Sophie hosts drinks at her place. She has an outdoor fire surrounded by comfortable couches and cushions and an actual bar. Her friends include some of the least pretentious and most likable expat women I've met in Kabul and, as always, it is a pleasure to catch up with them all.

As I curl up on the sofa with my friend Jan, I glance over to where Tim is busy stoking the fire and serving drinks. I wonder when I'm going to summon up the courage to make a move. Given my recent track record with men I'm not feeling confident. I fear that I may have used up all of my chutzpah on my email declaration. Maybe if I wait a little longer Tim will take matters out of my hands. I return to my conversation with Jan, but she has noticed my distraction and asks me what I'm planning to do about Tim. I'm as flustered as a schoolgirl and avoid the question. Jan smiles knowingly at me and for a moment I hope that she has come up with a plan to make this all happen for me. Then I remember that I'm thirty-five years old, not fifteen. If anything is going to come of my five-month-long flirtation with Tim, I'm going to have to do it myself.

Someone announces that there is a party at another house, the home of yet another Australian friend of mine, and that we are all invited. I would have been quite happy to stay by the fire, but everyone is moving out so I follow Jan into a car as well.

At the party I chat with people I know from when I lived in Kabul, but I'm not really in the mood for small talk. At one point Tim walks toward the couch where I'm chatting with a British private security contractor. He must sense something because he suddenly excuses himself, making room for Tim and me to finally sit together. We talk for a while about his research and my work and then the others from our house announce that they are heading on to yet another party. Tim asks me what I want to do. I realize that it's time to take action.

"We could continue this conversation at home," I say, feeling brave and a little brazen.

Tim doesn't hesitate for a second. "I like that idea," he says. "Let's go."

We climb into the nearest car and, despite both knowing only too well what grist this will be for the rumor mills of Kabul, tell our companions to drop us back at the house. When we get home Tim stokes up the outdoor fire and we sit on the couch. I lean in to him and, finally, feel the reassurance of his body, slowly relaxing into the unfamiliar sensation that I am with someone I can utterly trust. There may be an inevitability to our coming together, but when we finally kiss, nothing can detract from the thrill or the pure pleasure of this moment.

Tim and I spend the rest of the Eid holiday together. I move into his room, where we lie awake at night talking through the challenges of his book and then laze about in the morning playing Scrabble. He brings me coffee in bed and cooks eggs for our breakfast. We spend most of one day shopping for carpets for Tim and for ornately carved wooden Nuristani furniture for me. Initially I'm taken aback by the ease and comfort with which we seem to slip into each other's life. But then I realize that our emails have been building this intimacy for months.

I talk to Tim about my yoga practice without fear of mockery. He seems to understand what I'm trying to say when I explain what Pema's teachings mean to me. In his bedroom, I feel I can be utterly myself without fear or shame. There is great kindness in Tim's approach to me, and my soul soaks up that kindness like rain after a long drought. It may only have been a week since my final phone call to Joel, but it has been much longer since we were truly kind to each other.

Eventually the week comes to an end and it is time for me to fly out to California. I leave Tim knowing that his kindness, his love, have helped to equip me for saying my final good-bye to Joel. I'll be back in a couple of weeks and I've arranged to have another week in Kabul to finish up the UNIFEM report before I return to Ghor. This will be my last chance to spend time with Tim because he is due to leave Afghanistan. I have no idea what will come of our friendship, but for now I've enjoyed every minute of it.

43
Time to Go Home

November 2007: Ghor, Afghanistan

By the time I get back to Ghor I've cried my way through a final farewell to Joel in Portland, recovered in the company of Kate in New York and enjoyed a delightful week with Tim in Kabul.

Seeing Joel was harder than I expected. In the end, though, I felt better, lighter, and ready to wish him well.

Tim and I fell right back into the comfort of feeling truly safe with each other. Both of us had been through a long, hard few months of feeling unable to fully trust or rely on anyone around us. Tim may have plenty of journalist friends in Kabul, but there is a current of competition that runs through their relationships, which keeps him from sharing his doubts and fears with them. For me too, it is a powerful relief to feel able to be entirely myself with someone, without worrying about being judged or misunderstood.

Tim is leaving in just a few weeks, heading back to Australia to write his book. We don't even discuss the possibility of continuing our relationship post-Afghanistan, although I think about it. Tim never raises the subject, so I let it be. I have no idea what is coming next in my life but I feel clear that it is time for a change.

Back in Ghor I realize I can no longer put off telling Fahim that

I am leaving. I've been putting off telling all my colleagues in Ghor, but Fahim is going to be the hardest. It isn't just because we've become close friends. I think that Fahim, more than anyone else, relies on me.

It's an interesting turn, because I know how much I rely on all of them. I wouldn't have lasted a week in Chaghcharan without my colleagues. They showed me where to buy my bread and how to get credit for my phone. When they realized that I don't eat meat, they brought eggs from their village so that I had some protein. They told me who each of the men were who turned up at my office door and they explained to me how this warlord was connected to that politician.

Sure, there were things I did for them. I helped them navigate the UN administration, and taught them how to use email. Every day I gave someone a lesson in writing reports.

But I realize that Fahim relies on me for his sense of security in the office. After the murder accusations, Fahim returned to the office reluctantly and with understandable concern about his long-term future. I assured him that I would make sure he was given a fair deal. So far I've been able to deliver on my promise. But when I leave, he'll be vulnerable—or so I imagine.

One morning, Fahim and I are sitting in my office working on the weekly political report. I turn to him.

"I'm going to leave Ghor, Fahim," I say in English. "I'm going home to New Zealand at Christmas and I won't be coming back."

Fahim looks at me with genuine surprise and sadness. "Oh, Miss Marianne. We'll miss you."

"I'll miss you too, Fahim. I'll miss you all."

"You've been such a patient teacher," Fahim says. "We'll be lost without you."

Now he is flattering me. After two years in Afghanistan I'm used to this kind of flattery, and it no longer embarrasses me. I now understand its social value, even when it isn't entirely true.

"I'll be lost without you too," I say, quite truthfully. "But I need to go home to my own family."

"Yes," Fahim replies, gravely, "your family needs you. You've been here two years. It is time to go home."

And, just like that, I realize I'll have no trouble explaining to my colleagues why I am leaving. If I were leaving Afghanistan to go work for the UN in another country, that would be different. But I am going home. I am returning to my family. Afghans understand that. Indeed it was hard for them to understand how I could have left my family to come here in the first place.

"You are right, Fahim," I sigh, "as usual. It's time for me to be near my family." I stare at my report for a while, feeling the heaviness of my heart. "It's still hard for me to leave. The problems here are so big and there is so much work still to be done. I feel like I'm abandoning you all before we've finished what we set out to do together."

Fahim looks at me and smiles.

"This work will never be done, Miss Marianne. But there is also work for you to do at home. Go home. Let your father and mother stop worrying about you for a while. Spend time with your nephews and nieces. Then do what you can in your country to help people understand what is really happening here in Afghanistan. Help them see that our problems are their problems too."

I wish I could hug him. I promise to do my best, not really sure how I will keep that promise.

Within days of having this conversation with Fahim, I receive a request from a New Zealand journalist asking if he can come and visit me in Ghor. He wants to write an article about my life and work for a magazine in New Zealand. Perfect, I think; this is exactly what Fahim asked me to do.

44

Why Do You Talk Funny?

November 2007: Ghor, Afghanistan

*T*he night before Daniel, the journalist, arrives, someone throws a
grenade into the home of Massouma, the head of the Department
of Women's Affairs. I've been working with her for a long time and
know her well. The grenade lands just outside the window of her front
room and shatters the glass, sending deadly shards flying over the heads
of her sleeping children. The only victim of the attack is her dog; red
splatters of his blood still cover her front porch when I rush over to see
her the next morning.

It rattles me that the anonymous threats made against Massouma
in recent months were no bluff. I've become accustomed to living in
a town where there are constant threats of violence and even the occasional poorly aimed missile fired toward our compound, but this grenade came frighteningly close to hitting its target.

Massouma gives me a tour of the wreckage, calmly pointing out
the bullet hole in her own car from the shots she fired at her attackers.
She didn't see them, but as soon as the grenade exploded she checked
on the children, grabbed her husband's gun and ran out on the front
porch to shoot at whoever was responsible. I can't help smiling at the
image she paints of her firing wildly into the air as the invisible villains

fled into the night. She's certainly got plenty of spunk, even if her shots were far off the mark.

I ask her what she will do now. I want to know that she is going to protect herself and her family. After an earlier attack on her office compound, I supported her when she refused to close or move the office. "If we give in to this kind of violence," she had declared, "then we have given in to a reign of terror that may never end." After that attack an international NGO withdrew its funds from a women's conference she was organizing. They felt it was too dangerous. I applauded Massouma's courage. If she wasn't willing to give in to the scare tactics then I thought it was our job to stand behind her.

But this is different. This is personal.

This is not an attack on the Department of Women's Affairs. This is a grenade thrown into a private home. This is shards of glass barely missing the heads of sleeping children. Massouma may be unrepentant about her work for the rights of women in Ghor, but that doesn't mean she isn't afraid for her children.

She is scared and she is angry. "I'm going to move my children to my parents' home. I hope they will be safer there," she tells me. "And I'm going to find out why the police haven't yet made any arrests over the previous attack on my office. Will you come with me to meet the chief of police?" she asks. "I want to know what he is doing to catch whoever did this."

"Of course," I say, "I want to do anything I can to help. I want to hold these cowards to account. Who throws grenades at sleeping children? And what kind of a police force can't even find one damn suspect?" I am scared for her, but more than anything else I am angry.

We can't meet with the police until tomorrow so I go back to my compound to prepare for Daniel's arrival. Truth is, I'm in no state to be hosting him. Between the sadness of saying good-bye and the fury, fear and frustration I feel in the face of the attack on my friend's home,

I'm not sure I can offer a balance of emotions or opinions. Still, when he arrives I bury my agitation and show him the town as I know and love it. One of my colleagues offers to take the journalist home to his village, I accept and we travel to the Pashtun village that afternoon.

Throughout the afternoon I try to convey to this young urban sophisticate what life is like in Ghor. I answer his questions about the role of the Taliban in the attacks in the town, despite knowing that the complex truth is unlikely to survive his interpretation of it. I try to explain the subtle yet pervasive power of drug lords and war-lords in this town and their ability to effectively control senior public officials. I tell him what it feels like for me to live with the constant threat of a rocket attack or a roadside bomb. I look him in the eyes, making sure he is listening, and emphasize: "Any stress I live with pales in comparison to that experienced by my Afghan colleagues and neighbors."

That evening I cook up the last of my fresh vegetables for us to eat. The market in Chaghcharan is empty and I had to get a box of vegetables sent up to me in the last helicopter from Herat. This makes each one of the carrots spectacularly precious. Having been raised by farmers, schooled on hospitality by Bedouins in Gaza, and then cared for by Afghans, it doesn't occur to me to hoard them for myself. The fact that Daniel is in Ghor for only a day or two, and is hardly in need of the nutrients, doesn't register. I have a guest and that means bringing out the best food I have.

He gobbles up the vegetable stir-fry, which I consider to be the best meal I have had in weeks, without comment. I wonder if this is how my Afghan hosts feel when I force myself to eat their lovingly prepared lamb stews, never quite managing to entirely disguise my discomfort. There is no way for him to understand what a big deal it is to eat fresh vegetables in Ghor, but I can't help but feel deflated. Compared with the effusive thanks I receive from my Afghan guests for making them a simple cup of tea, his nonchalance, quite typical for a New Zealander, seems like ingratitude.

In this one simple interaction, I see a chasm, larger than I expected, open up between me and my own culture. As if to emphasize the point, my guest asks me why I talk so funny.

"You know," he says, "you don't have to talk to me in that strange pidgin you use with your colleagues."

I am standing at the bench in my tiny kitchenette with my back to him, so he doesn't see the look of pain that shoots across my face.

"I didn't realize I was doing it," I stammer. "I guess it's just because I spend all my time speaking to people who speak English as a second language."

No one else has ever commented on my speech before, so either I adapt quickly once I get among English speakers, or others have been too kind to say anything.

"Well, it sounds a bit ridiculous," he says. "You don't need to put it on for me."

"I'm not putting it on," I respond, a little stunned, "and I think it will probably just wear off if I have a couple of days talking to someone who speaks English."

But I don't want to spend several days speaking to him. Not even to restore my ability to speak the Queen's English. Accustomed as I am to the great care Afghans take to avoid causing offense, the once familiar frankness of my compatriot has caught me entirely off guard.

That night I lie awake for a while wondering if I really want to go "home." I have become fond of the Afghan approach to conversation and to life. The direct manner in which Daniel questioned and addressed me is not only unfamiliar, but it is making me extremely uncomfortable.

In the morning, as I get started on my working day, Daniel stays in his room writing his article for a well-known New Zealand current affairs website. Over lunch—a simple spread of naan and fresh white cheese—he announces the article is published online. "I've sent you the link," he says proudly.

I have a frantically busy day at work so I don't get to look at the post until after we have each retired to our rooms that night. I read it with a growing sense of dismay.

He jokes about "donkey-borne improvised explosive devices" and compares landing in Ghor to arriving in Tatooine, Luke Skywalker's home planet in *Star Wars*. I despair. I had wanted to help New Zealanders better understand and relate to the people of Afghanistan. Instead I have created yet another opportunity for the media to perpetuate the idea that Afghanistan is as alien to the rest of the world as a fictional planet.

It gets worse. He misquotes me on several points. What concerns me most is an allegation that the local governor is under the control of a local warlord. The difference between what I said, which is that the warlord was probably more powerful than the governor, and what he has written probably seems trivial to him, but I see the potential for cataclysmic misunderstanding if his words were ever to be read by people in Ghor.

By the time I get to the end of the article and read the posted comments, I have no trace of humor or goodwill for Daniel or his article. One commenter makes a joke about Daniel proposing to the very young girl he photographed for the article. The photograph is of my colleague's four-year-old daughter. I can't see anything funny in the comment. At least one other commenter seems to find it hilarious. Who are these morons?

When I finish reading the article I sit at my kitchen table and cry. I feel I have betrayed my colleagues and neighbors. I invited this man into their town, I showed him around. Because he was my guest, people welcomed him, even inviting him into their homes and allowing him to photograph their children.

In return he compared their town to an alien planet, joked about their greatest fears and called their governor a lackey. I read the article, not as his New Zealand readers will, but as an Afghan might. In that light it reads like an insult, and I feel personally responsible for it.

I am not sure what to do. This article isn't the real reason he is here. His real assignment is to write a feature article about me for a widely read New Zealand magazine. I no longer trust him to write anything I would be able to live with. I decide to pull the plug on the article.

The next morning I tell him I am unhappy with the piece he wrote. "I think it would be better if we forget about the other article."

He is surprised and, to his credit, concerned by my response to his writing. He assures me that he won't write anything more about me if I don't want him to. He smiles weakly and heads outside to take photographs, leaving me alone with my thoughts.

It takes me a long moment to recover from the sense that I did something terribly wrong by inviting this journalist to Chaghcharan. I suspect it will take me much longer to feel comfortable enough to allow my humor to come through in any of my own writing about Afghanistan. I never want to be the kind of person who jokes about an exploding donkey in a town where real explosions can narrowly miss killing children I know and care about. How long will it take me to find the courage to write about Afghanistan without fear of getting it horribly wrong? How will I ever be able to fulfill my promise to Fahim?

The next day, Daniel moves on to more accommodating pastures. A New Zealander in another part of Afghanistan is building wind turbines to deliver electricity to Afghan villages. It makes a great story and presumably comes without the kind of emotional complication I have presented. Meanwhile, I continue the hard work of preparing to leave.

Daniel's visit was probably a gift in many ways. It gave me a sneak preview of the gaping chasm I am going to have to negotiate when I get back to New Zealand. I will have to learn how to talk about

Afghanistan in a context where the reality of roadside bombs is so distant that people can't help but react to them as though they were televised melodrama rather than genuine human trauma. I will have to relearn how to get straight to the point rather than carefully skirting around the issue Afghan-style. I am even going to have to relearn how to speak English, placing verbs, objects and subjects in their "correct" order rather than using English words in sentences that follow Persian grammatical rules. Perhaps hardest of all, I will have to accept that Afghanistan, my home for the past two years, is a wildly alien place for most New Zealanders.

I am starting to appreciate just how difficult the task Fahim entrusted to me is going to be.

45
Saying Good-Bye

December 2007: Ghor, Afghanistan

For now, my biggest challenge is working out how to say good-bye to all my friends in Ghor without crying like a baby. Luckily for me, Afghan men are more comfortable with tears than men in New Zealand. My Afghan colleagues have taught me there is no shame in tears when they are shed for good reason. Sitting with a woman whose child has been kidnapped by a warlord is a good reason. Meeting a father who has no food for his children is a good reason. Whenever my colleagues see me in those situations, tears glistening in my eyes as I frantically scribble down all the information I need, they smile approvingly.

"Marianne is very compassionate," they announce to each other and to anyone who will listen. "She feels the pain of our people."

It is true. I do feel the pain of the people I meet in Afghanistan. And in that constant meeting of sorrow, I have learned that I don't need to fix their problems. That simple lesson, perhaps more than anything else, has finally allowed me to be fully present to the person in front of me. When my mind isn't racing ahead to think of what I can do to help, I'm able to give my full attention to the person who is talking to me.

There is an art to saying good-bye. There's a temptation, when you are preparing to leave a place you love, to begin to withdraw your heart from the place. It seems easier to leave quickly, with little fanfare and without really acknowledging the ways in which your heart is being torn in two. But I've learned that the good-byes you don't say will haunt you.

So I say good-bye to everyone. I don't pretend I will be back. I know that I will want to come back, desperately, but it is unlikely I will find a way to get back to Ghor in the foreseeable future. This is probably the last time I will see most, if not all, of them.

I say my good-byes to the governor, the chief of police, the commander of the PRT and all the heads of the different government departments I've worked with. I exchange long hugs and kisses with Massouma and her female staff. I say good-bye to Heida, whom I am going to miss terribly. I make my rounds of the orphanage, the provincial council and the office of the Afghan Independent Human Rights Commission. I say good-bye to Mr. Baluch—the English "mister" has become like an affectionate nickname between us.

I still haven't said good-bye to Fahim or any of the other men with whom I worked day and night for the past six months. How do I honor them for the fact that they opened their homes to me? How can I thank them for accepting and, most of all, for loving me?

We all sit around the table in the meeting room. Haji gives a speech. He thanks me for being a "patient teacher" and a "compassionate friend to the people of Ghor." Then he insists that I give a speech in response.

"Thank you for looking after me," I say, my heart pounding with emotion. "Thank you for supporting me and for doing the good work you are doing for the people of Ghor. I feel hopeful for Afghanistan because I know there are men like you." I pause for a moment. Tears are forming in my eyes and I know my voice is about to fail me. I breathe deeply and feel my feet on the earth, practicing a little yoga to get me through the speech.

"You have taught me what it means to serve," I say, "and you have shown me what real hospitality and generosity look like." I look around and see that I am not the only one with tears in my eyes. I am determined not to let my emotion keep me from saying what is in my heart. "It has been an honor to know you all, and to work alongside you. I will always pray that you and your families are kept safe, and that your country will know peace." I'm not really sure what I mean by a prayer, but I know that my heart's deepest desire is for these men, and everyone in this country, to be at peace and safe.

After my speech I insist on taking a photo of every man in the room. I want to be sure that I have at least one decent photo of each of them. Then we all stand out in front of the office and someone takes a photo of all of us together.

Soon after this photo is taken Mr. Baluch comes over from the Afghan Independent Human Rights Commission. By then my plane has landed and I need to make my way to the airstrip, so I don't have time to pull out my camera for a photograph with him. There isn't enough room in the cars for everyone and I want to stay with my colleagues for as long as I can, so Ahmad takes my suitcase over in the car and the rest of us walk to the airstrip. It isn't far but it is long enough for me to thank Mr. Baluch for coming, and to say good-bye again to each of my colleagues.

Before I climb into the tiny Cessna, my luggage tucked into the back, I embrace each of these men, men who may not have embraced any women outside their immediate families before.

Once I am in the plane I look out onto the tarmac. Lined up along the edge of the airstrip, like a guard of honor, are the men who taught me what it was I had to offer the world. In Afghanistan I learned the difference between working on the big picture of human rights—when it is possible and maybe even essential to focus on policies that improve life for the majority—and working one to one with the individuals who fall through the cracks in those policies. In Afghanistan I lost faith, for a time, in the possibility of a fairer world. But here, in Ghor, these men taught me that what still mattered was how well I loved and served the people right in front of me.

Epilogue

August 2012: Wellington, New Zealand

Three months after I leave Afghanistan, I get news that Mr. Baluch has been kidnapped by the Taliban while visiting his family in Kandahar. Initially I am hopeful that the Human Rights Commission will be able to negotiate for his release. I pray for him every morning, never sure to whom I am praying, but unsure how else to deal with my sense of helplessness. After a few weeks I learn that he has been killed. I'm devastated. I search through my photos for an image of him. I discover that I have none. Instead I find the photo that was taken on my last day in Ghor, just before Mr. Baluch arrived.

When I look at that photo, I see ten Afghan men gazing solemnly at the camera. It's winter, late December, and they are all wearing heavy coats and scarves over their cotton tunics. Their hands are tucked into their warm pockets or crossed demurely in front of their chests. In the center of the photo is a young woman with long black hair pulled back into a ponytail. She is dressed in jeans and a long black shawl. A bright red and pink scarf around her neck brings the only patch of color to the scene. Unlike all the others in the photo, she is smiling. Other than her smile, there is no sign of warmth between the people in the photo.

There is no clue that the man standing next to her, wearing a brown

coat over a crisp white cotton tunic and pants, has been one of her closest confidants for the past six months. There is no sign of the friendship that will continue to bind these two people together years after the
photo is taken.

As a souvenir of friendship, it is an entirely unsatisfying photo. But
I still like to look at it. It reminds me of a place I called home for a time
and the people who made it so.

It is now August 2012. I have been away from Afghanistan for four
and a half years. I've been back in New Zealand for twice as long as I
was in Afghanistan. I still keep in touch with Fahim and some of my
colleagues in Ghor and earlier this year I was able to go back to Ghor to
see them. They never fail to amaze me with their resilience in the face
of a deteriorating security situation.

Abdul-Karim wrote to me when his wife gave birth to their fourth
child, a boy after three girls. He didn't write about the food shortage or the harsh winter in Ghor or the challenges his office—my old
office—must be facing. Nor did he write about the increasing security
problems in his province, although I know they must be making his
work harder by the week. What he wrote was: "My wife M is fine with
our girls and our baby boy S. S is growing, he is a very lovely baby like
his sisters and all the time he is laughing. We are feeling well and things
are going well with us at the moment, hope you are also doing well."

Perhaps you have to have been in Ghor and seen the hunger and the
fear and the relentless daily struggle to really appreciate how extraordinary this email, from this young man, really is. Every day I am challenged and inspired by his gratitude.

Recently, the UNAMA office in Ghor closed, so Abdul-Karim and
Fahim have both been emailing me about their efforts to find new jobs,
not an easy task in Chegcharan.

Whomever Fahim works for, I know he will continue to do all he can
to promote peaceful resolutions to age-old conflicts in his province. He

still insists I taught him a lot during my time in Ghor, but I think he knows very well that I was the one who learned the most. He has always been as generous in word as he is in deed. When I was in Afghanistan this year, we sat on the balcony of my old house and drank tea. Both of us had tears in our eyes when we said good-bye again. Fahim is getting older, and I wonder if I'll get back to Afghanistan to see him again.

Suraya still heads Voice of Women, and its shelter in Herat has been joined by shelters in Badghis and Farah. When I visited her this year I was able to introduce her to a funder who was interested in paying to get a shelter open in Ghor as well. As the international community withdraws not only its military presence, but also much of its financial support from Afghanistan, women like Suraya are having more and more trouble finding funding for their work. At the same time, their work is becoming more and more important as the Taliban and others try to reassert repressive controls over the lives of Afghan women. I hope this book raises awareness of and support for Suraya's work helping women leave violent and abusive relationships and build new lives for themselves. For more information about ways to support Suraya and her work, see the Resources section at the back of this book.

My assistant Asiyah is now in the United States, studying politics and law. Her dream is to be the first female secretary general of the United Nations, so she can make real changes in the lives of women in countries like Afghanistan. From time to time I help raise a small amount of money to subsidize her scholarship, and anyone who would like to help her is more than welcome to get in touch through my website.

Joel stayed on in Afghanistan for another year after I left. He may not be one for talking about the stress of life in a war zone, but he seems to be able to process it all in his own way. From Afghanistan he moved to central Africa where he was valued for his levelheaded approach to complex emergencies. When the earthquake hit Haiti he was sent there for a few months. I called him in Port-au-Prince to see how he was doing. He told me, in his characteristically understated manner, that the security situation in Haiti wasn't as bad as the media was making out.

"It's not half as bad as Afghanistan," he told me.

I wasn't sure if he was being entirely honest or if he was trying to reassure me that he wasn't in danger. I wouldn't put the latter past him.

Months later, when he was back in Africa, we chatted online about this book.

"It's got some pretty intimate stuff in it," I warned him. "Maybe you should read it to make sure you are okay with it all."

"I don't care what you write about me," he said, "as long as you make me taller. And I'd like to play the trumpet."

I laughed out loud when I read his response. That was the Joel I fell in love with—a man who really doesn't care what anyone thinks of him and who maintains his sense of humor under even the most trying circumstances. If this story says anything about Joel, I hope it will be that he is a passionate advocate for the rights of those who are oppressed. He may have his flaws, like all of us, but he is undeniably motivated by a sense of justice.

Tim returned to Australia and wrote his book. Although nothing more came of our romance, we remained friends. Tim encouraged me in the process of writing this book and provided invaluable feedback on early drafts. I'm grateful for his support and I hope his book finds a wide audience; it is a vivid, engaging and very informative account of the pervasive effect of the opium trade on Afghan economic, social and political life.

In the four years since I left Afghanistan, the general consensus is that the situation has continued to deteriorate. In April 2011 seven UNAMA staff members were murdered in their office in Mazar-e-Sharif when an anti-American protest turned violent. The protests were sparked by reports of "kill squads"—groups of U.S. soldiers

in Afghanistan who carried out premeditated murders of Afghan
civilians—and by reports of the burning of a Quran by a Christian
pastor in Florida. News of the "kill squads" had sickened me and left
me wondering how things had been allowed to go so horribly wrong
in Afghanistan. The UNAMA killings then shocked and saddened me
deeply, not least because of what they tell us about the failure of our
peacekeeping efforts in Afghanistan.

How did we come to a point where members of the local Afghan
community in Mazar saw the UNAMA staff in their city not as impartial representatives of an organization committed to improving the
protection and well being of the civilian population, but rather as a
symbol of the United States of America? The answer to that question
could fill another entire book, but I can't help thinking it lies partly in
the concerns I expressed throughout this book about the blurred lines
between the international community's civilian and military efforts in
Afghanistan, internal tensions within UNAMA between political goals
and human rights/humanitarian values, and the controlling influence
on international efforts by the United States.

As well as a profound sense of sadness for what these killings tell
me about how UNAMA is now perceived by at least some factions of
the Afghan community, I also—obviously—felt deeply and personally devastated for the people directly affected by the murders. The
UNAMA security officer who came with me up to Ghor to help open
the new office was working as a security officer in the Mazar office
at the time of the murders. He wasn't at the office at the time of the
attack, but when we spoke, forty-eight hours after the murders, he
told me he had been crying for two days. I am stunned UNAMA
security officers were left without support from the Afghan National
Police (ANP) or the International Security Assistance Forces (ISAF).
UNAMA has never pretended to be equipped to defend its staff against
this kind of attack and has always relied on agreements with the ANP

and ISAF that backup and protection would be provided whenever they are needed.

These feel like dark times for Afghanistan. My friend Horia Mosadiq—with whom I worked in Kabul and who now works for Amnesty International—told me recently that she worries that human rights generally and women's rights specifically will be traded away by the political elite in exchange for some kind of compromise with the Taliban. As the international community scrambles to get their troops, and much of their money, out of Afghanistan, the rights of Afghan women, so often touted as a reason for U.S. intervention in Afghanistan in the first place, were described by one senior U.S. official as a "pet rock" that had become too heavy to carry.

I got an email from Fahim recently in which he said that Ghor has been very affected by drought again this year and that the central government and the international community seem to have forgotten the province.

"I still have in my memory," he wrote, "that forty years ago when I was in high school I found 38 people who had died from hunger, and I myself helped to bury them. I worry about 2013."

I too worry about Afghanistan in 2013 and wonder what more I can do to make it harder for the world to forget about Ghor.

On the brighter side, there has been growing recognition of the risk posed to civilians by increased military involvement in aid and humanitarian work and international military forces are focused on the transition of their security role to Afghan security forces. Almost everyone I spoke to about this in Afghanistan agreed: Afghan security forces must eventually take the lead in their own country, and development and humanitarian work should be Afghan-led and undertaken by civilian actors.

But are the Afghan security forces ready? Has enough been done to train, equip and prepare them for the challenge of maintaining security in the face of increasingly bold and violent attacks from the Taliban? And will the money currently spent on military engagement be reassigned to development assistance to Afghanistan? Will the international community heed the words of former UN High Commissioner for Human Rights Louise Arbor and dedicate more attention and resources to Afghanistan rather than less?

There is little reason to feel hopeful on that count. As the international military forces withdraw from Afghanistan, much of the international funding for nonmilitary activity appears to be leaving with them. When I talk to Horia, Suraya and others like them—Afghan women working for the protection and well-being of Afghan women—they tell me it is getting harder and harder to find donors to support their work.

Despite the grim prognosis for Afghanistan in the near future, the persistence and passion of people like Suraya, Fahim, Horia, Sima Samar and the entire staff of the Afghan Independent Human Rights Commission give me hope.

※ ※ ※

As for me, I had planned to stay home for perhaps a year, maximum, before I headed back into the field. Within days of arriving home, however, I fell in love with someone I'd known for years and, in doing so, found a reason to stay in New Zealand. Over the past four years I've learned that there are ways to be of service in this world other than being on the human rights frontline. I've worked for humanitarian and human rights organizations here in New Zealand. After my experiences in Ghor, I became active in environmental advocacy. I also studied psychology and yoga, and now teach yoga as a path to sustainable, conscious service. The lessons I learned in Afghanistan lie at the heart of everything I now teach to my yoga students.

I teach that we can't be of true service to anyone else unless we are prepared to face our own shadows. As I have learned, our own fears and even our best intentions can get in the way of our ability to serve others. Yoga, meditation, writing and walking continue to be my tools to process the fears that get triggered by the suffering I encounter in the world. These practices bring me face to face with my own human frailty, day after day, and I learn over and over to meet myself with the same compassion that I feel for all suffering everywhere.

In his extraordinary memoir, *The Translator*, Daoud Hari writes about the days he spent translating for the UN genocide investigators in Darfur.

> *Often, then, the stories would come pouring out, and often they were set down before us slowly and quietly like tea. These slow stories were told with understatement that made my eyes and voice fill as I translated; for when people have no emotion remaining for such stories, your own heart must supply it.*

I read these words about a year after returning to New Zealand, as I was beginning to write this book. I wished I had read them while I was in Afghanistan because they helped me understand in a new light that great bowl of sadness I carried for so many months after I interviewed those mothers in Shindand.

It's time to talk honestly about the emotional and psychological impact humanitarian work, especially human rights and protection work, is having on people. The rhetoric of "resilience" needs to be unpicked and stripped of its connotations of toughness. True resilience, in my view, includes the ability to allow our hearts, as Daoud Hari puts it, to supply the emotion for people who have none remaining. And it requires the support to talk, freely and without fear of judgment, about the impact that emotion will inevitably have on our own well-being.

For my part, I plan to keep writing and talking about the importance of self-care for aid and humanitarian workers. I plan to keep
teaching yoga and meditation to anyone whose commitment to serve
others—whether their children, their elderly parents, prisoners, homeless people or people affected by war—has taken a toll on their ability
to care for themselves. And I plan to keep looking closely at my own
motivations to serve, noticing when my "good intentions" are being
distorted by my personal demons.

Even in stable, predictable New Zealand, life still doesn't always
take the form I might imagine or plan. What makes it different for me,
after Afghanistan, is the understanding that I am in control of so much
less than I once imagined. There are many things that I cannot create
by determination or will alone. I've come to trust in the power of grace.

In the West we are taught to believe that we can craft our lives into
exactly what we want them to be. In places like Afghanistan the myth
of being in control is exposed as exactly that, a myth. Real peace, I
have learned, comes not from being able to control my life but from
accepting my life as it comes. Real happiness comes not from getting
everything I want but from embracing and deeply appreciating everything that I have. This is the beauty, and the power, of grace, surrender
and gratitude.

When I left Afghanistan I struggled for many months with a terrible
sense of guilt. As I walked through the woods above Wellington, or sat
in a café with friends, I would be overcome with the knowledge that
while my life was so comfortable and free, my friends in Afghanistan
still lived with fear and insecurity. It was Fahim who reminded me that
there was no point in my guilt.

"There is nothing wrong with you being able to walk freely through
the streets of New Zealand," he wrote. "There is nothing wrong with
being able to eat fresh fruit and vegetables. What is wrong is that we
can't do the same. No one should feel guilty for doing what everyone

should be able to do," he insisted. "Just be grateful. Always be grateful. And do what you can to make sure everyone enjoys those same rights. Just keep doing what you've always done, Marianne, and keep telling our story to the world."

I only hope Fahim will be happy with the story I've told.

Glossary

Al-Aqsa Intifada   popular Palestinian uprising that began in 2000 after a visit from Ariel Sharon to the site of the Al-Aqsa mosque in Jerusalem

bukhari   stove

jirga   tribal council

khareji   foreigner

madrasa   religious school

mujahedeen   literally "Muslims who fight in the 'path of God.'" In this context, mujahedeen were the Afghan opposition groups that rebelled against the incumbent pro-Soviet government during the late 1970s.

shalwar kameez   cotton suit, for men or women, made up of a long tunic and loose pants

sharia   Islamic law

shura   council

zinna   crime of adultery

Abbreviations

AIHRC Afghanistan Independent Human Rights Commission

ANP Afghan National Police

IDLO International Development Law Organization

IED improvised explosive device

ISAF International Security Assistance Forces

JSSP Justice Sector Support Program

MOSS minimum operating security standards

NATO North Atlantic Treaty Organization

NDS National Directorate for Security

NGO nongovernmental organization

PRT Provincial Reconstruction Team

PTSD posttraumatic stress disorder

SRSG Special Representative of the United Nations Secretary General

UNAMA United Nations Assistance Mission in Afghanistan

UNHCR United Nations High Commission for Refugees

UNICEF United Nations Children's Fund (originally the United Nations International Children's Emergency Fund)

UNIFEM United Nations Development Fund for Women (UNIFEM has since been dissolved and incorporated into the newly established UN Entity for Gender Equality and the Empowerment of Women [UN Women])

WFP United Nations World Food Program

Resources

Reading List

If you are like me, your good intentions to read hefty, learned tomes go largely unfulfilled. So this is a list of books about Afghanistan that I found compelling and easy to read. In other words, you don't need to be a scholar to read them.

Fiction

Ellis, Deborah. *The Breadwinner Trilogy*. Groundwood Books, 2009.

Hosseini, Khaled. *The Kite Runner*. Riverhead, 2004.

———. *A Thousand Splendid Suns*. Riverhead, 2008.

Rodriguez, Deborah. *A Cup of Friendship*. Ballantine Books, 2011.

Senzai, N. H. *Shooting Kabul*. Simon & Schuster/Paula Wiseman Books, 2010.

Nonfiction

Alexander, Chris. *The Long Way Back: Afghanistan's Quest for Peace*. Harper Collins, 2011.

Ayub, Awista. *Kabul Girls Soccer Club*. Hyperion, 2010.

Jones, Ann. *Kabul in Winter*. Picador, 2007.

Joya, Malalai. *A Woman Among Warlords*. Simon & Schuster, 2011.

Lamb, Christina. *The Sewing Circles of Herat*. Flamingo, 2003.

Rodriguez, Deborah, and Kristin Ohlson. *Kabul Beauty School.* Random House, 2007.

Salmon, Gregor. *Poppy.* Random House Australia, 2009.

Stewart, Rory. *The Places in Between.* Mariner Books, 2006.

Tzemach Lemmon, Gayle. *The Dressmaker of Khair Khana.* Harper, 2011.

Wahab, Saima. *In My Father's Country.* Crown, 2012.

Suraya's Organization

Voice of Women Afghanistan: www.vwo.org.af

Horia's Organization

Solidarity for Justice: www.solidarityforjustice.org.af

Aid Worker Well-Being

WhyDev: www.whydev.org/

Antares Foundation: www.antaresfoundation.org/

Mandala Foundation: www.mandalafoundation.org.au/

InterHealth: www.interhealth.org.uk/home/personal-health/

Garrison Institute: www.garrisoninstitute.org

Headington Institute: www.headington-institute.org/

Mindfulnext: www.mindfulnext.org/

Meditation

Pema Chödrön: pemachodronfoundation.org

Peter Fernando: www.monthofmindfulness.info

Sharon Salzberg: www.sharonsalzberg.com

Susan Piver: www.susanpiver.com

Shambhala meditation centers: www.shambhala.org/centers

Upaya Zen Center: www.upaya.org

Military and Veterans

Warrior at Ease: www.warriorsatease.com/

Veterans Yoga Project: www.veteransyogaproject.org/

Vets Yoga: www.vetsyoga.com/

Yoga for Vets: www.yogaforvets.org/

M-Fit Mind Fitness Training Institute: www.mind-fitness-training.org/tr_what.html

Yoga

Marianne's online yoga courses: www.marianne-elliott.com

Off the Mat, Into the World: www.offthematintotheworld.org

Richard Miller: www.irest.us

Yoga for depression: www.yogafordepression.com

About the Author

*M*arianne Elliott is a writer, human rights advocate, and yoga teacher. Trained as a lawyer, she helped develop human rights strategies for the governments of New Zealand and Timor-Leste; worked as policy adviser for Oxfam, a nonprofit international development agency; and spent two years working in human rights in the Gaza Strip prior to her time in Afghanistan, where she served in the United Nations mission (2005–7) with a focus on human rights and gender issues.

A popular blogger (www.marianne-elliott.com), Marianne writes and teaches on creating, developing, and sustaining real change in personal life, at work, and in the world. Marianne lives in a converted church above the zoo in Wellington, New Zealand, where she writes to the sound of lions roaring.

Online Guide

I've created a free guide to staying *Zen Under Fire*. It covers the key lessons I learned in Afghanistan about finding a place of inner peace even in the midst of war. The *Zen Under Fire* online guide is a four-week course in finding your own inner peace in the midst of whatever chaos, conflict, or simple day-to-day challenges you might be facing. It includes:

- One lesson per week (for four weeks) with a key learning from my experiences in Afghanistan and a simple exercise to help you apply the lesson to your life
- One practice per week (including yoga, meditation and writing) to help you put the lessons of *Zen Under Fire* into practice in your life
- Access to a private Facebook group where you can post updates, questions or insights from your own *Zen Under Fire* journey.
- One live Q&A call with Marianne (on Sunday June 9th)

Visit http://bit.ly/ZenUnderFireCourse or scan the QR code below to receive the free guide.